A PELICAN BOOK

What We Really Do All Day
Insights from the Centre for Time Use Research

JONATHAN GERSHUNY, ORIEL SULLIVAN,

KIMBERLY FISHER, PIERRE WALTHERY,

EVRIM ALTINTAS, JOOYEOUN SUH,

CHRISTOPHER PAYNE, GIACOMO VAGNI,

EWA JAROSZ, TERESA HARMS,

KILLIAN MULLAN AND JIWEON JUN

PELICAN
an imprint of
PENGUIN BOOKS

PELICAN BOOKS

UK | USA | Canada | Ireland | Australia
India | New Zealand | South Africa

Penguin Books is part of the Penguin Random
House group of companies whose addresses can
be found at global.penguinrandomhouse.com.

Penguin
Random House
UK

First published 2019
001

Text copyright © Jonathan Gershuny, Oriel
Sullivan, Kimberly Fisher, Pierre Walthery, Evrim
Altintas, Jooyeoun Suh, Christopher Payne,
Giacomo Vagni, Ewa Jarosz, Teresa Harms,
Killian Mullan and Jiweon Jun, 2019

The moral rights of the authors have been
asserted

Book design by Matthew Young
Set in 10/14.664 pt FreightText Pro
Typeset by Jouve (UK), Milton Keynes
Printed and bound in Great Britain by
Clays Ltd, Elcograf S.p.A.

A CIP catalogue record for this book is available
from the British Library

ISBN: 978-0-241-28556-5

MIX
Paper from
responsible sources
FSC® C018179
www.fsc.org

Contents

List of Tables

List of Figures

A Note on the Text

This book is written by the members of the Centre for Time Use Research (CTUR), the leading international specialist research institute in this field and originator of resources such as the American Heritage Time Use Study (AHTUS) and the Multinational Time Use Study (MTUS) – the latter harmonizing more than 90 national time-use studies from 25 countries, and including approximately 1 million days of time-diary data. It is predominantly based on data from the UK Time Use Survey of 2014–15. The UK historical data analyses and the cross-national analyses of Chapter 3 also utilize the MTUS.

Weights have been applied as appropriate to all figures and tables in the following chapters.

The Timeliness of Time Use
—
Jonathan Gershuny
Oriel Sullivan

Some of us may remember the Flintstones and the Jetsons; cartoon nuclear families, respectively stone-age and space-age, from 1960s and 1970s television. The stone-age Flintstones with their all-modern conveniences and fully fitted cave residence lived, from the viewpoint of the less affluent half of the British population, in a still-aspired-to future of American suburban luxury. They, and the Jetson mother and father in their orbiting satellite home, had just the same homemaker-breadwinner arrangements as our parents and grandparents did. The employed husbands left the cave or space station after eating a breakfast cooked by their wives, travelling to work and back in their foot- or jet-propelled private vehicles, and at night watched the same small TV screens placed in the corner of the cave or leisure-deck. Both families had the same reassuringly unchanging patterns of daily activity. The *lack* of change was the core running joke, of course, at the heart of both series. And, as the evidence presented in this book shows us – at least over the more than half a century of change captured by our time-use data, and despite the enormous progress of technology over that period – there is indeed a certain sameness about the daily round. The pattern through the day, from morning to night, changes somewhat, but in reality quite slowly.

Through much of the 20th century, people had a sense that 'in the future' daily life was going to be substantially transformed: less work, more leisure, and more equality in the distribution of these by gender, age and social stratum. The economist John Maynard Keynes, in a lecture delivered in 1924, forecast a future for his audience's grandchildren with a workweek of no more than a dozen hours or so. In predicting this he was following an idea central to John Stuart Mill's *Principles of Political Economy* (1848): that eventually societies would evolve into a 'steady state' in which all human needs could be met completely, through the operation of the economy accompanied by an ever-diminishing work-week. Technological change 'operating like compound interest' would increase productivity exponentially so as to satisfy all conceivable human wants.[1]

Nineteenth- and 20th-century socialists, liberals and conservatives all – if for a variety of different reasons – saw the reduction of working hours as the natural and proper concomitant of economic progress. Sociologists in the 1960s and 1970s interpreted the recent economic and social history of the developed world as progress 'towards a society of leisure'. Twenty years later, observers, noticing that work time in the USA was if anything increasing, assumed that the apparent end of progress towards the leisure society was a symptom of errors in the management of the US economy.[2]

But not everyone had taken this optimistic view. Keynes

himself (in the second half of the same lecture) identified what others in the 1920s and 1930s characterized as 'The Leisure Problem'. If work time diminished to this extent, what would a population not educated for leisure actually do with its unoccupied time? Worse, the vacant time left by a substantial reduction of work might actually be damaging. An influential group of European researchers studying the central Austrian village of Marienthal, where almost all the male population became unemployed as a result of the Great Crash in 1928, came to a clear conclusion: work provides a range of experiences (time structure, exercise, a framework for sociability and a sense of wider social purpose) whose loss produces real physiological and psychological damage. In some circumstances, winning freedom from the necessities of work is not necessarily a good social outcome.[3]

So, do we actually see the emergence of a leisure society in the UK over the past half-century? Or – a theme addressed in several chapters of this book – are we in fact getting busier? The UK population structure has changed quite markedly over the period from the 1960s to the first decade and a half of the 21st century: fewer children are born per family, marriage occurs later, and there have been significant increases in life expectancy. In addition, human needs at the various stages of the life and family cycles may be constant, but the ways they are met are transformed by technological innovations and new sorts of institutional arrangements. And over this period, important new technologies for meeting wants have diffused into UK households. But how has day-by-day life *actually* changed?

Time-use diary data

Time use is difficult to measure in conventional surveys. Like fish in water, we live in time. While we are aware of the *passage* of time, we generally do not remember *how much* of it we devote to each of our activities. For this reason, the sorts of direct questions about time use that are sometimes asked in conventional questionnaire surveys – for example, 'How many hours did you spend in your job last week?' – produce rather unreliable estimates. Unreliable in part because of a failure of recall. We do not, as part of our normal routines, undertake the various mental processes that would be necessary to answer this sort of question accurately: firstly, classifying activities into groups – deciding, for example, what belongs in the category of 'paid work' – then adding the duration of each successive episode to the accumulated total for that category. And finally, deciding what constitutes 'the week', and starting to accumulate a new total of time as a result. Not knowing the answer, we make a guess.

And guessing, we may perhaps be influenced to *represent ourselves* in particular ways, as, for example, the *sort of person* who works long hours at her job or cooks, or does not cook, who plays a sport or goes to the theatre, by exaggerating or reducing our estimates of the time we devote to particular activities. These two sources of error, respectively, measurement error and normative bias, are known to distort the responses that people give to these sorts of questions.

The approach taken in time-use diaries is different. We collect a form of information that does not require guesses about totals of time over a day or a week. We simply ask people to record the sequence of what they did over a specific day, together with approximate clock-times. This is a much simpler sort of exercise, which requires respondents to recall a continuous stream of activities, together with the times during which they did those activities. In addition, we ask them to record where they were when they did them, who they were with, and how much they enjoyed themselves. We are used to this sort of record-keeping in our daily lives. We have schedules of activities, often with fixed time points, that require us to keep track of when we are doing things. And we are used to answering questions about our schedules – from friends, parents and partners – about what we've done today, with whom, or how much we enjoyed what we did yesterday. It turns out that most people can record reasonably detailed and specific accounts of this sort. And the time-use researchers who collect these sequential narratives can classify the activities that people record into larger groups of activities (e.g. paid work, leisure and unpaid work), and calculate the totals of time spent in each – producing, strangely, information not immediately accessible to their informants!

A brief history of time-use diary collection in the UK

Details of the conduct of everyday life can be found (for example) in the diaries of remarkable mid-17th century individuals such as Samuel Pepys and John Evelyn, whose images of London daily life still capture the imagination. But the daily lives recorded in their diaries are certainly not in any sense representative of the society they describe – if only because the very act of keeping a diary renders the diarists themselves remarkable. In addition, the earliest diaries were simple free-form records of sequences of activities, often without detailed reference to timings. This makes it impossible to accurately calculate the aggregate time spent in different activities. The application of diaries to systematic social research depends on collecting carefully harmonized daily activity reports in large samples selected randomly from a population. Sociologists, economists and demographers can use the results of such time-use studies to describe and explain the factors that influence the chains of behaviours which comprise daily life.

Media-initiated surveys formed the first national-sample time-use surveys in many countries, including the UK, and their collection for these purposes spread quickly across the world. The first surviving large-scale UK sample of time-use diary-based data of this kind was the approximately 2,500 weeks of diary records collected by the BBC Audience Research Department in 1961, used to assist in planning the output of radio and television programmes. From the late 1930s, radio (or 'wireless') and early television providers needed to find a way to identify who listened to or watched their programmes. The BBC – and broadcasting companies worldwide – also wanted to know with whom listeners or viewers shared their programmes, as well as what else these people did at other times. This evidence could be used to inform future programming, reach out to new audiences, attract sponsorship for programmes and, in many countries (though not at that point in the UK), sell advertising by apprising potential sponsors about the demographic make-up of audiences at different points in the day or week.

The BBC drew the 1961 seven-day diary sample from electoral address registers in BBC regions. The first survey asked one person aged 15 or older in sampled households to keep a diary for one week in April 1961. The second surviving survey, in 1974–5, also sampled addresses with registered voters in BBC regions, but this time asked all people aged 5 and older who lived in the selected households to complete a diary. This whole-household diary design was quickly recognized as important for a variety of other research purposes. For example, in 1970 the British sociologists Michael Young and Peter Willmott collected a sample of time diaries from marital partners aged 25 to 45 in London as the basis for an early and influential study of the division of domestic labour (The Symmetrical Family[4]). Subsequent research from the 1980s and 1990s[5] further demonstrated the value of obtaining both partners' – and indeed whole households' – accounts of their daily routines on the same days. This enables complex analyses of how the activities of different members of the same household interplay and interact across the diary day, looking, for example, at the interaction of the activities of partners, and also how parents and children interact with each other in the home.[6]

In the early 1980s, the UK Economic and Social Research Council (ESRC) funded, for the first time, a British nationally representative time-use survey designed by academic researchers. It drew a stratified random national sample of addresses, asking all members of participating households aged 14 and older to complete a one-week diary. This survey collected 10,360 days of diaries from 1,601 people during the autumn and winter months of 1983–4. Subsequently, as part of the 1985–8 Social Change and Economic Life Initiative (SCELI) study, the ESRC also funded a time-use diary sample which, like the 1983–4 study, asked all people aged 14 and older in the selected households to complete a one-week diary. Just over 1,700 people from 912 households completed 11,332 day diaries during the spring and summer of 1987. Taken together, these two mid-1980s surveys offer a picture of life across most months of the year, and form the 1980s component of the historical sequence of UK time-use diary surveys we feature in this book.

In the mid-1990s, the UK Office for National Statistics (ONS) took up an interest in time-use diary surveys, expanding the field in the UK from the academic and commercial arenas to that of official statistics. At the same time, the European Statistical Office, Eurostat, began the development of the Harmonized European Time Use Survey (HETUS) programme, designed to provide comparable daily-activity statistics across the countries of the European Union. These comparable, nationally representative time-use surveys are designed to be run every ten years or so. They are intended to contribute to European policymaking in areas as diverse as gender equality, extended national accounts,[7] measuring hours of paid work,[8] and capturing the impact of work patterns on family life and overall national health.[9] The HETUS design incorporated the collection of diaries from all members of the household on the same days. Another important characteristic is that two diaries per person are collected, so that there is information from every respondent about how they spend one of their weekdays, and how they spend one of their weekend days, enabling, for example, the direct comparison of individual weekly and weekend working patterns. In addition, in order to provide a parallel measure to the European Labour Force Survey estimate of weekly hours of paid work, but based on something closer to a time-diary method, Eurostat also proposed a 'weekly work schedule' grid for inclusion with the HETUS surveys. This grid includes seven rows representing the days of the week, and 96 columns for quarter-hours through the day. Respondents mark this grid according to the times at which they undertake paid work across the selected week.[10] The ONS 2000–2001 national time-use diary survey formed the UK's first contribution to the HETUS programme, incorporating its guidelines. Based on a nationally representative stratified sample, 11,854 individuals in 6,414 households contributed 20,991 interviews and/or diaries.

The UK 2014–2015 Time Use Survey

The most recent survey in the UK historical sequence of time-use diary surveys is the UK 2014–2015 Time Use Survey (TUS), a collection of more than 16,000 diary days from 8,000 people in 4,000 randomly selected households. It was designed and organized by the authors of this book (the Centre for Time Use Research) during 2014–15,[11] and was funded by the ESRC. Like the previous 2000–2001 survey, the 2014–15 survey formed the UK's contribution to the HETUS programme and followed its guidelines (see above).

The diary instrument used in our UK study – shown in Figure 1 – has rows representing successive 10-minute periods, and separate columns in which respondents record their answers to: 'What were you doing?' (main or primary activity); 'Were you doing anything else at the same time?' (secondary

DAY 1

Use an arrow or quote marks to record that an activity lasted longer than 10 minutes

Time 7am–10am Morning (am)	What are you doing? Please write down your main activity	If you did something else at the same time, what else did you do?	Did you use a smartphone, tablet, or computer?	Where were you? Location, or mode of transport	Were you alone or with somebody you know? Mark all relevant boxes								How much did you enjoy this time? 1=not at all 7=very much
					Alone	Spouse/partner	Mother	Father	Child aged 0–7	Other person	Others you know		
7.00–7.10	Woke up the children			At home									5
7.10–7.20	Had breakfast	Checked emails	✓										6
7.20–7.30	" "	Talked with my family											5
7.30–7.40	Cleaned the table	Listened to the radio											4
7.40–7.50					✓								
7.50–8.00	Helped the children dressing	Talked with my children											
8.00–8.10	" "												
8.10–8.20	Went to the day care centre			On foot									1

10

THE TIMELINESS OF TIME USE

activity); 'Where were you?' (location); and 'Where you alone or with somebody you know?' (co-presence). An innovation of this particular survey was that we added two columns recording whether the respondent was using an electronic device (screen, tablet or smartphone), and how much she/he enjoyed each 10-minute period. The two activity columns are each coded into over 250 distinct activity categories (the 'own words' format means that they can be recoded into more detailed classifications if future research demands it). And since respondents often enter more than one distinct activity into these columns (e.g. 'made breakfast listening to the radio'), we can record anything up to four simultaneous activities when we process the handwritten responses into electronic form for analysis.

Each of these simple or complex activity time-slots shown in the diary describes part of a day. The essence of time-use analysis is using one, some, or conceivably all, of the diary fields to produce a classification of each of these intervals of the day which together sum to the 24 hours (1,440 minutes) of the individual's day. These individual classifications can then be averaged across the sample as a whole, to produce the 1,440 minutes of the population's 'Great Day' (described in Chapter 2).

A large, nationally representative sample of randomly selected diary days collected from whole households provides a uniquely broad and varied analytic potential.[12] The same diary study might be used at one point to produce a classification that relates to issues of paid-work time done during unsocial hours (Chapter 4) or the domestic division

Figure 1
The UK 2014–2015
use diary

of labour (Chapter 5), at another to estimate the amount of time that family members spend together in each other's company (Chapter 7), at a fourth to measure the extent of ICT usage during the different activities of the day (Chapters 10 and 11), at a fifth to assess the wellbeing or 'rushedness' associated with the use of time or to estimate the total enjoyment (or utility) generated across the whole day (Chapters 13 and 14), at a sixth to assess life balance among the elderly (Chapter 12), at a seventh to produce a classification of the activities of the day into different levels of physical exertion (as in Chapter 9), at an eighth to measure the social and spatial context of eating (Chapter 8), and at a ninth to estimate the total value to the economy of unpaid work (Chapter 6). The range of possibilities is limited only by the creativity of the analyst.

PART ONE

Fifty Years of Change in UK Daily Life

Fifty Years of Change in UK Daily Life at a Glance
—
Jonathan Gershuny
Oriel Sullivan

We start with the most intuitive representations of changes in the sequential pattern of our daily lives. When we write an ordinary diary or daily 'journal', we are typically recording a *sequence* of activities, events or feelings – often all of these together. This daily sequence, the way we progress from activity to activity and place to place, meeting different people at different times – at work, for lunch, in the evening – is also the way in which respondents to time-use diary surveys record their daily activities. However, this sequential progression of our daily lives tends to get lost in the aggregate statistics of time use. Aggregate statistics typically average the amount of time that we spend in different activities, in different locations, and with different people (an average 8 hours per day at work, and 2 hours watching TV with family, for example). They have an important place in research into changes in time use, as we will show in Chapter 2, but they do not have the same intuitive appeal as the visualizations of the sequences of our daily activities that we present here. Strangely, this more intuitive, sequence-based, method for analysing how people record their daily lives in diaries is a relatively recent addition to time-use diary methodology. A rapidly growing body of research now moves beyond the analysis of aggregate time-use statistics to examine how time is structured *sequentially*.[1] These newer sequential approaches study not just what people spend their time on, but also the *order* and *timing* of their activities. The order and timing of people's daily lives matter for important social processes such as coordinating household divisions of labour, productive activity, and the scheduling of social contacts. Putting together these sequential accounts of daily life gives us an insight into how individuals' activity sequences are aligned throughout the day.

Analysing time-use diaries as sequences has led to new breakthroughs in the measurement and modelling of everyday time. An example, enabling the comparison of daily sequences for different individuals or groups, is Andrew Abbott's classical optimal matching approach, where we can envisage sequences of activities as strings of events that can be compared in the same way that strings of DNA or protein sequences are compared to each other.[2] This allows the computation of similarities and dissimilarities between pairs, or clusters, of activity sequences. Using developments of this method we can compare differences, for instance, in the sequence of activities between those who have standard and non-standard work shifts, or between men's and women's work/family schedules. In addition, since we can compare when and to what extent individuals' activity sequences intersect, we are able to analyse activities that take place at particular times as part of the larger networks of social action that connect individuals through space and time.

We use our historical sequence of UK time-use diary surveys here to compare activity sequences for the whole population from the 1960s through to the second decade of the 21st century, giving us a unique perspective on changes in the sequential patterns of activities of the UK population over a 50-year period. This technique provides the most visually intuitive, detailed and comprehensive picture of broad changes over the past half-century in the national population's patterns of daily activity sequences.[3]

Tempograms: the way through the UK day

The sequential activity 'tempograms' we illustrate here show the proportions of the population engaged in various activities through the 10-minute episodes of the day from the early 1960s to the second decade of the 21st century.

Figure 1.1 illustrates the temporal sequence of primary activities for the whole UK for the population aged 16–64 (working-age population), from the earliest (1961) to the latest (2015) time-use surveys. This provides us with a picture of the activities that diarists are doing in successive 10-minute time slots throughout the day. The tempogram shows the time of day charted on the horizontal axis, and the percentage of the population engaging in a range of activities on the vertical axis. We have simplified the activities of the day into nine distinct sorts of activity: 1) sleep, personal care and eating at home; 2) paid work and education – the latter for those identified as being full-time in school, further or higher education; 3) unpaid cooking, cleaning or DIY; 4) shopping; 5) childcare; 6) out of home leisure and recreation; 7) exercise; 8) watching TV, video, audio and reading; and 9) other

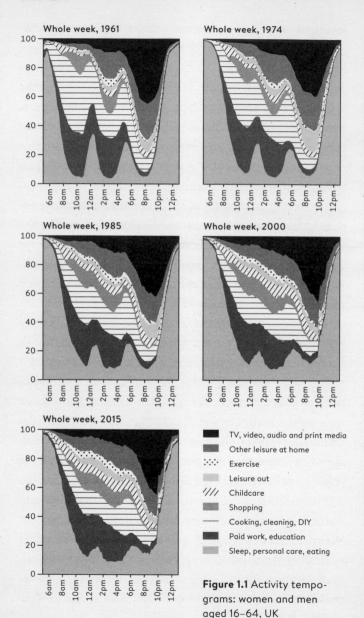

Figure 1.1 Activity tempograms: women and men aged 16–64, UK (1961–2015)

leisure at home.[4] The differently shaded areas are proportional to the average time devoted to each of these activity categories through the day.

By simply eyeballing the areas representing the different activity groups across the five graphs we get a preliminary overall impression of *historical change* in how time is used across the 24 hours of the day. The graphs as a group show substantial changes over the period from 1961 to 2015. Perhaps the most striking change is the gradual, but historically consistent, fading away of the division of the waking day by the three peaks which marked mealtimes (shown by the lightly shaded areas at the base of the graphs). In 1961 we see two prominent peaks, at 1pm and at 5.45pm. Averaging across the whole population aged 16–64, 30 per cent or more of men and women were eating at these times, and 80–90 per cent were involved in some eating within an hour of each of these peak mealtimes. The peaks determine the overall shape of the 1965 graph. By 2015 it is evident that they have substantially diminished in size, and the graph has a distinctly 'flatter' (less 'peaky') profile. But, as we will see in subsequent chapters (in particular Chapter 8), this does not mean that eating itself is disappearing. Rather, it points to a combination of the desynchronization of mealtimes, and the spread of between-meals 'snacking'.

On the other hand, there are also some remarkable continuities evident in the historical succession of tempograms. We are frequently assured that the emergence of the '24/7 society' has led to a substantial reduction in sleep. However, little evidence for this is apparent (lightly shaded areas at the beginning and end of the day). Indeed, Chapter 2, which looks at aggregate statistics for sleep time, shows a small *increase* of time spent in bed, most clearly through the more recent period, which is precisely when the supposed decrease is supposed to have occurred. The disappearance of work as envisaged by the sociological prophets of 'the leisure society' is likewise not evident. While the area of the graphs relating to (traditionally feminine-defined) tasks like cooking and cleaning (see horizontal stripes) has reduced in size somewhat over the period since 1961, the overall area devoted to other categories of unpaid work – shopping, childcare – (horizontal stripes and the area immediately above) has increased. Similarly, a casual impression of the area devoted to leisure (both indoor and outdoor) suggests that there has not been that much change in leisure time over successive decades.

Admittedly, when we dig down further according to gender and across the days of the week, which we do below, we do see some more substantial changes. However, the main point here is that when we use this unique body of sequential evidence to examine many of the more dramatic prognostications of change in the broader patterns of the day – work, leisure, sleep – they simply vanish away.

Delving deeper into some of the differences we find if we look separately at particular subgroups of the population, we distinguish in the next sets of figures between tempograms for women and men, and for weekdays, Saturdays and Sundays. Weekdays usually resemble each other quite strongly in terms of time use due to the structured sequencing imposed by traditional weekday patterns of work, while Saturdays and Sundays are usually rather different, both from each other and from weekdays.[5] Here we restrict the figures to show only tempograms from the first (1961), middle (1985) and last (2105) surveys of the UK time-use diary sequence.

The first group of tempograms (Figure 1.2) shows women's and men's weekdays. Most strikingly, and emerging throughout this and the next chapter, we see a convergence over time between the weekday tempograms of women and men. In 1961 women's weekday pattern was really very different to that of men, with much of the main part of their weekdays – up to 5pm or thereabout – being largely devoted to the unpaid work activities of cooking, cleaning (in horizontal stripes), shopping, and childcare, with the corresponding portion for men being almost exclusively devoted to paid work. Focusing in on these changes in paid and unpaid work by gender, in the three graphs for men we see a quite sizeable reduction in those parts of the weekday spent in paid work across the period 1961 to 1985. But this reduction ceases when we compare men's paid work from 1985 to 2015. If anything, over this second period we have a picture of a slight increase in the part of the day occupied by men's paid work (with less time devoted to meal breaks). And in parallel, over both the 1961–85 and 1985–2015 periods, and pretty much throughout the weekday from morning to evening, we see small but growing increases in the areas representing men's cooking and cleaning, shopping and childcare.

The series for women shows some complementary changes. Over the two time periods between 1961–85 and 1985–2015, we see significant reductions in those areas of the weekday tempogram devoted to cooking and cleaning activities (horizontal stripes). The area indicating women's paid work time

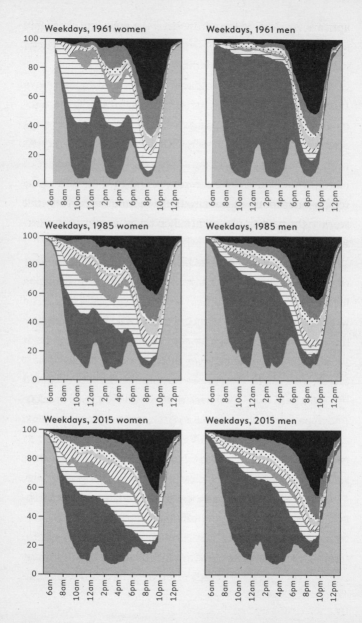

Weekdays, 1961 women

Weekdays, 1961 men

Weekdays, 1985 women

Weekdays, 1985 men

Weekdays, 2015 women

Weekdays, 2015 men

appears, as expected, to grow between 1985 and 2015. But, as is the case for men, this area actually somewhat *decreased* in size over the earlier period between 1961 and 1985. How does this apparent discontinuity square with what is known from other sources to be a continuous growth in the rates of women's participation in the labour force through the 55 years covered by these graphs? The answer is that it reflects both the effects of the general reduction in hours spent in all full-time paid jobs between 1961 and 1985 (shown in the tempograms for men), but also the predominance of *part-time* work in the paid employment taken up by women in this earlier period.

The Saturday tempograms (Figure 1.3) remind us of a mostly forgotten achievement of the mid-20th century: the invention of the two-day weekend. If we follow the historical sequence for men, we see a dramatic reduction in the area of the tempogram devoted to paid work on Saturdays. This was, it seems, a post-Second World War development in the UK. Until the 1930s, in the UK paid work for the employed usually occupied six of the seven days of the week. Our UK time-use data series starts about halfway through the process that transformed Saturday into a day more resembling a day of leisure, shopping and unpaid work.

By 1985 we see, apparently compensating for the end of the Saturday morning 'at work', a considerable increase in the amount of unpaid work

TV, video, audio and print media

Other leisure at home

Exercise

Leisure out

Childcare

Shopping

Cooking, cleaning, DIY

Paid work, education

Sleep, personal care, eating

Figure 1.2
Weekday activity tempograms: women and men aged 16–64, UK (1961–2015)

23

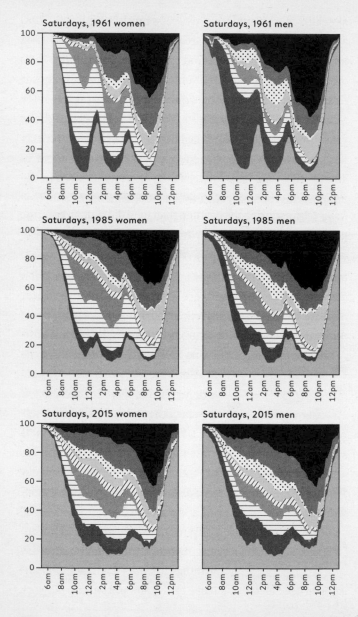

(cooking and cleaning, and growing most rapidly, shopping) done by men. And between 1985 and 2015, the area representing men's cooking and cleaning continues to increase, while the equivalent area diminishes somewhat for women: suggesting perhaps an actual gendered *transfer* of work, with men seemingly taking some unpaid work in a category previously done almost entirely by women. In relation to leisure time on Saturday, in 1961 it appears that men had more *out-of-home* leisure, particularly during Saturday afternoon, than did women. Correspondingly, women had much more *at home* leisure during the daytime than men did. But by 2015, the gender specialization in daytime Saturday leisure had disappeared. In fact, the disappearance of men's paid work on Saturday mornings seems to lead to an even more marked historical gender convergence than we saw in the case of weekdays. The Saturday tempograms in 2015 have a distinctly similar appearance for men and women (although men still do somewhat more paid work and women more unpaid work).

Finally, linking the tempograms for Saturday and Sunday, the area of the tempogram representing women's and (more particularly) men's Saturday shopping increased remarkably, particularly during the afternoon, over the first part of the 55-year period, but remained hardly changed – or even slightly reduced – from 1985 to 2015. Why did this happen?

TV, video, audio and print media
Other leisure at home
Exercise
Leisure out
Childcare
Shopping
Cooking, cleaning, DIY
Paid work, education
Sleep, personal care, eating

Figure 1.3
Saturday tempograms: women and men aged 16–64, UK (1961–2015)

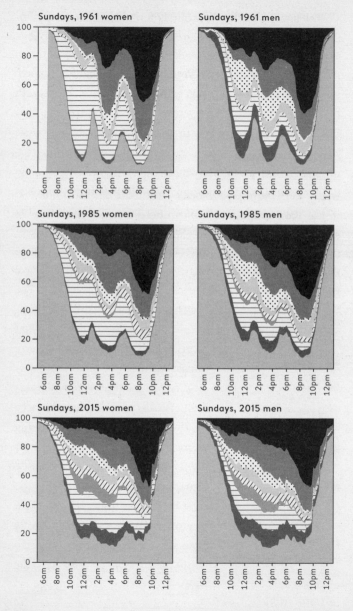

The answer to this question is found in the Sunday tempograms (Figure 1.4). Weekday and Saturday shopping have shifted to Sunday. Gradual changes in legislation governing the opening of shops on Sunday ('Sunday trading') from the 1970s onwards introduced a whole new category of activity to Sundays in the UK. In the 1960s only a very few specialist shops (off-licence shops selling alcohol, some do-it-yourself equipment shops, and shops catering for ethnic or religious minorities with restrictions on shopping on other days of the week) were permitted to open during the day on Sunday. So in the 1961 tempogram we can detect only a tiny sliver of shopping activity through the morning. By the mid-1980s, the number of exceptions to the Sunday trading restrictions had increased, showing up in a little more shopping activity throughout the day. But major changes to the Sunday trading laws came only at around the start of the present century. As a consequence, we see a dramatic growth in Sunday shopping between the 1985 and the 2015 tempograms. Just 4 per cent of our sample went to church on Sunday in 2015, while 25 per cent went shopping. In the UK, clearly, shopping rather than church now emerges as the major act of Sunday worship.

Other quite dramatic changes specific to Sundays emerge from Figure 1.4. In 1961 substantial amounts of exercise, particularly for men, took place on Sunday mornings and afternoons: this largely involved sports

TV, video, audio and print media
Other leisure at home
Exercise
Leisure out
Childcare
Shopping
Cooking, cleaning, DIY
Paid work, education
Sleep, personal care, eating

Figure 1.4
Sunday tempograms: women and men aged 16–64, UK (1961–2015)

participation in team games. By 2015 the dominance of team sports on Sundays was gone, and exercise had become more evenly distributed both across the day, and between men and women. At pretty much the same times on Sunday mornings in 1961, while the men were out playing sports, the women were doing housework, the weekly wash, and making Sunday lunch. In 1961 something approaching half the adult population were having their Sunday lunch *at the same time of the day* (represented by the peaks of light shading).

With respect to at-home leisure activities, in 1961 on Sundays there were small surges of media participation before and after Sunday lunch – this was one of the high points of weekly radio listening in 1961: 'family favourite' musical performances and comedy programmes on the BBC's Light Programme. And then, substantial time devoted to home leisure on Sunday afternoons – digesting the unusually heavy midday meal, and then starting mid-late afternoon television – which was in 1961 on the cusp of its diffusion across British households: by 1967, 88 per cent of British households had television licences, while only 48 per cent had them in 1957.

In summary, over the three successive day graphs spanning the 55 years of Sundays, we can identify some really striking historical changes. The prominence of mealtimes, which in 1961 were even more strongly delineated on Sundays than on weekdays or Saturdays, is substantially eroded. Media activities and exercise have spread more evenly across the day, though with the peak of concentration – now overwhelmingly television viewing – in the evening. Whole new categories of activity have come to prominence, in addition to the previously mentioned Sunday shopping. For example, childcare, which hardly signified in 1961, but by 2015 was reported as a significant Sunday activity by both men and women. And, most remarkably, the gender convergence in activities. The essential characteristic of traditional gender relations, the dependence of men on women's immediate supply of timely domestic services through the day – caring for the youngest children, cleaning and preparing the lunches while the men are out at work or playing – can be seen from the 1961 Sunday tempograms. The equivalent pair of 2015 tempograms still show some gendered disparity in work time, with men doing somewhat more paid work than women, and women a bit more unpaid work. But, 55 years on, it seems that all our days are now much less strongly differentiated by gender.

CHAPTER 2

Adding Up and Fitting Together
The UK's Great Day across Time

—

Jonathan Gershuny
Oriel Sullivan

Adding up: summing the Great Day

Time is a fixed quantum, and everything we do happens in time. For one person, there is one day of just 1,440 minutes, into which all our activities have to fit. A society has its equivalent, the Great Day, also with 1,440 Great Minutes, within which all the activities of that society's whole population must fit. The Great Day is calculated as the total of the population's time, across the 24 hours (1,440 minutes) of the day. It involves summing across all the day's sequential activities shown in the previous chapter's activity tempograms to produce the average quantity of time spent in each activity across the population. It summarizes the activities for a society in a comprehensive way, providing an integrated and exhaustive account of the way in which this society spends its time. These aggregated accounts, though, are simply abstract statistics – they are directly derived from the sequential activity patterns of our daily lives, and the way that these sequences of activities across the population have changed over time.

Take the distribution of paid and unpaid work. Once, just a few years prior to the first of the UK time-use surveys in 1961, our mothers (or grandmothers) would walk to a local shopping parade and discuss the family's weekly food requirements with the grocer. This was, from our mother's perspective, unpaid work, but also coincided with the shopkeeper's paid work. He would pack into a basket the product of various farm, transport and manufacturing workers' work – that had been transferred from a food manufacturing establishment (which had itself acquired food products from farms and import agents) to a wholesale warehouse some days before, then in turn delivered to his shop by a wholesale services transport worker – and a junior employee would cycle to our homes and deliver the order (more paid work). Our mothers would unpack the produce into a larder (unpaid work), maybe giving her children one segment of the Five Boys chocolate bar (her unpaid childcare, their consumption time), then bake a cake for tea.

Thirty years on, we ourselves might drive to the supermarket (which has been stocked by some process not dissimilar to the way the wholesale warehouse was stocked 30 years before), park, then walk up and down the aisles collecting our own baskets (our unpaid work, replacing the paid work previously done by various transport, wholesale and retail service workers), then drive home. We unpack the goods, and might cook for our families, perhaps producing rather less elaborate meals than our mothers managed!

How will things change from now onwards? What will our children and grandchildren do, should they start families of their own? Some of the time currently spent using IT devices in unpaid work (see Chapter 11) is devoted to retail purchases, including some grocery shopping, but this is still a small part of overall shopping time (10 per cent of all mentions of shopping in the 2014–15 diaries involved the internet, up from less than 0.5 per cent in 2000–2001). We would expect much more of this sort of activity in the future, with rather complex effects on time-use patterns. Certainly, the increased efficiency of web-based retail shopping may have directly negative effects on the numbers of retail staff in shops and supermarkets. But it may also imply positive effects for the employment of delivery workers – or alternatively for designers and builders of robotic delivery devices.

So the Great Day provides precise and detailed information on a critical component of national economic activity, the overall time spent in paid work, which is more conventionally covered by money-based statistics on national income and wage rates. It also allows us to estimate – and then put a value on – the extent of *unpaid* economic activity, the work that goes on in households, in voluntary work, and in community groups. In addition, time-use diaries tell us about the full range of activities *outside* work, the leisure, consumption and self-care (sleep, washing and dressing) that occupies the remaining two thirds of the day. Most importantly, they can show us how these various sorts of activities are distributed among members of the same households, and among different sorts of people: men and women, the young and the old, the rich and the poor. The additional information about each activity included in the diary – its social context, its location, and the extent to which it was enjoyed, allows us to build a complete portrait of the society's Great Day. This portrait provides a comprehensive and multidimensional description of that society's use of time, potentially providing a much richer picture of the sources of wellbeing in the society than we can get from conventional economic statistics.

We begin with the broadest summary of all (later chapters delve deeper into specific activities, illustrating trends and differentials in greater detail). The nine activity categories shown in the tempograms of Chapter 1 are here aggregated into four broad activity categories and averaged across diary days to give us a general picture of the changing aggregate distribution between paid work, unpaid work and leisure of the UK population's time across successive time-use surveys from 1961 to 2015. Unlike the sequences of the tempograms shown in Chapter 1, these aggregations allow us to focus on changes in the *overall* amounts of time spent by the UK population in the different activities. The four activity categories are paid work, unpaid work, leisure and time spent in necessary activities (sleep, personal care and non-social eating). They correspond to the four-fold typology of activity originally introduced by the sociologist Dagfinn Ås, who distinguished between activities necessary to human functioning ('necessary' activities); activities committed to various types of unpaid work and care ('committed' activities); activities associated with paid work ('contractual' activities); and leisure and consumption activities ('discretionary' activities).[1]

Figure 2.1 includes only men and women aged 16–64 (controlling to some extent for the consequences of the demographic changes that have taken place over the 55-year timespan covered by the UK time-use surveys). The vertical axis shows minutes of the Great Day spent in the different activities, and

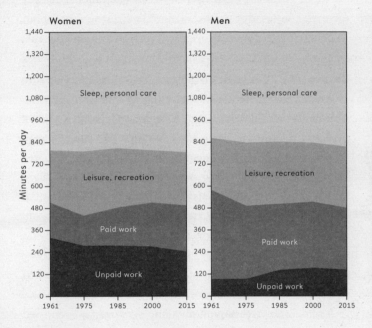

Figure 2.1
The UK Great Day (1961–2015), average minutes per day
for women and men aged 16–64

the horizontal axis shows the UK sequence of time-use surveys from 1961 to 2015.

These aggregated totals tell us that, for men, the category of sleep plus personal care increased by an average three-quarters of an hour over the whole period, from 577 minutes per day (about 9 hours and 45 minutes) in 1961 to 623 minutes (about 10 hours and 30 minutes) in 2015. Average time spent in this category for women was greater, but increased less over the period, from 634 minutes to 647 minutes (10 hours and 30 minutes to 10 hours and 45 minutes). Leisure time increased by three-quarters of an hour for men, but by only five minutes for women, so that, while in 1961 men's and women's leisure time was relatively equal, by 2015 men enjoyed over half an hour's more leisure on average per day than women. Which brings us to the vexed category of 'work'.[2] Work is most helpfully identified by what economists call the 'third-person' criterion: *could* you – irrespective of whether you *actually* do so – sensibly pay some third party to undertake the activity for you? If, like washing a floor, you could do so, it is classified as work. If, like going to a concert, you couldn't, it is not work.

The overall total of paid plus unpaid work (as identified by the third-person criterion) shows a considerable *advantage* of an hour's less work per day for women in 1961 (their average was 511 minutes of all work, where men averaged 573 minutes). Men's daily work total reduced by an hour and a half over the 55-year period, while women's reduced by only 17 minutes. The result is that by 2015 the advantage in favour of women had transformed into a penalty (albeit much closer to gender equality than in the 1960s), with women doing an average of 494 minutes of total work compared to men's 483.

Over the period 1961–2015, women's average unpaid work time reduced by over 1 hour and 10 minutes per day, while men's increased by three-quarters of an hour. Due to the simultaneous increase in women's average paid work time over the period, this meant that the proportion of women's work taken up in unpaid work reduced from 63 per cent to just 50 per cent of all their work time. For men, who experienced a reduction in paid work time, the equivalent proportion rose from just 16 per cent in 1961 to nearly 30 per cent of their total work time.

Fitting together: the components of the Great Day

There is more than mere adding up in the constitution of the Great Day out of the combined days of the members of the population. There is also an important accounting constraint. More time devoted to one activity by individual members of a society must mean less time available for other activities. Put simply, *more consumption*, for one individual person, means *less work*. But, crucially, the activities of the members of a society also *fit together*. Time devoted to some activities may enable or inhibit time spent in others. More consumption for some means, necessarily, more work for others to do, to supply the commodities used in that consumption. Work (paid and unpaid) and leisure must both *add up* for the individual and also *fit together* for the society.

Consumption takes time. A film, or a restaurant meal, takes two hours, plus time to travel to the venue. A football match, allowing for extra time and the interval, might take three hours. Given our employed work time, to which we are contracted, and our household work, childcare and so on, to which we are committed, and our sleep, a necessity, do we actually have time for leisure – to go to the match or meet friends at the cinema or restaurant?

For each of us individually, this is a matter of accountancy. This is not, however, simply a question of *time* accountancy: it also involves *money*. To pay for the ticket to the match or the cinema, or for the meal, we need access to money, which we generally acquire through some form of employment. For people on low hourly wages there may not be enough time in the day to earn enough to pay for the ticket to the Premier League match. Or conversely, the time we spend working to pay for the activities to which we have committed ourselves (e.g. children's clothes or education) may leave us with insufficient time to go to the match. There are straightforward arithmetical relationships based on coefficients such as wage rates, or durations of consumption activities, which link the amounts of time *spent in* consumption to the amounts of time *available for* paid and unpaid work. We refer to these three broad categories of time – paid work, unpaid work and leisure – as the 'life-balance triangle', and these relationships constitute the micro-economics of time.[3]

Less familiar to economists – necessarily so, since time in consumption is so difficult to measure, and hence so underrepresented in economic statistics – is the corresponding macro-economics of time. One person's consumption time is another's employment. As well as occupying the consumer's time, each purchase or act of consumption also pays for the time of the workers who are producing the commodities that are involved in that act of consumption.[4] At any given historical juncture there are, in addition to the micro-economic coefficients, also coefficients that describe the relationships between, on the one hand, the various acts of consumption, and on the other, the various sorts of paid work that provide the commodities that are consumed. Therefore, unlike for the individual, *more consumption*, for the society as a whole, means *more work*.

These two sets of coefficients – the micro ones which relate to individuals' choices about the make-up of their own time allocations, and the macro-coefficients which relate everyone's consumption time to everyone's work time – constitute, in effect, a system of constraints on the combinations of paid and unpaid work and leisure that are possible in a society. Once we know how many trained cooks there are in the population, and where cooks' wages lie in the distribution of wages of other workers with other sorts of work skills, we are quite a long way to understanding how much time is spent eating out, how much time spent cooking at home, and how many jobs there are in the restaurant trade. These coefficients fit together in a simple set of equations that describe which combinations of work and leisure are arithmetically possible and which are impossible, as well as the possibilities for historical trajectories of change.[5]

Figure 2.1 showed the broadest meaningful summary, dividing the day's activities into four large categories: paid work; unpaid work; leisure/recreation; and sleep. And from this comprehensive summary we saw rather surprisingly small changes over time in the overall mean time spent in these broad categories of activity (with the exception of a change in the distribution of paid and unpaid work). This is perhaps

remarkable given the extent of the changes in the organization of daily life that we know have taken place over the past
half-century. It seems, though, that when added up and aggregated into these broad activity categories, the half-century
of change that we might have expected to see in our daily lives
has not in fact been so revolutionary after all.

However, by looking at more detailed breakdowns of these
aggregated changes over time we begin to see where some of
the changes that we expected to see do appear. As before, we
focus on the working-age population, and divide the figures
for women and men. We start with the unpaid work category,
dividing it further into three categories: general household
work (including both cooking and cleaning, but also household maintenance, etc.), shopping and care-giving.[6]

Figure 2.2 shows that over the period men substantially
increased their contributions to two of the three categories of
unpaid work, albeit from a very low initial level in each case.
Firstly, their general household work time remained essentially unchanged from the start to the end of the period at
around 70 minutes (though it rises, and then falls back again
from 2000 to 2015). Their shopping time, on the other hand,
rises from 12 to 37 minutes per day, and their child- and adult-
care time almost triples, from 11 to 30 minutes per day. In contrast, women's daily time spent in general household work
declines remarkably over the period, from 243 minutes, or just
over 4 hours, to 133 minutes, under 2 hours and 15 minutes. In
the same way as for men, though, the other two unpaid work
categories increased, from 44 to 52 minutes shopping time,
and from 32 to 63 minutes (almost doubling) for care-giving
time. These latter increases are proportionally less over the

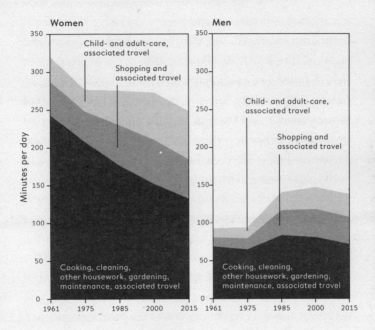

Figure 2.2 — Three categories of unpaid work: average minutes per day for women and men aged 16—64, UK (1961–2015)

55-year period compared to the equivalent increases for men, but the amount of time spent in these activities by 2015 is still substantially greater for women than it is for men.

The sleep and personal care data provide us with one of those surprises which only come when we first make good quantitative estimates of phenomena that have never previously been measured. In Figure 2.3 we divide the sleep and personal care activities, allowing us to see how sleep times have changed over half a century. We had been told by sleep experts that (in effect) the nation's sleep had been murdered by the advent of '24/7 society' – the emergence of round-the-clock, throughout-the-week consumer services.[7] But their expertise resides in sleep medicine, not in the collection and analysis of social and economic statistics. One very eminent sleep specialist, questioned as to how he knew that sleep time has been reducing over recent decades, told us that he asks people whether they sleep less now than they did previously! Plainly – and on the assumption that a good proportion of the people he asked are anyway only talking to him because they are suffering from sleeplessness – the answers he gets will not necessarily very reliably represent the general population. And in any case, as we discussed earlier, without a purposely collected diary, it is difficult to estimate how much time one spends in bed in any given week – let alone provide a reliable comparison with some previous time!

In fact, the really important issue may be to do with the effect of 24/7 society on sleep *quality*. The diary evidence does not necessarily provide a completely accurate picture of sleep itself, since some people may fail to record (or even remember) time spent 'tossing and turning' in bed or getting up to

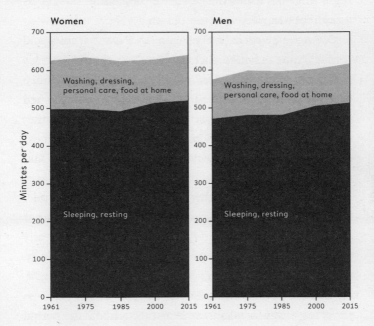

Figure 2.3
Sleep, rest and personal care: average minutes per day for
women and men aged 16–64, UK (1961–2015)

comfort a crying child, or answering the calls of nature.[8] And in particular, the 1961 and 1974–5 diary collections excluded the 'small hours' of the night, so that the approach that we use to compensate for this exclusion probably leads to a slight overestimate of sleep time for these years (insofar as it assumes that sleep is not interrupted).

So, in the 'sleep' category, Figure 2.3 shows 'sleeping and resting' (time in bed) rather than just 'sleep'. And what we see in the chart really does not fit the '24/7 society murdered sleep' metaphor at all. Women's 496 minutes in bed (8 hours and 15 minutes) rises gently to around 519 minutes, or 8 hours and 30 minutes in 2015 (including a small apparent growth through the very same 2000–2015 decade and a half during which the 24/7 society really took hold). Men show a more substantial growth from 467 minutes in 1961 – 7 hours and 45 minutes – rising to 8 hours and 30 minutes in 2015. These last two surveys in 2000 and 2015 are nearly identical in design, and they in turn match the 1985 study insofar as they provide direct evidence throughout the night. So the best available comparisons we have show sleep time (or at least time in bed) increasing through just the period that many informed observers have told us that we should expect it to decline.

We do not propose a full explanation for this unexpected result. But we do know that over the period the spread of the different times across the population that people go to bed and wake up has become more varied, and less concentrated around the 11pm to 7am hours. So perhaps the effect of 24/7 is to spread sleeping time out a little more, rather than decreasing the total. And it is possible that this 'spreading out' means increased daily variation in bed-times, leading in some people to more difficulties in getting to sleep, and hence increasing the ratio between time in bed and actual sleep. In short, the generally rising trend of time spent in bed might be consistent with a roughly constant sleep total.

Minutes devoted to washing, dressing and other personal care, throughout slightly higher for women compared to men, rise and then decline, so that over the 55-year period they remain roughly constant for men at around 110 minutes, and decline by 10 minutes for women (from 138 to 129 minutes/ day). This category also includes eating at home (classified as a necessary activity), and, as we discuss in greater detail in Chapter 8, this is an activity that declines substantially over the period. All in all, the general image of an increasingly frenetic society with less and less time for sleep and self-care simply does not fit the evidence. We discuss the general issue of the 'speed-up society' at more length in Chapter 13.

At first glance the evidence presented in Figure 2.4, showing changes in leisure time spent at home, might suggest that time spent watching and listening to media has somewhat reduced over the last couple of decades. For men, media time (TV, video, radio, audio, print) rose from 174 to 190 minutes per day between 1961 and 1985, then fell away quite sharply, particularly from the year 2000, reaching only 158 minutes in 2015 (this drop is masked in Figure 2.4 by the rise in the 'other home leisure' category over the same period – see below).[9] For women, more modest changes in media time are seen, but the same general pattern is similar, rising from 141 minutes per day in 1961 to 158 minutes per day in 1985, then falling back to 139 minutes in 2015.

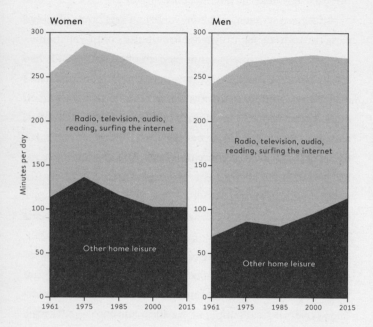

Figure 2.4
Leisure at home: average minutes per day for women and men aged 16–64, UK (1961–2015)

But this is not the whole story. These calculations, showing only modest changes, are based on a fixed set of media technologies – this restriction is necessary to allow us to compare media activities over more than a half-century. This is the problem with the cartoon comparisons of stone-age and space-age lifestyles with which we began this book. The diaries started to register the use of computers in private households in 1985, when only a few per cent of all households had access to this equipment. By 2015, we had three new classes of device – laptops, smartphones, tablets – actually the stuff of 1961 science fiction, and in 2015 most households had at least one of each of these new devices. In this chapter, for the sake of backwards comparability with previous decades, we have categorized the use of home computers, together with use of the other new devices, in the 'other home leisure' category.

The 2015 diaries, unlike the earlier surveys, contained information on the use of tablets, smartphones and laptops in conjunction with other activities. Where (in Chapters 10 and 11) we use this extra information to try to disentangle exactly what ICT is being used *for*, we show, among other things, that screen watching, not on televisions but on those tablets, smartphones and laptops, increases the estimates of the 'new media' by more than an hour. This explains much of the increase in men's 'other home leisure' that we see in Figure 2.4. But in turn it sets up another puzzle; why does women's total of 'other home leisure' not increase at all over the same period? It seems that some of the answer to this is provided by looking at women's out of home leisure time.

In 1961 men had much more overall out-of-home leisure

time than women, but the gap erodes over time (Figure 2.5). Time devoted to sport and exercise (including all walking) rises for both men and women, but while men maintain a small edge over women in absolute terms (30 minutes per day as against 23 minutes in 2015), women's more than four-fold increase over the period is somewhat faster than men's trebling of theirs. The 'other out-of-home leisure' category behaves in a less straightforward fashion. In general, we see a slight rise of 5–10 minutes per day devoted to this category between 1961 and 1985, then a falling off from 1985 to 2000, and a partial recovery from 2000 to 2015. This may reflect an increase in (particularly male) pub-going through the 1960s to the 1980s, followed by, as the trade statistics confirm, a reduction over the subsequent quarter-century. Eventually, though pub-going continued to decline (and the number of pubs in the UK reduced as a consequence), there was a growth again post-2000 as eating out to some extent substituted for drinking out as an out-of-doors leisure activity.

Eating out partly substitutes for eating at home. Just as the tempograms above demonstrated the progressive loss of whole population-synchronized meals at home, we also see a substantial increase in eating out (included in Figure 2.5 in the 'out-of-home' leisure category). On an average day, only 14 per cent of the adult population ate or drank away from home in the 1960s, but this had risen to 28 per cent by 2015. The large gender gap, with women much less likely to eat or drink out of home in 1961, had virtually disappeared by 2015.

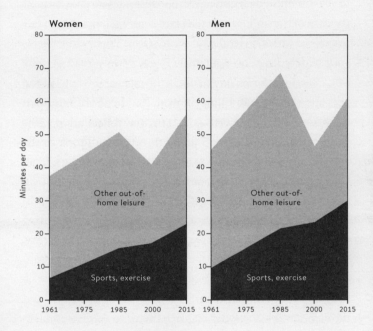

Figure 2.5

Out-of-home leisure: average minutes per day for women and men aged 16–64, UK (1961–2015)

Historical changes by gender and social position

One of the more remarkable findings to emerge from our historical time-use data concerns the 'class/leisure gradient'. At the turn of the 20th century, leisure time was unambiguously associated with superordinate social status. Thorstein Veblen's very widely known – but rather less widely read – book *The Theory of the Leisure Class* is the origin of what Veblen perhaps rather pompously dubbed the 'theory of stratified diffusion' – or alternatively, 'the principle of emulation'. This is the proposition that consumption patterns diffuse downwards, from the superordinate to subordinate classes, from the higher orders to the lower.[10] For Veblen, writing in 1899 at the start of the massive 20th-century US industrial expansion, the superordinate capitalist class saw itself as inheriting the social position previously held by the landed aristocracy, which, in his account, identified itself by 'conspicuous abstention from work'. Leisure, in his illuminating phrase, was 'the badge of honour' for the previous superordinate class, and the capitalists who would displace them would also emulate their leisurely lifestyle. Here was another source for Keynes's 'leisure society' prediction: it wasn't simply that technical innovation would allow the satisfaction of human wants with less labour, but also that 'not working' could be construed as itself honourable by association with the leisurely habits of a once-dominant social class. This section discusses how the population's Great Day varies by social position, in addition to gender. We use a rather straightforward conceptualization, which simply identifies an individual's social position as measured by their level of education in years. Generally, those with high levels of economic, cultural and social capital also have high levels of education: for this reason, economists and sociologists often use years of education as a proxy for social position.

And we do see some trace of that leisure class/working class contrast in paid work in our very earliest surviving time-use data: in 1961, both men and women with higher education (leaving education at ages 21 and over) spent an hour or more *less* time per day in paid work as compared with those who left school at or under age 16, reflecting Veblen's positive class/ leisure gradient.

But fast forward 55 years to 2015, and we find an almost reversed relationship. Higher-educated women now do on average an hour more than the least educated. They are now more likely to be employed than non-employed, and more likely to be employed full-time than part-time. Men with no formal educational qualifications now spend less time on average in paid work per day than the better educated. This is partly because they are more likely to have no job, but, even on work days, well-educated men work slightly longer hours at their paid jobs than those with low levels of education, while the best-educated women have a margin of three-quarters of an hour more paid work than the less educated on work days.

The pattern for total unpaid work is rather different. For women, there is an even more convincing reversal, in which the most highly educated women in 1961 were doing half an hour *more* unpaid work than the least well-educated, but 20 minutes *less* unpaid work than less well-educated women in 2015. The reasons for these changes in unpaid work are further discussed in Chapter 5. Here we only note that they relate in complex ways both to women's progressive entry into the paid labour force during this period, and to the parallel development of gender-political debate about gender equality and discrimination (both in the workplace, but also within households), leading ultimately to progressive changes in law and public policy.

Our focus in this chapter is the consequences of these changes in paid and unpaid work for work in total. Paid employment on its own is important as the major source of money income. But our wants and needs are actually met *both* by the combination of the things that we can buy from the economy and the additional work we do to use these purchases to satisfy our wants. We need to do both sorts of work: the work time contracted within the economy, and the work time committed to the provision of needs outside it. So, most importantly, it is the two sorts of work *together* that will influence our feelings of work pressure.

When we add together the paid and unpaid work totals, and look at the outcomes according to educational level, we see the second half of the century-long process that has transformed the positive status/leisure gradient of the turn of the 20th century into the negative status/leisure gradient at the start of the 21st century. Figure 2.6 shows that in the 21st century, by a not inconsiderable margin, more highly educated men, and particularly, women, work on average, the longest total hours. According to Veblen's process of stratified diffusion – the *principle of emulation* – leisure, as the characteristic of the privileged class, was once the envy and hence the goal of the underprivileged. But now, the richest and most successful do

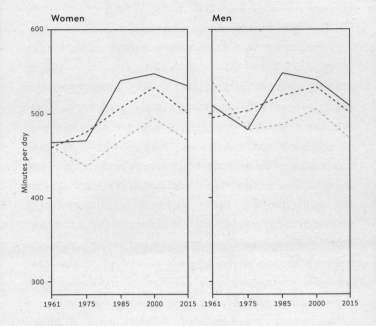

Figure 2.6
All work by school-leaving age: average minutes per day for
women and men aged 16–64, UK (1961–2015)

----- Left ≤ 16
----- Left ≤ 17–20
——— Left ≥ 21

not the least, but, by a considerable margin, the *most* work. Could this be, by that same principle of emulation, the ultimate source of the apparently growing reported feelings of time pressure related to 'busyness' in the UK (and indeed across the developed world)?

Time-diary materials, collecting exactly the same evidence on the allocation of time in both paid and unpaid work, are uniquely useful in allowing the 'all work' summary shown in Figure 2.6 – and also the overall gender work balance presented in Figure 2.7.

Various commentators have presented what is shown in Figure 2.7 in a relatively optimistic light as 'isowork' (the term is due to the US economist Daniel Hamermesh, and the general finding itself goes back at least to the British sociologists Michael Young and Peter Willmott in the 1970s).[11] In the more recent period, since the turn of the 21st century, men and women tend to do, on the aggregate, a reasonably similar broad total of work (this similarity is even more pronounced if just husbands and wives are analysed). Women's proportion of all work has increased slightly from below parity (46–48 per cent) in 1961 to parity by 2015 for both the lower-educational categories. However, for the highest-educated women, the proportion of total work by now slightly exceeds parity (at closer to 52 per cent).

But it is important to note here, in contrast to the more optimistic visions of 'isowork', that gender 'symmetry' in work time (this is the term that Young and Willmott used instead of 'isowork') is not gender equality. The key capabilities that determine life chances relate to paid work. Paid work capabilities are built up, and demonstrated to potential employers,

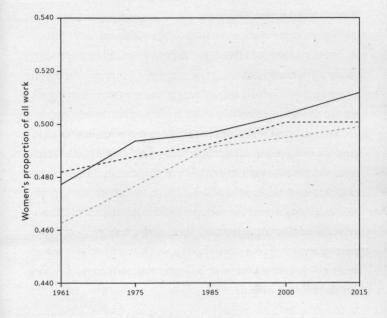

Figure 2.7
The women/men work ratio, by educational level, UK (1961–2015)

- - - - - Left ≤ 16
- - - - - Left ≤ 17–20
——— Left ≥ 21

by *participation* in employment. Paid work skills and, more important, reputations, are accumulated through time spent in work. Gender symmetry in the UK still means that men do a lot more paid work than women, while women do a lot more unpaid work. This means that women accumulate less paid work experience over time, and so are less well paid on average, and are less likely to be promoted, all contributing to the gender pay gap.

In addition, while the gender differences shown in Figure 2.7 are nowadays relatively small on aggregate, there are nonetheless clear and systematic changes in direction across time. And these aggregated averages hide much larger imbalances once we compare men and women at specific life stages. In particular, at the family formation stage in the 20–40 age groups, well-educated women with careers and children still find themselves with a multiple burden. Shouldering a disproportionate part of the total of a household's work at a crucial stage in their employment can have severely negative consequences for their future careers.

Comprehensive accounts of wellbeing: the importance of time

We have discussed how all of the consumption time, and all of the production time, in each society can be comprehensively described by representative time-diary samples. Time-use evidence provides the basis for thinking about chains of provision for the entire range of human needs in a more concrete and practical way than does the partial coverage of conventional economic statistics. By comprehensively summarizing the information provided by time-use diaries, the

Great Day forms the basis for a new approach to social science, more inclusive than either traditional economics or traditional sociology. It can integrate accounts of what goes on in 'the economy' with information on the division and balance of the 'extra-economic' activity more usually studied by sociologists. The minutes of the Great Day provide a time-based metric allowing direct empirical comparison across the full range of human activities, social contexts, locations and feelings of enjoyment, only a very few of which may be accounted for in money terms.

It also allows us to consider the *uses* of households' purchases of commodities in further production located strictly outside the money economy (whose output is included in the National Accounts). In the introduction to this chapter we mentioned several examples of economic activity moving out of conventional economic statistics – such as supermarket trips replacing the paid activities of retail workers – as well as movements in the opposite direction, in the shape of new jobs in the home delivery of internet orders, or, alternatively, in the shape of even newer well-paid work for designers and builders of home-delivery drone systems. A major area of research for national statistical institutes across the world is the design of systems for 'national income extension accounts'. There are several different sorts of these, covering various issues which are otherwise excluded from the conventional United Nations System of National Accounts – such as natural resource depletion and pollution effects of economic activity, both of which are ignored in conventional National Product accounts (such as GNP). One of the more important of these – important particularly given the strongly gendered distribution of unpaid work – involves valuing unpaid house-hold production (see Chapter 6).

The same diary evidence that we use for understanding the chains of provision for consumption provides materials that can contribute to other sorts of national accounts. The walk to the shops made by our mothers may have been one of the more enjoyable times of their days. The same sort of diary evidence that allows us to calculate durations of activities through the day is also, in our 2014–15 UK survey, used to collect direct evidence of the enjoyment or utility derived from the activity. We ask respondents, in addition to what they are doing at each point in time, to record how much they are enjoying what they are doing. This provides evidence from which we can calculate not just overall totals of enjoyment through the day, but also differences between the enjoyability of different activities for different people. As we see change in the distribution of different activities for different sorts of people over historical time, so, in Chapter 14, we find possible explanations for historical changes in the population's feelings of enjoyment or wellbeing that are related to their mix of daily activities rather than to their wealth.

That same walk to the shops also provided our mothers with exercise, of a sort that is lost when we drive to the super-market. So, in turn, the same data allow us to consider the consequences of lifestyle changes in physical activity for public health (Chapter 9). And the record of the number, frequency and spacing of meals (see Chapter 8) in diaries from different eras can give us clues about historical change in general nutrition status.

The Great Day, therefore, in summarizing everything done

by everyone in the society, provides the evidential basis for various new sorts of accounting for historical change. It allows us to produce economic accounts, extended to include the product of work that is not undertaken as part of any sort of exchange activity, and the exactly balancing (according to the theoretical definitions of economic inputs and outputs) value of the consumption that takes place outside the broadly drawn sphere of work. It also provides the raw material that allows us to estimate the extent of time devoted to nutrition and to all the various sorts of exercise and sedentary activity. It enables us to consider feelings of wellbeing and enjoyment, and their relationship to all the things we do during our days and nights. And we can in principle use these historical accounts and descriptions, in turn, as the base material for grounded speculation about the future – in the hope that in doing so we might help to promote better health, more wealth and greater wellbeing. We are now turning our minds to some serious economic and sociological futurology. But in this book, we seek merely to provide the prequel to this future: the most concrete and comprehensive recent description of each of the elements of time use that come together to constitute the Great Day of a society.

CHAPTER 3

The UK in Cross-national Context
—
Jonathan Gershuny
Kimberly Fisher

Is the UK population unusual in the way it uses its time? Can we draw conclusions from the analyses using UK data presented in this book to make wider inferences about changes in the daily lives of people in other, similar countries? We might think that we know roughly what the differences are between the UK and other countries in the time that we spend in paid work, in leisure time, or in housework, but how much of what we think we know is based on fact, rather than on assumptions (or, even, simple prejudice)? Here, we take a brief 'time out' from our UK narrative to fit UK daily-time use into the wider international picture. The following sections of this book delve deeper into some of the issues raised in the previous two chapters in relation to the UK historical sequence of time-use diary surveys. Here we present some snapshots of where the Great Day of the UK stands in relation to other similar countries in the necessary, committed, contractual and discretionary activities introduced in the previous chapter.

Alongside the UK data collection, the Centre for Time Use Research (CTUR) has brought together detailed diary descriptions of more than one million days, in around 90 different time-use surveys from 25 other countries into the Multi-national Time Use Study (MTUS). We have reorganized and harmonized these as far as we are able, to make them internationally comparable. In the following pages, the diary collections from a sample of a dozen of these countries – chosen because they provide a reasonably long-term historical picture of change across a wide variety of developed societies – are used to provide an international context for UK patterns and trends in the use of time. A range of quite different countries are featured, though all are relatively wealthy. Two large Anglophone nations are included, the USA and Australia, in addition to the UK. There are three mid-continental European countries: France, Germany and the Netherlands; three Scandinavian countries: Denmark, Finland and Norway; three southern European countries: Spain, Portugal and Italy; and (for the moment) a sole representative of the ex-COMECON developed nations, Slovenia. Because some of the earlier samples have somewhat restricted age ranges – and also to avoid the complications imposed by the general ageing of population structures – all the graphs in this section are based on populations aged 20–60.

Necessary, committed, contracted and discretionary activities across countries

We saw in the UK case in Chapter 2 that the expected recent decline in sleep time, predicted by some on the basis of the '24/7 society', simply did not happen. This also seems to be the case for the other dozen countries of our analysis. Figure 3.1 shows sleep time for all 13 countries (the UK and the 12 comparator countries). Sleep represents the largest component of the time necessary for human functioning (in fact, sleep time is described by the diarists as time spent in bed for naps or the night's sleep). There are some apparent sharp declines in sleep times for the first decade for which we have evidence (the 1960s). French men and women, for example, apparently reduced their sleep time by an average of 20 or 25 minutes between the 1960s and 1970s. But the surveys these estimates are based on have reached us with only rather limited documentation and we are uncertain whether this apparent change reflects real shifts in time use or, alternatively, differences in the way some activities are classified.[1]

By contrast, the evidence from the 1980s onwards in most of the other countries, as in the UK, suggests that sleep time has remained rather constant, or has been somewhat increasing. For these more recent decades, and for most of the surveys covered, we have quite high-quality documentation and are more certain of how the activity categorizations have been made. The UK shows a particularly large dip in sleep time from the 1970s to the 1980s that might reflect some problems related to the selection of the 1980s UK sample. But if we ignore this and look just at the 1970s, 2000s and 2015 time points in the UK, we see a gentle rise; for men from 487 minutes to 504 minutes, for women from 500 to 513 minutes. The changes seen during the last decade and a half are barely statistically significant. And this UK trajectory is similar to that of most other countries: generally, constant or gently rising sleep time over recent decades.

In absolute terms, time in bed for the Danish population seems to lie a clear 10 (for women) and 20 (for men) minutes below that for all the other countries. We have no explanation for this, but suspect it may be an as-yet-undetected difference in the procedures used for coding the diaries. But, generally, the range of national mean sleep times lie within a remarkably narrow band, between 480 and 510 minutes on average, and country by country remains relatively constant, with overall changes (mostly increases) of no more than 10 or 20 minutes.

One striking regularity emerges when we compare the two sub-panels of Figure 3.1, for men and women respectively. It appears that women, across our multinational samples, have just a little more sleep time than do men. Women have less sleep than men in only three of the 48 surveys in our 13-country comparison. Women's sleep advantage over men is small but regular – ranging from 1 per cent to 5 per cent. This persistent gender difference in sleep time is only observable by comparing historical diary studies and is essentially impossible to detect except with a large collection of time-use studies of this kind.

As far as we know, this result has not been previously identified. The small size of the margin, compared with its very high level of persistence, suggests that it is unlikely to reflect a general sociological cause such as women focusing more on the domestic sphere as compared to men. If this were the explanation, we would expect to see more variation in the scale, reflecting other intervening national differences in, for example, the proportion of women in employment – or indeed systematic national differences in the way men and women report their sleep time. Could there be a physiological explanation, an underlying genetically determined requirement for sleep, producing an approximately constant requirement for sleep, with a small but regular addition associated with being female?

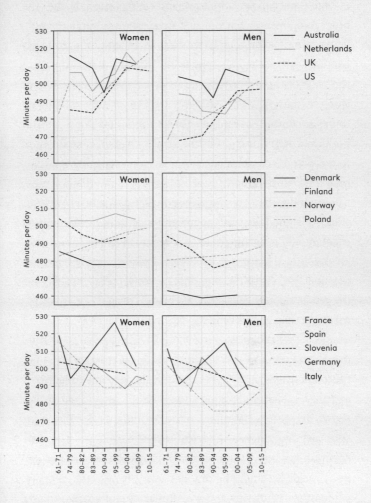

Figure 3.1
Necessary time: sleep in 13 countries

Time spent in personal care and eating time at home (the other components of 'necessary' time)[2] shows a similarly regular pattern of advantage to women, again with only three exceptions across the 48 surveys (not shown). But in this case the scale of the difference is rather larger, and the range of women's margin over men is much more variable, ranging up to 15 per cent in Finland in the late 1990s and 12 per cent in both the UK and the US in the 2010s. Overall, time devoted to this pair of activities has either remained roughly constant or somewhat declined (at around 2 hours per day for men, 2 hours and 30 minutes for women). Given that in most countries, as in the UK, time spent eating at home has declined substantially over this period for *both* men and women, women's additional margin of time in this activity clearly relates to personal care (bathing, dressing, personal toilet): in this case the gender difference is more likely to be related to a sociological rather than a physiological explanation.

Altogether the most remarkable long-term change in time use, in the UK and the 12 comparator countries alike, is in the 'committed' time represented by the 'general housework' category (cooking, cleaning and household maintenance), as shown in Figure 3.2. Women in the UK and the US – the countries with the longest historical series of time-use surveys – spent on average 1 hour and 30 minutes or 2 hours per day less time doing this type of work over the past half-century, while other countries show a similar rate of change over a shorter window of observation. Women in the UK appear to lie quite squarely in the middle of the pack in this respect.

One thing that patently does *not* explain the reduction in women's general housework time is men's general housework

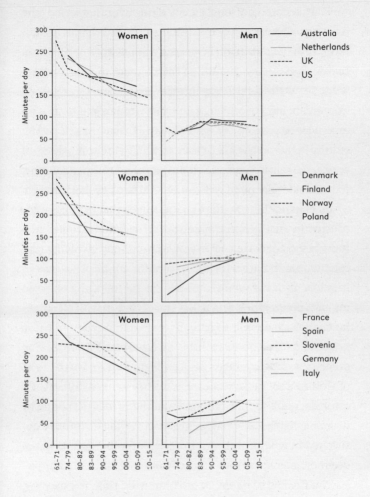

Figure 3.2
Committed time: unpaid cooking and cleaning and other
domestic activity

time. This rises in almost all countries over the period, and more than doubles in some. But it starts from a much lower level, with the reduction in women's housework occurring at two or three times the rate of the increase in men's housework. So, while it is the case that the gender balance of general housework has become less unequal, women still do in general twice as much or more of this work than men do. Noteworthy in this is the case of Italy, in which (in the most recent survey currently available to us) women still spend almost four times longer per day doing general housework than men.

Of course, there is more to the committed time category of activities than general housework activities. The largest additional element is care-type activities, mostly involving care for children, but also including care for adults. These activities take up 30 to 50 minutes per day for men, and 60 to 90 minutes per day for women. But since barely half of all households include people to care *for*, men and women in those households that do *any* caring spend around twice as long doing it as these averages suggest. Figure 3.3 shows the ratio of women's to men's time spent in care work. Again, we see some decrease in most countries in the proportion done by women over the past half-century, with the UK roughly positioned in mid-table, both in terms of level and of rate of decline.

The final large category of committed time is shopping, involving 20 to 25 minutes per day for men, and 30 to 35 minutes per day for women, but in this case (unlike for care time) it is an activity done by almost all households. As for care time, in the women to men ratios shown in Figure 3.4 we see some gender convergence, with, in most countries, women's

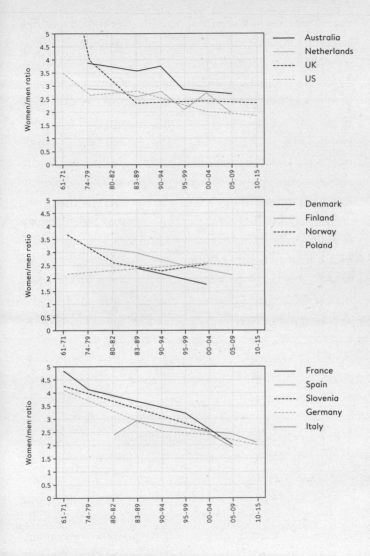

Figure 3.3
Women/men ratio in child and adult care

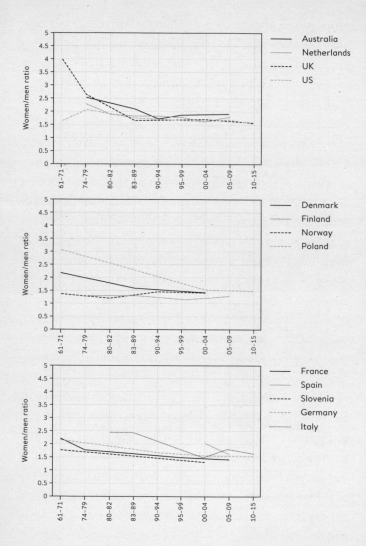

Figure 3.4
Women/men ratio in shopping time

proportional contribution declining to around 50 per cent higher than men's. Here again, with a women/men shopping time ratio of 1.5, the UK is placed pretty much in the centre of the group of comparator countries.

To sum up, although all three of the broad categories of committed time show gender convergence, all three still also display a substantial remaining gender disparity, with men doing, overall, much less unpaid work than women.

Figure 3.5 shows the changing totals of paid work for men and women (it also incorporates time in education, to take account of the enormous growth of higher education in most of these countries over the 55-year period). Trends in paid work time by gender to some extent present the mirror image of the trends in general housework time shown in Figure 3.2 (although this isn't entirely so because, while time spent in general housework is by far the largest component of women's unpaid labour time, the same is not the case for men, for whom shopping and caring time represents a much larger proportion of unpaid work time).

We again see a quite striking consistency between the UK and the 12 comparators in Figure 3.5. This is upset, once again, by the mid-1980s UK sample – without which we would find a smoothly declining total for men's paid work among 12 of our 13 countries: from around 400 to 450 minutes per day of paid work in the 1960s to around 300 minutes paid work per day in the 2010s, with UK men located pretty well in the middle of the group. (We might alternatively consider that the UK men's paid work estimate in the mid-1980s is rather similar to that of the Netherlands, and that subsequently men's paid work time in the Netherlands quite closely tracks that

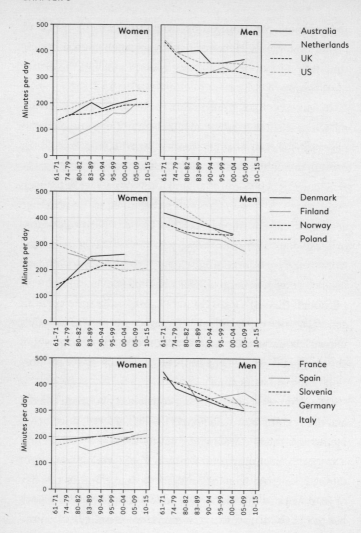

Figure 3.5
Contracted time: average minutes per day in paid work or full-time education

of the UK.) Nevertheless, the general story for men's paid work is quite clear: a slow general decline in average work time, of perhaps 20 minutes per decade. Women's paid work time by contrast (and with the singular exception of Portugal) either rises, or remains relatively steady. Women in the Netherlands, virtually all outside the paid labour force at the start, are now almost exactly converged with UK women's employment levels (and with a similar prevalence of part-time work). Again, the UK finds itself pretty much in the middle of the comparator countries.

Figure 3.6 adds together all the leisure and consumption activities to display trends in 'discretionary' or 'uncommitted' time. It shows a surprisingly tightly bunched plot of leisure trends across the 13 country samples. With the exception of Australia, which (for reasons we still do not fully understand) shows an overall decline in leisure time since the 1990s, we see a reasonably straightforward pattern of gender convergence, at around 400 and 350 minutes per day for men and women (who are part compensated by extra time spent in sleep and in personal care) respectively. The overall trend resembles not so much an inverted-U shape, as a shallow inverted J-shape. It appears that leisure and consumption time – the residual once 'necessary, committed and contracted' time has been account-ed for – was generally increasing from the 1960s to the 1980s. But over the following 30 years leisure time seemed to stabil-ize, or even gently decrease. The UK has a relatively high level of leisure time, but its total has also been falling slowly since the mid-1980s. So we get back, finally, to the issue we raised in the introductory section to this book: is there any evidence at all that we are moving towards a society of leisure?

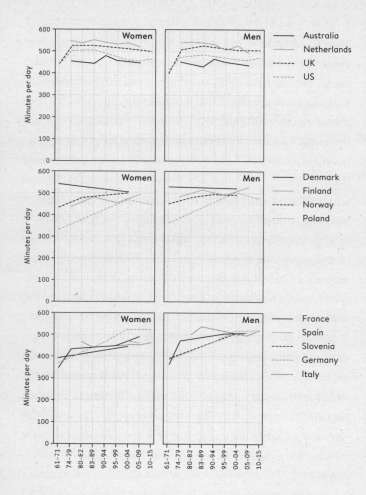

Figure 3.6
Discretionary time: average minutes per day in all leisure and consumption

Summarizing the Great Day

Here we can take full advantage of the 'adding up to 24 hours' characteristic of time-use data representing the population's Great Day. We have discussed the evolution of sleep and personal care. We have discussed paid and unpaid work. We have discussed leisure and necessary personal care. We can bring all these different sorts of time together into a single analysis, in the form of a 'life-balance triangle' graph. Figure 3.7, showing the central part of this triangle, plots paid work, unpaid work and non-work time into the two dimensions of the graph. Twenty-six trend lines, each representing the time trend for men or women from each of our 13 countries, are plotted on to the graph. In the vertical dimension, up and down the page, we have the split between work and non-work time (non-work time is calculated by adding together sleep and personal care, and all leisure time), expressed as a ratio of all time. The further up the vertical dimension, the greater is the proportion of the Great Day spent in non-work, as opposed to work. The horizontal axis of the triangle is calculated as the ratio of paid work to the total of paid plus unpaid work. The further along the horizontal axis, the greater the proportion of paid work time, as opposed to unpaid work time. To avoid confusion in the graph, only the first and last survey data points for each country are plotted.

Firstly, we see two distinct clusters of lines, one on either side of the 0.5 vertical dimension running up the centre of the graph (indicating the proportion of all work time spent in paid work). To the left are the lines for women, and to the right those for men. This simply reflects the fact that, on

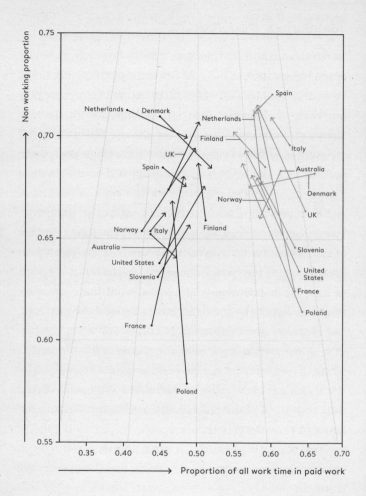

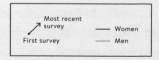

Figure 3.7
Less work time (mostly) and
more gender equality

average, men do mostly paid work, and women mostly unpaid. Second, we can see that both groups of lines lie roughly between the 0.6 and 0.7 level of the vertical non-work as opposed to work proportion – which corresponds nicely to the expectation that the Great Day should be divided roughly equally between work, leisure and rest, with the slight emphasis on leisure and rest (including sleep, of course). Third, the men's and women's lines are approximately at the same level on the vertical axis – with the men marginally higher, indicating a slightly higher average of leisure and rest time.

Of the 26 arrow-lines, 23 indicate movement towards lower levels of gender segregation in overall work patterns. Twelve of the 13 lines for men indicate movement from higher proportions of paid work towards lower – i.e. moving to the left of their initial positions (the exception here is the Netherlands). Similarly, 11 of the 13 women's arrow-lines indicate movement to the right away from unpaid work in the direction of a higher proportion of paid work – the exceptions here being Portugal and Finland, both of which show small shifts towards unpaid work. The intermediate survey points in the data series, not plotted in Figure 3.7, do not change this account in any substantial way.

Movements in the vertical, work/non-work, dimension are more divided. Nine of the 13 men's, and (from the same countries) nine of the 13 women's arrow-lines move upwards from the base of the triangle, indicating a reduction in overall work time. And, given that we saw only small changes in the totals of sleeping, eating and personal care in Figures 3.1–3, this indicates a general increase in leisure time. The four exceptions are Netherlands, Spain, Denmark and Australia, all of which experienced a decrease of non-work (leisure and rest) time.

In the case of the work/non-work distinction, when we include all the intermediate observations between the earliest and the latest survey dates, we see reversals in the directions of change, with sometimes larger, sometimes smaller, proportions of time spent in work – not apparent in the simple plot shown in Figure 3.7. So, while the first of the two trends – the reduction in the gender segregation of paid and unpaid work (horizontal dimension) – is a strong regularity, the trend towards a reduction in the overall proportion of work is less convincing (vertical dimension).

Finally, compare the arrowheads for women and men for each country. These mark the data point for the most recent survey for each country. For every country except Denmark and the Netherlands, the men's arrowheads are higher than the women's, indicating an overall advantage in access to leisure and rest for men over women. In most cases this advantage is not all that large, a matter of one or two percentage points. But we should take note of Italy, where the difference is something like 5 per cent, and Spain, where the difference is around 4 per cent. In these cases, the excess of total work for women is still a significant reality. But arguably, even in these cases, the division of work and non-work time is perhaps not the *most* important issue. Compare the gender differences for each country in the up–down dimension, with the large gap between women and men on the left–right dimension. The latter measures the relative degree of engagement of men and women in paid work time, or the money economy. The wider the left–right gap, the higher on average is men's paid work experience relative to women's. Pay and promotions are both to a considerable degree determined by work experience. So, even where the vertical difference in the total of work time compared to non-work time is small, the wider the horizontal distance between men and women in any given country the higher we might expect the gender wage gap there to be. Once the 'vertical' difference between men's and women's overall work time has dwindled, this horizontal difference in the paid/unpaid work balance becomes the central key issue for gender equality.

PART TWO

Paid and Unpaid Work

Our Working Lives
Paid Working Time

—

Pierre Walthery

The question of how much paid work is carried out in the UK is more complex than it may appear. For a start, we have to decide what to include in the definition of work.[1] Our working lives are made up of multiple intertwined sets of routines, rhythms and trajectories that are not easy to measure and describe.[2] Furthermore, these routines and schedules are determined within a web of social relations that also involve micro- and macro-economic as well as technological dynamics.[3] Time-use diaries have the considerable advantage of recording the working time of respondents in quasi real-time, as most people complete their diaries on the day of their diary. This undoubtedly represents a significant improvement on the instruments that experts have previously relied upon, such as the Labour Force Survey, which have involved recall-based, self-assessed estimates of respondents' weekly hours of work.[4]

In time-use diary data, paid work is for the most part recorded as a single activity, the distribution of which may be analysed across days and weeks. But there is also some differentiation of the time we spend at work; we can distinguish between main and second jobs, work breaks and other work-related activities. These additions represent a clear improvement over the data supplied in conventional surveys.[5]

How much do we really work?

We can get a sense of the magnitude of paid work in national daily life by noting that, on average, work-related activities in the UK in 2014–15 represented more than 19 per cent of the total time reported by men and 12 per cent of the time reported by women, excluding sleep. Figure 4.1 shows four work-related activities: working time in the main job; working time in a second job; work breaks; and other work-related activities according to gender, and whether the work happened during the week or at weekends. Not surprisingly, 'working time in main job' represents the lion's share of paid work-related time that is reported.

As expected, the overall average time spent in paid work at the weekend was shorter than during weekdays, with the exception of working time in a second job for men, which was higher at the weekend. It seems that second jobs for men tend to involve weekend work. Breaks at work (for coffee, tea and meals) lasted between 40–45 minutes on average, and the time didn't vary by gender, or between weeks and weekends. The gap between men's and women's working day stands out – the working time of men in their main job lasted on average 45–50 minutes longer than women's, both during the week and at the weekend. Women also spent longer overall doing a second job than men (although this difference is only statistically significant during weekdays). Both at the weekend and during weekdays, men spent more than twice the time travelling for

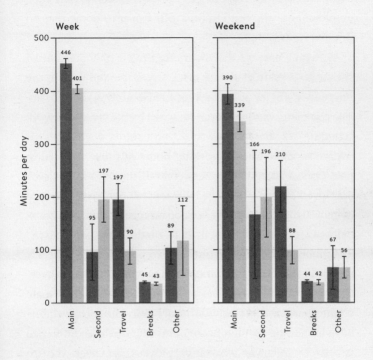

Figure 4.1

Paid daily working time by work-related activity type: women and men aged 16–64, UK (2015)

■ Men
■ Women

work. While this may appear to contradict the widely held idea that couples tend to move to be closer to 'his' job, it is in fact likely to reflect the high proportions of women in part-time employment, who tend to find jobs closer to home that do not involve travelling.

However, average daily working time is only one side of the story. Weekly hours are also important, and remain the reference point for policymaking and labour-market analyses. The complete weekly records provided by the seven-day work schedule associated with the time-use diary provides an overview of the weekly working hours of those engaged in paid work. Distinguishing between full-time, part-time, self-employed and employed respondents shows that full-time employed men and women work on average 40.2 and 37.3 hours per week respectively, as against 26.1 and 23.8 for part-timers.[6] The gender gap in working time is also confirmed at the weekly level: full-time and part-time working women work on average 3 hours and 2 hours and 30 minutes less than their male counterparts respectively (although only the former difference is statistically significant). Another obvious difference is between men who work as employees and those who are self-employed. On average the latter work over 3 more hours per week, feeding into the image of the hard-working self-employed small business man. This difference, however, is not found among women.

On the accuracy of weekly working-time estimates from time-use diaries

The accuracy of instruments used for measuring paid work time is of great importance given the significance of such estimates for policymaking. The UK 2014–2015 Time Use Survey (TUS) provides us with an opportunity to look at differences between estimates produced using the week-long work schedule and stylized estimates from the TUS questionnaire and other surveys, such as the Labour Force Survey (LFS), in which respondents are asked to provide an estimate of their total weekly paid work time. We compared both stylized and work-schedule measures from the TUS with the 2015 Annual Population Survey (APS), in effect an annual version of the Labour Force Survey, which is the main source for labour-market analysis in the UK. The APS has a large sample size (N>300,000), and asks respondents to estimate the actual hours they worked during a reference week. We found two outstanding differences between the traditional questionnaire- and work-schedule-based estimates of working time. In general, full-time work both for men and women seems to be overestimated in the APS, whereas the opposite is true for part-time work. Men who worked full-time reported 42.9 weekly working hours in the APS, versus 40.2 hours in the weekly work schedule, while full-time women reported 39.3 hours compared to 37.3 hours in the work schedule. Self-reported weekly hours of work from the TUS stylized question were, however, closer to the APS estimate than that derived from the work schedule. On the other hand, women working part-time reported 20.1 hours in the APS compared to 23.8 hours in the weekly work schedule (and 21.6 hours in the stylized TUS question).

It appears that some of the explanation for these contrasts may be found in the variability and predictability of weekly schedules. For example, when only APS respondents who stated that their working time tended not to vary from week to week were included in the analysis, the differences between them and the UK TUS 2014–15 respondents disappeared. Ongoing research has also revealed that for a small number of key occupations, significant differences between the LFS and the TUS exist by gender: women in elementary, as well as in caring and leisure occupations, and men in associate professional occupations tend to overestimate their weekly working time by several hours.[7] This in part confirms previous findings by the Office for National Statistics.[8]

Do we work more or less over time?

The accepted wisdom is that *annual* working time has decreased at least since the Second World War, while average weekly working time has remained stable.[9] The implication is that people are working less throughout the year (perhaps taking more holiday or sick time), playing into a rhetoric of decreasing productivity and a 'lazy' workforce. However, these assessments were based on estimates from traditional surveys, and, as discussed above, we have the opportunity here to compare these estimates with those based on time-diary data.

Figure 4.2 shows the long-term evolution in weekday and weekend daily working time from 1961 onwards using the UK historical time-use survey sequence. For both men and women, the time spent doing paid work at the weekend (dashed grey line) has risen since the 1980s, with some tailing off in the rate of increase from the turn of the 21st century. Over the same period the average daily working time during weekdays for those men who were working full-time (the great majority, represented by the plain black line) rose until the turn of

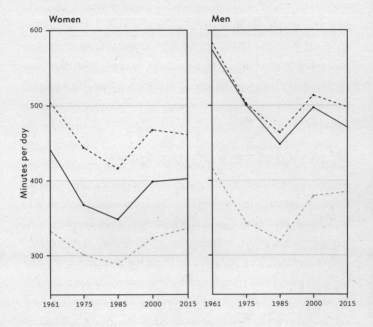

Figure 4.2
Trends in average daily paid working time: women and men
aged 16—64, UK (1961–2015)

——— Weekdays
----- Weekdays (full-timers)
----- Weekend

the 21st century and then fell somewhat subsequently. The change at the turn of the 21st century is clearly gendered: while men's daily working time decreased sharply, that of women remained more stable (although there was a greater decline for full-time employed women than for part-time). These differences may be due to the increase in atypical work contracts for certain socio-demographic groups of men. Overall, if current trends continue, we could see increasing convergence of the daily working time of men and women in the coming decades.

If we focus in on the period between 2000 and 2015, spanning the economic crash of 2008, we find considerable differences in these trends according to employment status. Overall, employed men's daily working time remained stable at just under 500 minutes of paid work per day (not shown). Employed women's daily working time rose by half an hour from 408 to 438 minutes per day, an increase that is largely due to more paid work time among part-timers. In contrast, the average daily time spent in paid work by the self-employed decreased over the first 15 years of the 21st century – by half an hour on average for men (from 478 to 443 minutes per day), and by an hour on average for women (from 361 to 301 minutes per day). This trend is likely to be associated with the increase in less secure forms of self-employment that followed the economic recession.

This declining trend in average daily hours of paid work is also matched by a decrease in weekly working time between 2000 and 2015 for men, from an average of 42.0 to 40.7 hours per week (not shown).[10] The bulk of this change occurred among men working full-time, whose weekly hours of work decreased. On the other hand, no statistically significant change in weekly working time was visible among women working either full- or part-time. Putting all this together across the days of the working week, Figure 4.3 shows that, when all work-related activities are included, the overall decline in men's working time results from a decrease in the average duration of the working day during weekdays (with, in contrast, an increase of about 30 minutes at the weekend). In particular, average working time on Mondays and Tuesdays has shrunk more than during the rest of the week. These changes amount to what would appear to be an erosion of the traditional working week for men since the turn of the 21st century. For women, the only statistically significant change occurs on Wednesdays, when work times have increased. Interestingly, though, the stability in overall working time across the week among women is due in part to an increase in the time spent in second jobs. When only time in the main job is taken into account, a decrease not dissimilar to that of men is seen. All these changes point to a process of erosion in traditional working patterns; in the following section we investigate how these changes have played out across different occupations and educational levels, representing different social and economic subgroups of the population.

Occupation, education and work in the 21st century

Figure 4.4 shows gender differences in daily and weekly working time across Standard Occupational Classification

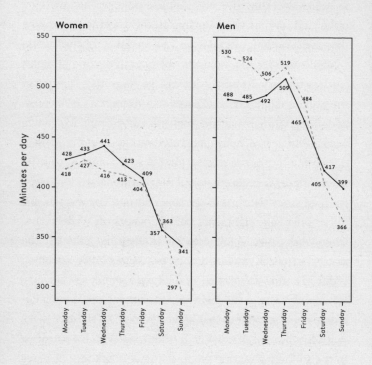

Figure 4.3
Paid daily working time (all work-related activities) by day of
the week: women and men aged 16–64, UK (1961–2015)

----- 2000
——— 2015

(SOC2000) occupations for men working full-time and women working both full- and part-time (part-time men were excluded due to low sample numbers). Focusing first on daily working time (left-hand panel of Figure 4.4), men employed full-time as machine operatives worked for an hour longer on average than those employed in professional and managerial occupations (8 hours 53 minutes on average per day as against 7 hours 49 minutes). For women employed full-time, the longest average day was also observed among machine operatives (8 hours 38 minutes), while the shortest day was for those in the skilled trades (7 hours 7 minutes). The duration of the working day for women employed part-time was shortest for those working in elementary occupations (4 hours 36 minutes), and longest for managers (6 hours 38 minutes).

The right-hand-side panel of Figure 4.4 shows the average length of the working week from the weekly work schedule. There is a difference of almost 8 hours across occupations between the longest and shortest working weeks for women employed full-time. Female managers and professionals, at one extreme of the occupational hierarchy, had the longest average working weeks, at 40–42 hours, while the shortest average working weeks were recorded among administrative occupations and skilled trades (32 hours). For men working full-time, the difference between the occupation extremes was narrower – 4-6 hours – ranging between those employed in caring and leisure (44 hours on average), those employed in sales and customer services (40 hours) and those in administrative occupations (around 38 hours). While women employed part-time also worked fewer average hours over the week, those in skilled or elementary trades had the shortest

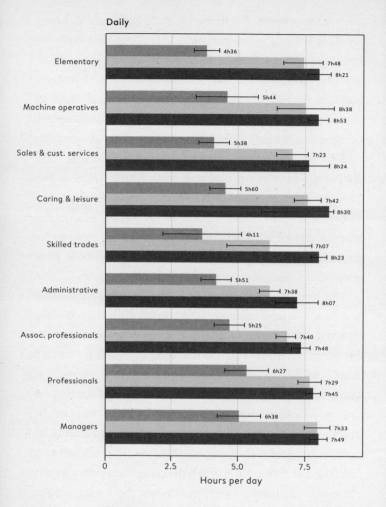

Daily

Figure 4.4
Daily and weekly paid working time by occupation:
men and women aged 16–64, UK (2015)

■ Part-time women
■ Full-time women
■ Full-time men

Weekly

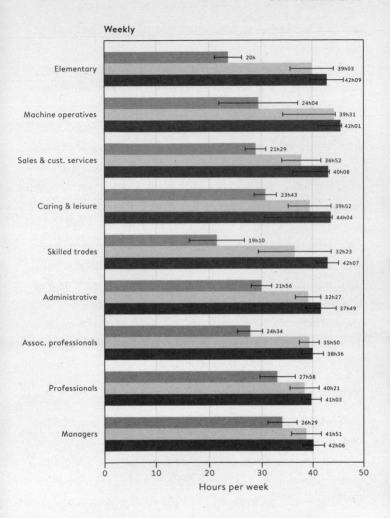

Elementary	20h / 39h03 / 42h09
Machine operatives	24h04 / 39h31 / 42h01
Sales & cust. services	21h29 / 36h52 / 40h08
Caring & leisure	23h43 / 39h52 / 44h04
Skilled trades	19h10 / 32h23 / 42h07
Administrative	21h56 / 32h27 / 37h49
Assoc. professionals	24h34 / 35h50 / 38h36
Professionals	27h58 / 40h21 / 41h03
Managers	26h29 / 41h51 / 42h06

0   10   20   30   40   50

Hours per week

Part-time women
Full-time women
Full-time men

working weeks (19–20 hours), compared to professionals or managers (26–28 hours).

Figure 4.5 shows differences in working times by educational level. Particularly notable in relation to daily working time (top panel), women with no secondary school qualifications employed part-time had significantly shorter days than equivalent degree holders (5 hours and 31 minutes against 5 hours 50 minutes). Differences in weekly working time by education were more marked than for daily working times, both within and between genders: low-qualified men in full-time employment reported working on average one hour and a half more per week than degree holders (41 hours 49 minutes compared to 40 hours 20 minutes), while, in contrast, only among part-time employed women did those with degree qualifications work longer hours than other women. Thus, the gap between the weekly working times of employed men and women grows wider as one moves from higher to lower levels of educational qualification.

Who works unsocial hours?

In terms of subjective experience, the schedules people follow over their working week may be more important than the daily or weekly average amount of time they spend at work. A recurrent question has been the extent to which the 'standard working week' (understood as a nine-to-five or eight-to-four working day over five weekdays) is being eroded by the gradual emergence of atypical work patterns such as zero-hours contracts or flexible working arrangements.[11] In this section we describe patterns of atypical work among respondents of the 2014–15 TUS, with the focus on 'unsocial' hours. These

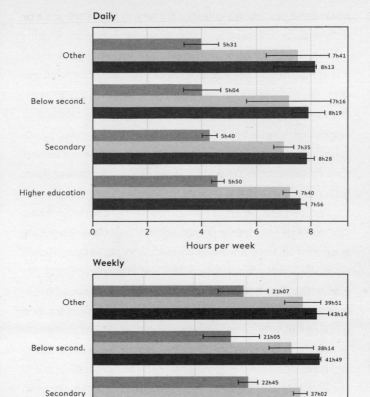

Figure 4.5
Daily and weekly paid working time by education:
men and women aged 16–64, UK (2015)

■ Part-time women
■ Full-time women
■ Full-time men

hours have particular relevance for health and work-life balance policies. Unsocial hours are generally defined to include working early in the morning, late in the evening, or at the weekend.[12] If we take a definition of standard hours that encompasses any work between 8am and 6pm during the week, and no work at the weekend – we find that, as a percentage of respondents' total weekly working time, working during unsocial hours is still quite limited in extent, with overall more than 77 per cent of respondents' working time taking place within standard hours.

The top panel of Figure 4.6 shows the time spent working any unsocial hours as a percentage of total weekly working time for full-time men and women, and part-time women from the weekly work schedules. For example, only 15 per cent of the time that women employed full-time spend working takes place during unsocial hours. The equivalent for men working full-time is 19 per cent.

On the other hand, we also find that between two-thirds and three-quarters of respondents report at least *some* unsocial hours during the week of their work schedule. The bottom panel of Figure 4.6 shows the percentage of respondents who report working at least one hour in any one of the categories of unsocial working hours: before 8am, after 6pm, and at the weekend. It also shows the percentages involved in *any* category of unsocial hours, as well as the percentage who work standard hours. Firstly, men working full-time are the most likely to work outside standard hours at some point during the week; 76.6 per cent of such men record some unsocial working before 8am, after 6pm or at weekends. This contrasts with 68.5 per cent of women working full-time. Women

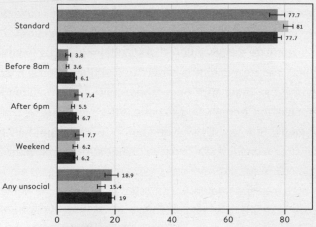

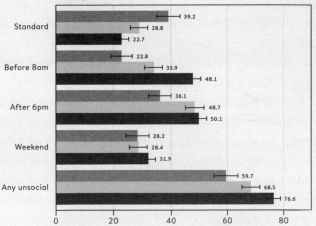

Figure 4.6

Standard and unsocial paid weekly working time:
men and women aged 16–64 who worked during
the week, UK (2015)

- Part-time women
- Full-time women
- Full-time men

working part-time were the least likely (59.7 per cent) to work unsocial hours (they are also the group known to have the lion's share of childcare duties within their households).[13]

In terms of the percentage of respondents involved (bottom panel), the most common pattern of working unsocial hours involved working after 6pm (about half of full-time working men and women, and 36 per cent of part-time working women), followed by working before 8am (again, half of full-time men, but only between one quarter to one third of women). Weekend work was reported by around 30 per cent of both men and women. On the other hand, part-time women spent a slightly higher percentage of their working hours working after 6pm and at weekends than either full-time men or women (see top panel). In relation to gender differences, the general conclusion is that full-time employed women are less likely to work unsocial hours than equivalent men, with part-time women spending a higher percentage of their working time during unsocial hours.

Focusing in on how unsocial hours are related to dimensions of inequality such as occupation and education, there is a clear relationship to occupational hierarchy, with additional differences by gender (see Figure 4.7). Men at the bottom of the social scale of occupations – that is, those in elementary occupations; machine operatives; those employed in caring and leisure; and those in sales and customer services – spent between 28 per cent and one third of their weekly working time during unsocial hours. This contrasts sharply with the working time of professionals, managers and administrators, who spent between 10 and 18 per cent of their weekly working time working unsocial hours. The trend is similar among

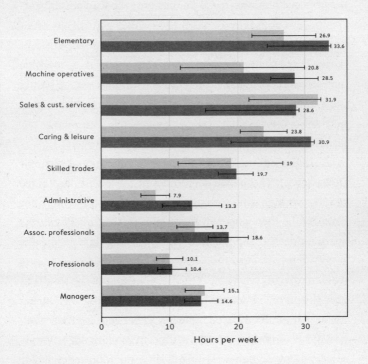

Figure 4.7
Unsocial paid working time by occupation: populations aged 16–64 who worked during the week, UK (2015)

Women
Men

women, with differences ranging from 31.9 per cent of working time spent in unsocial hours for those in sales and customer services occupations, to 7.9 per cent for those in administrative occupations. On average, the gender gap within occupations tends to be wider at the lower end of the scale of occupational status: at one extreme men employed as machine operatives reported spending close to 10 percentage points more of their working time during unsocial hours than women machinists (28.5 against 20.8 per cent), while little gender difference was found among professionals and managers.

A similar picture is seen across the educational gradient (not shown). Those with degrees spent the lowest percentage of their working time working unsocial hours (15.5–18.3 per cent), while men who didn't complete GCSE qualifications spent more than 27 per cent of their working time during unsocial hours. An even more extreme gradient is seen among women working part-time. Only 18.3 per cent of the time that part-time women degree holders spent working was during unsocial hours, compared to nearly 37 per cent for those who had only completed GCSEs. Differences were slightly narrower among women working full-time, but followed a similar trend. A clear age gradient (not shown) is also present, with young people spending a higher proportion of their working hours before 8am, after 6pm or at the weekend.

By including similar data from the weekly work schedule for 2000, we are also able to discern changes in the percentage of employees working unsocial hours in the UK across the first decade of the 21st century. To summarize, there is an increase in the percentage of people – especially women – reporting unsocial work hours, with a concomitant decrease in those working standard hours. These overall changes reflect two opposing trends: a smaller percentage of respondents worked at the weekend in 2015 than in 2000, especially among those working full-time, but at the same time there was an increase in the percentage either working after 6pm or before 8am In 2000, for example, 45.3 per cent of full-time men worked after 6pm, compared to nearly 48 per cent of women. By 2015, the percentage for both men and women had risen by more than 7 percentage points, to 55 per cent for full-time women and 53.8 per cent for men. An even larger increase occurred for female part-timers over the same period. In general, these findings are consistent with the thesis of an erosion of the standard working week and a growth in atypical working patterns over the period framing the 2008 economic recession.

To sum up, a number of interesting features of the current configurations and trends in working times in the UK today are revealed by these analyses. Firstly, gender differences in the intensity of participation in the labour market remain entrenched, with women in many cases working shorter days and weeks than men. At the same time, however, women continue to catch up with men, both in terms of their overall daily and weekly working times, as well as in their propensity to work at the weekend, early in the morning or in the evening. Secondly, there remains a clear divide in both daily average working times (calculated from the time-use diary) and weekly hours (calculated from the weekly work schedule) along the dimensions of gender, occupation and education. Lower-qualified men and/or those working at the bottom of the occupational pyramid tend to work longer days and spend a greater percentage of their working time during unsocial hours. In contrast, more highly qualified women tend to work longer weekly hours. However, as for men, those with lower qualifications spend a greater percentage of their working time during unsocial hours. Thirdly, there has been a clear increase in the number of men and women working unsocial hours since the turn of the 21st century, pointing to the erosion of standard work patterns over the period of the economic crash.

On the methodological side, systematic differences were found in relation to working time estimated from recall- and work schedule-based instruments. Our results confirm that there is an overestimation of work time in traditional surveys for full-time employees, but also point to a possible underestimate among part-timers. The fact that work-time estimates obtained with stylized questions in several surveys all contrast with the seven-day work schedule included in the 2015 TUS hints that the latter may indeed be capturing something that has previously been missed in official statistics.

CHAPTER 5

Dividing Domestic Labour and Care

—

Oriel Sullivan
Evrim Altintas

The division of domestic labour refers to the division of unpaid household work and care between household or family members. It is part of, and is related to, the wider domestic division of labour, which describes the division of paid and unpaid work between family members.[1] In common parlance, it's about the 'who does how much of what around the house' question that forms the focus of so many marital discussions, negotiations and disputes. In fact, who does the housework has long been recognized as being a major source of emotion and conflict about fairness and equity within partnerships.[2] A recent BBC *Woman's Hour* online survey tool, to which the Centre for Time Use Research contributed, allowed partners to assess their own domestic divisions of labour. With this tool, respondents rate their own and their partner's contributions to domestic chores like cooking, cleaning, laundry and grocery shopping. Jane Garvey of *Woman's Hour* put it this way: 'Anecdotally women say, "We are exhausted and he's lazy!" But is it true? If you are in charge of putting out the bins, does that mean you get off the ironing? How many rows are rooted in anger and resentment about who does what in our homes and how often?' The so-called 'Chore Wars calculator' shows how much interest, and emotion, this subject can generate.

When feminist sociologists started to look within the 'black box' of the family in the 1960s and 70s, they revealed the hidden burden of 'women's work', and the boredom and isolation that went with having main responsibility for looking after the home.[3] Up to that point, the division of the paid and unpaid work necessary to the functioning of a 'typical' (heterosexual nuclear family) household had been treated in academic research as relatively unproblematic. Economists had tended to see it in terms of rational decision-making – it was rational that the person who could earn the highest wage (at that time, almost always the man) should be in paid employment, while the person with lower qualifications and potential wages (almost always the woman) would look after the home. Since that time, the extent and significance of this 'women's burden' has become a major area of sociological research, and a recent focus of media attention, with many column inches devoted to persisting gender inequality in the home, and how it might be remedied. It has also been a topic of great relevance to the development of national policies around parental leave and childcare. In addition, the growing awareness of the contribution of unpaid domestic work to national economies has meant that the valuation of unpaid work and care within the home is now in many countries becoming an important feature of national accounting (see Chapter 6).

Research into the division of domestic labour and care over the past half-century in all areas of the world has shown that women still do the vast majority of family work in heterosexual couples, and that, despite some changes in the direction of greater gender equality, this pattern persists in the face of increasing female employment. However, while the cross-sectional gap in the domestic labour and care done by women and men is still large, the main trends that have been observed over the past half-century are: 1) a substantial decline in women's domestic work time; 2) a slight increase in men's domestic work time; and 3) large increases in time devoted to childcare for both sexes. The overall result of these trends has been a convergence in the direction of greater gender equality in the division of unpaid work and care.[4]

Of course, overall trends across the whole population can hide a myriad of differences between various population sub-groups. Researchers who have reviewed the factors affecting unpaid work across the previous decades agree that, among the major factors affecting the amount of time that women and men spend in domestic work and care are family and employment status, and educational level.[5] In general, those who are employed do less housework and care than those who are not employed (particularly less than women who are staying at home to care for children), while paid work hours among the employed are negatively associated with time spent in domestic work in a straightforward way (the greater the hours spent in employment, the less time spent on housework and care). Family status is also highly influential in determining time spent on both housework and childcare. Both the fathers and, especially, the mothers of young children spend more time in domestic work and care than those without children. This effect is, of course, particularly strong among mothers staying at home to care for children. Among socio-economic factors, educational level has perhaps the most important effect; overall the higher the level of women's education the less housework they do, while the opposite is true for men. In distinction to this contrasting trend by gender, the higher the level of education, the *more* childcare both men and women do.

There are known to be many other factors that come into play in the determination of time spent in housework and care activities. For example, gender ideology (couples where both agree that men and women should share career and family responsibilities equally have more equal divisions of domestic labour and care); the absolute and relative financial resources of spouses (in general, the higher the absolute and relative income of one spouse, the less housework they do); and the sexuality of the couple (lesbian women have been shown to be the most equal in their division of domestic work, ahead of gay men and heterosexual couples). There is a huge literature about the complicated effect of all these factors, separately and in combination.

In this chapter we first give an overview of trends in women's and men's time spent in domestic labour and care using the UK time-use data series. We then illustrate, according to the arguments made above, the variations in domestic labour and care time for women and men in different family and employment statuses, and with different educational levels. In the latter part of the chapter we focus particularly on men's contributions. In an international context of increases in women's paid work time and corresponding overall declines in their housework time, whether, and in what circumstances, men are doing more is crucial to understanding the direction in which the gender gap in unpaid work is heading. For example, and following on from the findings of the previous chapter in relation to the growth of non-standard employment schedules, a growing body of research suggests that non- and irregularly employed fathers are likely to spend more time caring for children than their employed counterparts.[6] Obviously being at home creates more opportunities for spending time with children, and, when combined with the general increase in the time that fathers seem to spend with their children, this is an intuitively likely outcome. Non-employed fathers consist mainly of unemployed men and those on non-standard employment contracts, but they also include a small but growing percentage of full-time carer fathers. Both these subgroups have been increasing over the 21st century due primarily to higher levels of male under-employment. An analysis of US fathers who were 'highly involved' with their children (measured in terms of the time they spent in childcare activities) found that highly involved fathers were nearly twice as likely not to be in employment as non-involved fathers.[7]

The second issue we address in relation to fathers' contributions to childcare is differences by educational level.[8] A significant increase in parental time spent in childcare is observed, starting from the 1990s. This is the period when the social ideals of *intensive* patterns of parenting and, in particular, *involved fathering* spread widely.[9] Research has shown that highly educated parents are likely to provide not only more basic physical care for their children, but also to spend more time in developmental-related childcare activities, such as reading and playing with children. These findings match the theoretical expectation that highly educated parents are more likely to focus their time on activities that improve their children's social and cognitive skills, perhaps with an eye to aiding access to prestigious educational establishments. The overall result is a growing gap in the time spent in childcare between those with high levels of educational attainment and those with lower levels.

Setting the scene: the UK historical trend

An interesting question when we consider the UK TUS data series is whether we can observe a 'stall' in the process of convergence in the direction of greater gender equality in unpaid work, as discussed in an international context in Chapter 3. The idea of a 'stall' in gender convergence emerged in the US at the end of the first decade of the 21st century in response to several factors: a slow-down in mothers' labour force engagement; a slow-down in women's entry into male-dominated college subjects; and some apparent increase in conservative attitudes. These trends, together with evidence from other countries for a slow-down in the proportions agreeing with statements supporting gender egalitarian attitudes, seemed to offer support for the idea that the trend towards gender convergence in the division of labour had slowed. Large-scale analyses based on time-use data also seem to show that there was a slowing of gender convergence from the late 1980s in those countries where men and women's time in housework was already more equal, with steeper gender convergence continuing in those countries where the gender division of housework was less equal.[10] The media have been quick to seize on the idea, presenting the idea of a 'stalled revolution' as meaning that we've got as far as we're going to get with the gender revolution.

Figure 5.1 shows trends in the average (mean) minutes spent

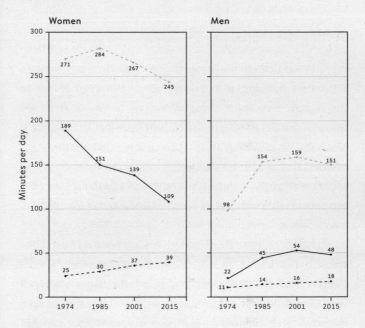

Figure 5.1
Average minutes in domestic work tasks: women and men aged 18 and over, UK (1974–2015)

```
----    All domestic work
——      Core domestic work
- - -   Childcare
```

in domestic work and care for the UK from the 1970s through to 2015.

Core domestic work in Figure 5.1 includes cooking, cleaning and clothes care. Childcare includes all forms of childcare, plus child-related travel, and 'all domestic work' includes all these categories, plus other domestic work like gardening, DIY and shopping (including shopping-related travel). For UK women aged 18 and over, there was a steep decline in the average time spent doing core domestic work, from 189 minutes per day in 1974 to 109 minutes per day in 2015. Time spent in childcare rose from 25 to 39 minutes over the same period (averaged across mothers and non-mothers). Time spent on all unpaid work tasks combined also decreased over the period, although not as steeply as the trend for core domestic work.

For men, on the other hand, there has been an overall increase in the time spent in housework. This increase, from 22 minutes in 1974 to 48 minutes in 2015, however, does not match the magnitude of the decrease in women's housework and, moreover, all happened during the period 1975–2000, declining slightly over the first decade of the 21st century. This kind of slow-down is exactly what has led some commentators to ask the question: 'So who *is* doing the housework?'! The overall time men spent on childcare showed a slight increase over the period, from 11 to 18 minutes (again, averaged across fathers and non-fathers). Men's overall average time in all forms of unpaid work rose until 2000, then fell again by 8 minutes by 2015.

On the basis of these overall trends, then, there appears to be some evidence in support of the 'stall hypothesis' in the

UK: there has been a slight decrease in men's contributions to housework and overall unpaid work since the year 2000. Women's contributions, on the other hand, continued to fall in the 2000s (again with the exception of childcare time, which rose somewhat). In terms of men's *share* of all unpaid work tasks, this has risen steadily since the 1970s, from 27 to 38 per cent of all unpaid work. Their share of core housework has increased even more steeply, from a much lower base (10 per cent in 1974) to close to a third in 2015 (31 per cent). However, it is important to note that the overwhelming reason for these overall increases in men's share has been the decline in the time that women spend in these activities, rather than increases in the time that men spend doing them. Men's share of childcare time has remained relatively constant at just under a third of all time spent in childcare throughout the period. This is because time spent in childcare has been rising for both men and women (unlike the case for core domestic work, where women's time has fallen steeply).

These trends paint a somewhat depressing picture from the perspective of gender equality, and seem to lend support to the idea of the 'stall hypothesis'. However, it may be that the level of generality shown here is misleading. If we focus in more detail on what is happening to different population groups within this overall picture, more nuanced findings emerge that may offer some hope for the continuation of the move towards gender convergence in domestic work and care.

Differences by family and employment status

This section illustrates contemporary variations in the time spent in domestic work and care between different population subgroups. The idea is to put the spotlight on those groups who are most likely to be under the most intense pressure of time due to their combination of family and employment commitments. Accordingly, Figure 5.2 shows average minutes spent per day on core housework and childcare for three subgroups of parents: full-time-employed spouses with children aged under 18 in their household; employed single parents of children aged under 18 in their household; and non-employed spouses with children aged under 18 in their household. The first two of these groups are likely to be under more pressure of time trying to combine employment with childcare. In contrast, the final group (non-employed spouses with children) are likely to have more available time to do different kinds of family work, including domestic work and looking after children. For comparison, we also show the same results for the whole population aged 18 and over.

The most striking thing about this figure is the differing amounts of time spent in these activities by men and women. In general, as we saw above, women do more core housework, childcare and overall domestic work. Nonetheless there are some interesting distinctions when we focus in more closely on the different subgroups of parents. For example, we can see that those who are likely to be under the greatest time pressure (full-time employed partnered parents and single employed parents) spend less time in core housework than

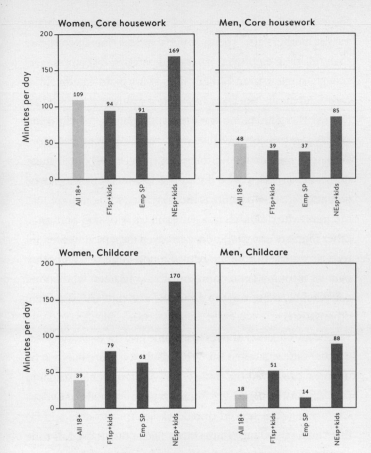

Figure 5.2

Average minutes per day in housework and care
tasks: selected family and employment groups by gender,
UK (2015)

All 18+ — comparison with whole population aged over 18
FTsp+kids — full-time employed, married or living
as married, with children under 18 in the household
Emp SP — employed single parent with children under 18
in the household
NEsp+kids — non-employed, married or living as married
with children under 18 in the household

the average for all those aged 18 or more. Employed single-parent mothers also spend somewhat less time in childcare than full-time employed partnered parents. By comparison, though, single-parent fathers spend very little time in childcare (and much less than full-time employed partnered fathers). This may be because they are paying for childcare services, or possibly because relatives are helping out. Non-employed parents spend the most time overall on all these domestic activities. The difference between non-employed parents and other parents is most striking for non-employed mothers, who do much more unpaid work overall both than other mothers and than non-employed fathers. However, interestingly, the difference between non-employed and other parents also applies to non-employed fathers, who spend considerably more time in domestic and care activities than other fathers.

The introduction of *paid* work time into the equation poses a rather different question. Which subgroups are likely to be the most pressured for time, when we sum both unpaid and paid work time together? Figure 5.3 shows totals of overall work time (all paid and unpaid tasks) for mothers and fathers in the three subgroups identified above: those full-time employed, married with children aged under 18 in their household; employed single parents with children aged under 18 in their household; and those non-employed, married with children aged under 18 in their household. The total for all women and men aged 18 and over is also shown for comparison.

Figure 5.3 shows that, for both women and men, those who spend the longest time working (and, correspondingly, have the least rest and recuperation time) are those combining

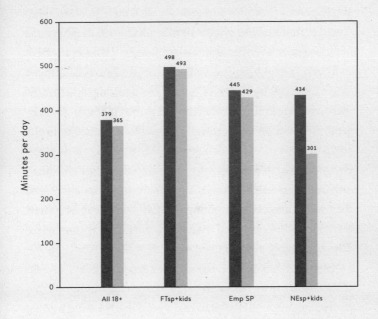

Figure 5.3
Average minutes per day in all work: selected
family and employment groups by gender, UK (2015)

All 18+ — comparison with whole population aged over 18
FTsp+kids — full-time employed, married or living
as married, with children under 18 in the household
Emp SP — employed single parent with children under 18
in the household
NEsp+kids — non-employed, married or living as married
with children under 18 in the household

■ Women
■ Men

full-time employment with parenthood. They are followed by single-parent mothers and fathers, with little to choose between them in terms of overall workload. Both these groups of fathers spend longer hours in employment than equivalent mothers, but they do less unpaid work and care. Employed single mothers, by contrast, spend less time in paid employment and much more time in unpaid work. Finally, all the subgroups shown do substantially more work overall than the population averages for their gender, with the exception of non-employed married fathers. By definition these fathers spend only minimal amounts of time in paid work, so almost all their work time consists of unpaid work. The same, of course, is true for non-employed married mothers, who nonetheless do considerably more unpaid work!

Figure 5.3 makes clear the existing gap in mothers' and fathers' overall work times, in particular among non-employed married parents. However, we can get a feel for what's going on in relation to the vital question of changes in fathers' contributions by looking more closely at trends across time for these groups. Figure 5.4 shows trends for two subgroups: one likely to be under considerable pressure of time (full-time employed partnered parents), and one with more time availability (non-employed partnered parents). Summing up all the work (paid and unpaid) done by fathers and mothers in these categories, the trend lines in Figure 5.4 show the share (percentage) of *overall* work time done by fathers in these subgroups.

We can see that for those men who are under the greater pressure of time, i.e. full-time employed partnered fathers, there wasn't much change in their overall share over time (a slight increase, from 48 per cent to 50 per cent of all paid and

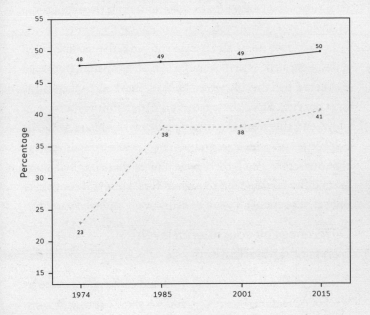

Figure 5.4

Men's share (percentage) of all work time: selected family and employment groups, UK (1974–2015)

——— Non-employed, married or living as married with children under 18 in the household

----- Full-time employed, married or living as married with children under 18 in the household

unpaid work). The overall work done by full-time employed fathers today equals that done by full-time employed mothers, and this trend appears to have been relatively consistent over time. The picture looks quite different, though, for the group of fathers with more time availability, i.e. non-employed fathers. In 1974 non-employed partnered fathers contributed only 23 per cent of the overall work done by non-employed partnered parents. However, by 2015 this had risen steadily to 41 per cent. Since these fathers are by definition not in employment, this work is entirely made up of unpaid activities like housework, childcare and other domestic work. It appears that non-employed fathers have almost doubled their share around the house (even though in total they still contribute only 41 per cent of all work done by non-employed parents).

Differences by educational level: trends and polarization?

Turning to trends in domestic work and care differentiated by level of education, Figures 5.5 and 5.6 show average minutes spent in core housework and childcare according to educational level for women and men respectively. Level of education is shown amalgamated into three groups: those with low (incomplete secondary education), middle (complete secondary level) and high levels (above secondary level education). From Figure 5.5, for women, we can see differences in the trend over time when we contrast core housework with childcare. Highly educated women do less housework, although housework time declines noticeably over time for women of all educational levels. On the other hand, childcare time has in general increased over the period 1974 to 2015, and more highly

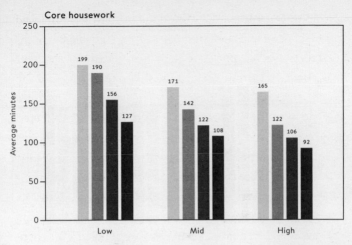

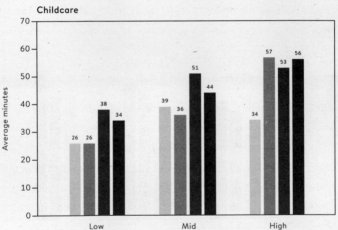

Figure 5.5

Average minutes in core housework and childcare by educational level: women aged 18–65, UK (2015)

■ 2015
■ 2000
■ 1985
■ 1974

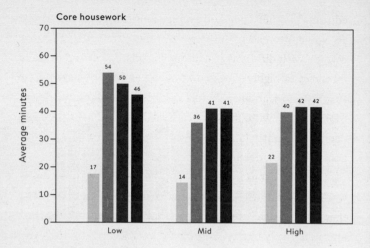

Core housework

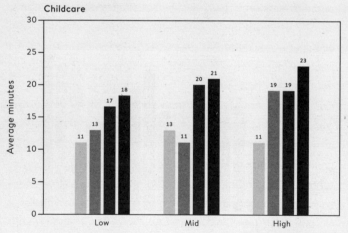

Childcare

Figure 5.6
Average minutes in core housework and childcare by
educational level: men aged 18–65, UK (2015)

■ 2015
■ 2000
■ 1985
■ 1974

educated women spend on average longer in childcare. There are some interesting differences in these trends, though, for women with different educational levels. The main increase for the most highly educated women seemed to come between 1974 and 1985, and has thereafter been more stable, while for those women with lower educational levels the main increase occurred slightly later, in the 1990s (between the 1985 and 2000 surveys), declining somewhat thereafter.

The fact that more highly educated women do less housework is well known, and in part at least reflects the reality that they are more likely to have jobs – and within that category they are more likely to have full-time career jobs. In general, the higher the income that people have, the less housework they do. Women with lower levels of education are more likely to be in part-time employment, and to have more available time for housework. However, the reverse picture for childcare tells us that the distribution of paid employment by educational level cannot be the whole story. In the case of childcare, women with the highest levels of educational attainment, who are most likely to be in full-time career jobs and therefore under greater pressure of time, do more childcare than their counterparts. This finding corresponds to results from other countries, so it is not just a UK phenomenon. It probably relates to something described earlier: the ideology of intensive childcare as the 'ideal' form of parenting is more prevalent among those with higher educational levels. The higher aspirations that highly educated parents may have for their children's educational futures also leads to increased time being spent in childcare of the kind thought to promote such futures (i.e. 'developmental' childcare).[11]

We see some broadly similar trends in men's average child-care time by educational attainment (Figure 5.6). Both more highly educated women and more highly educated men do more childcare – probably for the same reasons. But, interestingly, the pattern for men shows a steadier increase in childcare over time for all educational levels, rather than levelling off in the first decade of the 21st century as it does for women. Furthermore, the increase between 2000 and 2015 is most pronounced for the most highly educated men. It may be that more highly educated men are increasingly exposed to ide-ologies about intensive fathering and that this continues to have an effect in greater amounts of time spent in childcare activities.

Trends in core housework for men also differ by educa-tional level. While, from the 1980s, those with the lowest level of education did progressively less housework over time (starting from a higher level), those men with middle and high levels of education are doing somewhat more over time. Here we are unable to draw upon materialistic explanations relating to career employment, since highly educated men with career employment spend more time in paid work now than they did in the 1970s (see Chapter 4). Instead, we might rely on gender ideology as at least a partial explanation; for ex-ample, higher levels of education among men have been shown to be increasingly associated over time with attitudes that are more supportive of gender equality.[12]

We return here to an issue that was identified earlier on in this chapter: 'involved fathering'. We have seen that more highly educated men are spending more time in childcare; we now ask whether father care time is increasing generally, or whether we can identify particular groups of fathers who are spending more and more time in childcare over time, in a process that has been described as the 'polarization' of father care.[13] For this analysis the focus is on fathers aged under 50 with children aged 12 and under, who spent 15 or more minutes per day in childcare, comparing them to all fathers of the same ages with children of the same ages. The first group we refer to as 'involved fathers', since they do at least make what might be considered some meaningful contribution to the daily care of their children (enough time, at least, to change a nappy, or read a story).

In fact, the percentage of involved fathers according to this definition more than doubles over the 40-year period from 1974 to 2015, from 31 per cent to 64 per cent. In other words, on average twice as many men are actively involved in care of their children (where active involvement is defined as spending at least 15 minutes a day in childcare). However, what is noticeable is that while this *percentage* has increased relatively modestly since the 1980s, there was a far more marked increase in the average *time* that these involved fathers were spending in childcare. So while in the 1980s 52 per cent of fathers of this age did at least 15 minutes per day of daily childcare, the average time these 52 per cent spent on childcare was 74 minutes per day. By 2015 the percentage of involved fathers had increased to 64 per cent, but the average minutes these fathers were spending in childcare had increased much more, by over half an hour, from 74 minutes to 109 minutes – i.e. from approximately 1 hour 15 minutes per day to 1 hour 50 minutes per day. It does seem, therefore, that we may be observing a polarization effect over recent decades, whereby the percentage of involved fathers has increased comparatively slowly, while for those fathers who are actively involved, the average time that they devote to childcare has been increasing more rapidly.

The main findings of this chapter confirm that UK women's housework time continues to decline. For men there was a slight rise, but then a levelling off since 2000. Time spent on childcare per day on the overall level has risen by 14 minutes since the 1970s for women, and by half that for men (see Figure 5.1). Therefore, the increase in men's share of housework and overall unpaid work shown in Figure 5.2 is largely driven by declines in women's time in these activities, rather than notable increases in men's contributions. The effect of these trends is to create a levelling off in the process of convergence towards gender equality in housework, a phenomenon common to many countries where levels of gender equality were already relatively high by the 1990s. In this sense, the UK data lend support to the idea of a stall in the movement towards gender convergence in housework.

Against this rather pessimistic conclusion at the overall level, there are some indications of more positive signs when we break the data down into subgroups of the population. Since the stall in the process of gender convergence seems primarily to be about men's contributions, we have focused on these. Firstly, non-employed men are spending markedly more time in unpaid work and care over time (Figure 5.4). Increases in the number of non-employed men since the turn of the 21st century, largely due to the recession, combined with this increasing trend in the time spent in unpaid work and care, give hope that men who spend more time at home will continue to devote increasing amounts of that time to domestic work and care. Although still representing only a small minority, there are also growing numbers of households in which the woman is the main economic provider, and fathers take on the carer role. It is likely that the changes in gender ideology that support this arrangement (in particular, the increasing popularity of the idea of the 'involved father') will in time become more diffused within the general population.

One of the mechanisms that might help to promote this diffusion is increasing levels of education, particularly to degree level. The positive gradient of the relationship between time spent in childcare and education level for men is most pronounced in 2015 (Figure 5.6). As education levels increase, the known relationship between higher educational levels and attitudes in favour of greater gender equality should hopefully lead to an increase in gender ideologies that favour both equality and involved fatherhood.

Finally, we observe suggestive evidence for an increasing polarization in father care. It seems that the percentage of 'involved' fathers with children aged 12 and under is growing steadily over time. However, increasing even more rapidly is the amount of time that such fathers devote to childcare. Nearly 2 hours a day on average is a substantial amount of time. The signs are that an increasing percentage of fathers are making efforts to spend significant amounts of time with their children. This finding, too, accords with previous research. More highly educated parents are devoting increasing amounts of time to promoting their children's education. And in fact higher educational levels are also associated with increasing time spent in core housework over time (Figure 5.6), suggesting that an interpretation relating to increasing gender egalitarian ideologies among the highly educated may have more salience than those based on more materially directed arguments.[14] The hope is that, through processes of social diffusion,[15] ideologies in support of gender egalitarianism will spread more widely through the population. The big question will be whether social policies and managerial cultures that equate time spent in the workplace with effort and worth will be able to adapt sufficiently to support such changes.

Unpaid Work Matters
Valuing Household Production Time

—

Jooyeoun Suh
Christopher Payne

A woman in a quiet suburb is starting another weekday. After washing and dressing and rushing to prepare and eat breakfast, she does the dishes. While she washes the dishes, her three-year-old son is tugging at her leg, so she tries to entertain him by talking and singing to him. She puts the dishes away and drives to the supermarket with her son. She consults her shopping list, and purchases groceries and other household necessities accordingly, comparing the prices of different brands. When she returns from the supermarket, she first puts the groceries away, while talking to her son. Then she prepares lunch using what she has brought home with her. She and her child both eat lunch. After lunch, she collects the dirty laundry to be washed.

On the same morning in the same quiet suburb, and at a similar unearthly hour, a woman of an identical age awakes and begins her midweek morning routine. After washing and dressing, she runs down the stairs and does nothing but reach for the bunch of keys on the telephone desk before tugging the heavy front door closed behind her. For this woman, a job in the city beckons and while she could open the cupboard to prepare some food she prefers breakfast 'on the dash'. So she grabs a bagel as she continues her hurried commute from the tube station exit before arriving outside a shining glass office block fully fed and with appropriate levels of caffeine for her to feel the last wisps of sleepiness blow away in the wind. After courteous 'hellos' and 'how are yous' she switches on her laptop to begin responding to email requests and queries from those who need her services as a professional.

In these contrasting examples a different set of tasks occupies each woman's time. While they both have 1,440 minutes in their day, they spend those minutes consuming and producing goods and services from, and for, entirely different groups of people. But perhaps there is less difference than there initially appears to be? What they have in common is that they are both producers and consumers in their own right. If you reconsider the tasks listed in the initial 'home' example, these are all tasks which could be contracted out. For example, a nanny could have been employed to take care of the three-year-old son. Or a shop- or food-delivery service could have been used to replace home meal preparation, which would also have taken care of the dishwashing by means of eating from the throwaway packet. The point here is that all the tasks are productive activities. The work in the office is paid and delivered to a group of consumers from other households, whereas the work in the home is unpaid and delivered to a group of consumers inside that household. This work can be performed by oneself (do it yourself) or it can be contracted out (do it for me). Nonetheless, the first type of work is generally unpaid, and the lack of a currency transaction therefore places it outside conventional understandings of what 'counts' as work.

Although, economically speaking, work can be performed without pay, nevertheless most of it (i.e. conventionally defined 'work') takes place in profit-maximizing firms. Work is considered productive only if it is explicitly exchanged for money. Despite this artificial division between market work (in the paid workforce) and non-work (in the home and community), the essence of each type of activity is the same. Indeed, non-market work is not only productive, but also crucial, and also should be recognized as contributing to the economy. Families are producers, not just consumers.

How can we assess the value of unpaid work? Before we explore this question, it may be useful to review two common objections to the very notion of making this assessment. Efforts to assign market values to unpaid work have sometimes been stymied by various sorts of conceptual resistance. One widespread concern is that estimation is too rudimentary. Thanks to the availability of time-use data, we now have good measures of the number of hours devoted to market work and non-market work, but we cannot directly assess from such data the *value* of the hours devoted to non-market work. As a result, while approximations based on market rates for comparable types of paid activity have been made, they have often been considered too crude to be reliable. Yet, strangely, many of those who would dismiss such efforts have had no problem in assigning a value of zero to non-market work for the purposes of computing gross domestic product (GDP). We believe that valuations resulting from carefully constructed approximations would be an improvement on an arbitrary assignment of zero.

Another objection is that the assignment of market value to non-market work undermines the hallowed aspect of some forms of unpaid work, like mothering. Mothering is so sacred, the argument goes, that it can't and even shouldn't be, valued in monetary terms, and that to do so diminishes its inherent worth. This argument is extended to discourage the monetary valuation of any work with a care component (i.e. non-market work in general, and care work in particular). This objection, however, overlooks the reality that those engaged in many paid caregiving occupations are not purely motivated by money; in fact, paid care workers embrace motivations not dissimilar to those usually attributed to parents.[1] If we count the market value of the work of paid carers, why should we object to assigning market values to the efforts of unpaid carers?

This 'imputed' valuation of unpaid work, added to GDP so as to properly recognize aspects of a society's production that are otherwise invisible, is the focus for this chapter. Throughout, the terms 'non-market work', 'unpaid work' and 'household production work' are used interchangeably.

Why should we measure and value unpaid work?

As noted above, conventional measures of GDP value all non-market work activities (including production of goods and services in the household for one's own use, volunteer work, and so on) at zero.[2] But non-market work is quantitatively significant, at least in terms of time. Figure 6.1, a daygraph similar to the tempograms of Chapter 1, shows the percentage of

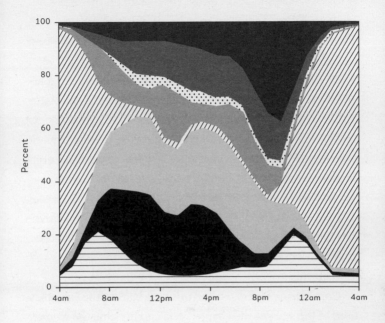

Figure 6.1
Unpaid and paid work tempogram (weekdays): women and
men aged 18–65, UK (2015)

- TV, radio and computer
- Leisure
- Civic and voluntary
- Eating
- Sleeping
- Unpaid work
- Paid work
- Personal care

people aged 18 to 65 engaged in different types of activities across weekdays in 2015 (from 4am to 4am on the next day). Eight activities (adding up to 24 hours a day) are considered: TV, radio and computer; leisure; civic and voluntary work; eating; sleeping; unpaid work; paid work; and personal care. The light-grey section of Figure 6.1 represents the percentage of people who are engaged in unpaid work, and the black-coloured one below those who are engaged in paid work. As is clear, the overall amount of time devoted to unpaid work even during weekdays is quantitatively large. And indeed, even though the majority of employed people do not do any paid work at weekends, the time devoted to unpaid work stays more or less the same then, indicating that there is a relatively constant – and substantial – percentage of people engaged in unpaid work on all days of the week, both on weekdays and at weekends.

Considering Figure 6.1, and thinking back to the examples used at the start of the chapter, one can imagine the woman working in the office leaving her place of work around 5.30pm as the percentage of the UK population at work begins to diminish, and people start to engage in either leisure or unpaid work activities. For the mother with the three-year-old son, her unpaid work continues into the evening as she prepares the family dinner. We see this element of unpaid work reflected in Figure 6.1, in the fact that the percentage of the UK population engaged in unpaid work (in light grey) does not decrease at the same rate as paid work over the early evening period.

Figure 6.1 has shown that, in terms of time, both paid and unpaid work make important contributions to daily life. But what exactly is the value of their contribution? The time spent in different unpaid activities can be valued in monetary terms by reference to some market equivalent, such as an hourly wage. Efforts to ascribe accurate monetary valuation of unpaid work inevitably yield only approximate estimates, but, as noted previously, they can be done with care, attention to detail and academic rigour. They are likely to provide a more accurate account of the true value of unpaid work to the economy than the arbitrary assignment of a value of zero. Done correctly, therefore, they can illuminate an otherwise hidden dimension of GDP.

The importance of these efforts can be illustrated in relation to the movement of women into paid employment, which represents one of the most important labour force trends of the last 40 years. Fifty-three per cent of women aged 16 to 64 in the UK engaged in paid work in 1971, but this figure had risen to 74 percent by 2014.[3] As women increased their average hours of paid work, they also decreased their average hours of unpaid work. While men began doing a bit more unpaid work over the same period, this increase has not been sufficient to fully take up the slack created by women's decrease in unpaid work. As a result, the increase in GDP since 1970 may have been, at least in part, driven by the increase in women's paid employment, while failing to take into account the average decrease in their non-market work. Thus, improvements in families' living standards as measured through GDP may long have been overestimated.

In addition, the continued reliance of public policy on family income to define economic welfare and eligibility for public assistance may also lead to distortions. For example, there is a great difference in living standards between families with the same income but different amounts of time to devote to unpaid work. Consider two households of identical composition (two parents and two young children) with identical after-tax market incomes of £25,000. The first household consists of one full-time wage earner and one stay-at-home parent. Compare this to a similar household in which both parents work full-time for pay, each making about £12,500.

In terms of household income these households are equally well-off by conventional measures. However, the first family (one full-time worker and one stay-at-home parent) enjoys the benefits of the unpaid housework and childcare services provided by a stay-at-home parent, allowing them to minimize purchases of paid services such as childcare.[4] A stay-at-home parent typically devotes more than 40 hours a week to unpaid work. On the other hand, dual employed parents like the second family (both working full-time with an income of £12,500 each) often need to purchase childcare services during the times when neither of them is available to provide such care. In other words, we ignore the fact that working in the market also *costs* money – the money required to purchase substitutes for family care.

In sum, measuring and valuing unpaid work deserves more attention. Unpaid work is invisible to conventional definitions of productivity, but time-use data can be utilized to underline how significant it can be. To examine how much unpaid work is worth, we here outline a valuation method that can provide a lower-bound estimate of the value of unpaid work in the UK since 1975.

Time-use data and the measurement of unpaid work

Time-diary data provide a unique way of measuring the time devoted to unpaid work because it covers such a wide range of unpaid work tasks. Here we consider 12 primary unpaid activities: physical childcare, developmental childcare, supervisory childcare, travel related to childcare, adult care, cooking and cleaning, laundry and ironing, home repairs and maintenance, shopping, gardening, pet care, and travel related to housework. In order to simplify the picture, these activities are condensed into four major categories: care work, core housework, household management, and travel and shopping. For the purposes of clarity, no secondary activities are considered for the analysis, a fact that will bias downwards our estimates of the total value of unpaid work.[5]

In this chapter, as first discussed in Chapter 2, our selection of what activities constitute unpaid work is made with reference to the 'third-person criterion'. According to Margaret Reid, a pioneer of studying household production, work can be defined as an activity that one can pay a person to perform.[6] She states:

> If an activity is of such character that it might be delegated
> to a paid worker, then that activity shall be deemed
> productive . . . [H]ousehold production . . . consists
> of those unpaid activities which are carried on, by and
> for the members, which activities might be replaced by
> market goods, or paid services, if circumstances such as
> income, market conditions, and personal inclinations

permit the service being delegated to someone outside the household group.

According to the third-person criterion, many forms of housework, including childcare, are considered unpaid 'work' because one could hypothetically hire someone else to perform them (regardless of whether or not one enjoys doing them). The criterion is not without its own problems. The degree of substitutability between money and time has its limit. Employed parents are often willing to pay for childcare as a substitute for their own working time. But it is usually either too costly or not considered desirable to hire someone to take care of one's own children for 24 hours a day.

We base our calculations on the average daily time that adults aged 18 and over in the UK allocated to these four categories of unpaid work from 1974 to 2015.[7] Despite the differences in levels and trends by gender shown in Figure 6.1, for the purpose of arriving at a valuation of all unpaid work across the population we need to average the time devoted to these activity categories across women and men. Overall, the total *average* time devoted to unpaid work did not change much between 1975 and 2015, ranging from 193 minutes per day in 1975 to 216 minutes per day in 2000. Among unpaid work activities, care work including childcare and adult care increased on average from 19 minutes per day (10 per cent of total unpaid work time) to 30 minutes per day (15 per cent of total unpaid work time). The increase in care work is mostly driven by childcare time, since average adult-care time has not changed since 1975 (on average 2 minutes per day including those who did not engage in any adult-care activities).[8]

Similarly, overall time devoted to core housework, including cooking, cleaning and laundry, decreased over time, but more dramatically between 2000 and 2015. Household management time, on the other hand, increased primarily due to growth in time devoted to pet care (2 minutes in 1975 compared to 10 minutes in 2015). The biggest increase, however, among the types of unpaid work shown in Figure 6.1, has been in travel time. While the average recorded unpaid work-related travel time in 1975 was 1 minute per day for adults aged 18 and over, by 2015 that figure had increased to about 17 minutes per day. Average shopping time, meanwhile, remained steady at around 27 minutes per day.

The total value of unpaid work in the UK

Under international law, the United Nations System of National Accounts is a regulated approach to the measurement of the value of all paid work within an economy. It omits nearly all of the unpaid productive activity described in this chapter.[9] Yet, as we have argued, all these forms of unpaid work represent an important contribution to the UK economy. So how can we calculate their value? The approach to solving this puzzle is to utilize methods borrowed from the core System of National Accounts. Such valuation can take the form of either an input-based valuation or an output-based valuation. In the calculation of GDP, both methods are used in a process called 'supply-use balancing' to pinpoint an exact value and reduce uncertainty related to different data sources.

The first technique, input-based valuation, requires the estimation of a range of different economic components – the sum of all inputs (typically labour, raw materials and capital) required to generate a product or service. Conversely, output-based valuation requires the volume of units of the good or service to be estimated and the application of a price per unit. The output-based valuation method uses a market price that includes the elements of labour, profit, taxes, subsidies, capital and materials, making it helpful for consistency with valuations made in the core System of National Accounts. However, one problem is that it does not give any detail about the size of each of these sub-components.

Let us revisit the two women at the start of the chapter. Once the woman from the office has arrived home, both women are in their respective households at 6pm on that evening and they are both in the mood for a cooked meal (say, a pot of lentil soup). The woman who works in the office decides to order soup online from a restaurant food-delivery service. If we break down the input components required for her to have her soup delivered, it requires the cook's time (labour), a pot and gas cooker (capital), and some ingredients like lentils and spices, plus gas to cook with (raw materials). Then there is the cost of delivery, and of course the taxes and subsidies to which the restaurant is subject.

Instead of ordering in, the mother with the three-year-old son has a homemade lentil soup recipe, and she gets to work making soup herself. In her situation, she has bought the materials, and has capital in the form of her cooker, but the value of her labour is not yet calculated. What is the best way to calculate this? Let us set capital and raw materials aside for a moment to simplify the picture. In order to estimate labour input value, there are two methods that can be applied – the 'replacement-cost' method and 'opportunity-cost' method.

In the replacement-cost approach, one can ask what the homemade soup would have cost if the woman was to hire a specialist cook (adjusted as much as possible for quality) on an hourly basis in the market to cook her soup for her. If the wage for a cook is £8 an hour and the woman spends an hour in her day to make lentil soup, the value of her time would be £8. However, beyond the market cost, while the woman could hire a cook to make the soup, perfect substitutes are hard to find as the woman is not only the cook when she prepares the soup, she is also a caregiver. She has relationships with those she cooks for and person-specific knowledge and skills that increase her value as a caregiver. For instance, she knows that her son has severe food allergies that require her to keep an eye on him while they eat in case of a bad reaction. Finding a paid caregiver who can match her parental knowledge and level of performance would be difficult.

Another concern with the replacement-cost method is quality control. What is the appropriate quality adjustment? Is a cook's wage suitable to estimate a mother's labour cost? It is possible that a mother is either a terrible cook whose value should not be considered on a par with a hired cook's wage, or a terrific cook whose value should be rated as higher than that wage. This issue has not been resolved fully in the calculation of replacement costs, but a 25 per cent deduction in the wage of specialists for some unpaid services like cooking, home repairs and so on has been suggested. However, this deduction is not thought to be appropriate for care-giving activities due to the lack of perfect substitutes (as in the example in the paragraph above).[10]

The opportunity-cost method, on the other hand, asks what

a woman who made a pot of lentil soup could have earned in the labour market if she had spent that time working for pay. While this approach is relevant to estimate the individual cost of specializing in unpaid work, it has its own shortcomings. If a neurosurgeon who makes £100 per hour cooked a pot of lentil soup, under the opportunity-cost method the value of the soup would be £100. But one can readily imagine that the neurosurgeon's soup might well be inferior in quality to a pot made by a cook who earns £8 an hour.

An output-based valuation approach estimates value by asking what the price would be per unit of goods and services if purchased from the market. In other words, if you have two children, how much does it cost per hour to put each child in a nursery? In the soup example, how much did the woman pay for her soup when she ordered it from the restaurant delivery service? How many soups did she order? The benefit of using the output approach is that it encompasses all elements which are included in the market price, and as such yields a comprehensive value of unpaid production if it were to be contracted out to a market service. Unfortunately, it does not show how that price breaks down into wages, profit margins, overheads, and so on. While it does not require measurement of who produces the soup and how long they spend cooking, it also provides no information on who, in the workforce, is responsible for the unpaid production.

Applying the input-based valuation approach, and within it the replacement-cost method, yields estimates of the value of unpaid work that reflect the market-equivalent paid wages that an employee would receive if she were contracted to carry out the work. The benefit of this is that it can be easily compared to the wages she might receive if the work was done for someone else. Furthermore, the valuation is not complicated by components that would feature in a market price (such as profit margins). For these reasons, the valuation estimated in this chapter employs the input-based valuation approach using replacement costs, as demonstrated below.

In order to use the replacement-cost method, the correct wage rates of specialists are required. We retrieved these from the occupation codes for specialists drawn from the Annual Survey of Hours and Earnings (ASHE) collected by the Office for National Statistics. According to ASHE, care workers for children and adults earned a median hourly wage of £0.78 in 1975 and £10.6 in 2015. Among caregivers, primary- and nursery-education teaching professionals earned the highest hourly wage (£1.23 in 1975 and £20.79 in 2015). The lowest wage earners were those in occupations related to laundry, dry cleaning and ironing (£0.66 in 1975 and £6.66 in 2015).

Following the replacement-cost method, we use a measure of the time devoted to the unpaid work activities listed earlier. Multiplying the average hours per person per week by the number of persons aged 18 and over in the population and the number of weeks per year yields an estimate of the total value of time devoted to unpaid work of about £26 billion in 1975 and £449 billion in 2015, respectively (see Figure 6.2). The value of unpaid work estimated here only accounts for labour input, ignoring intermediate goods, capital and raw materials. Nonetheless, when placed in the context of GDP, the value of unpaid work for adults 18 and over using this

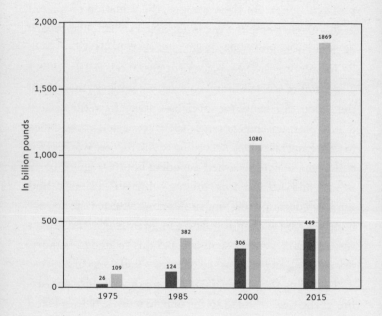

Figure 6.2
Values of unpaid work compared with GDP, UK (1975–2015)

GDP
Value of unpaid work

estimation is about 25 per cent of GDP in the UK. This is almost certainly an underestimation as we have used primary activities only, and measured only labour inputs.[11]

The digital revolution in unpaid work

This chapter has provided examples of the valuation of unpaid work based on traditional types of unpaid work which are commonplace in the wider economy. However, there are now a vast range of activities which could be legitimately contracted out to a third party and hence classed as a form of unpaid work – and many of those activities are much less traditional. People are engaged in so many practices which were formerly the preserve of the professional but have recently become opportunities (and/or burdens!) for the amateur due to the digital revolution. Indeed, the latest thinking is that modern advances such as the internet are encouraging people to produce greater amounts of unpaid work for themselves, a kind of digital Do-It-Yourself.[12] This is because the internet has allowed many of the services which used to be carried out by a paid employee to be done by the consumer for themselves – online. The well-documented example of this is where consumers might have gone to a travel agent in the past, they may now research and book flights, accommodation and car hire themselves without getting off their sofa.

On the other hand, when we consider the cultural and economic shifts created by this kind of digital DIY revolution, it is also important to recognize that productive consumer activity (where the consumer plays the role of an unpaid participant in the production chain) has always existed. The use of holiday brochures is one such pre-internet example. However, the extent to which the consumer now has the tools to produce many of the services which were previously contracted out has changed. Websites enable individuals to be their own estate agent or own bank clerk, freeing up valuable disposable income to pay for goods or services one would rather spend money on. In combination with traditional forms of unpaid work, increases in the value of other productive activities which are not paid will be a certainty for the foreseeable future. This movement of services online may allow the consumer to replace jobs (a process known as digital disintermediation) in a process by which they themselves handle services previously provided to them in exchange for money. But crucially, the online services/tools used by consumers also create jobs (such as in the technology sector), as consumers change the pattern of the services which they choose to pay for and those which they decide to do for themselves.

It's unpaid work, not unproductive work!

By accounting only for the value of goods and services that are bought and sold in the market, GDP provides only a partial measure of economic wellbeing. Both paid and unpaid work contribute to sustainable economic progress. Imagine what would happen if those providing unpaid work to family members decided to withdraw their services today. It would be impossible to fill the gap through already overloaded paid care services. In addition, when it comes to childcare, it is not just children who benefit from the care of their parents. All of society gains from those who devote their time and resources to their children, who will become the next generation of workers and taxpayers.

Productive activity has always existed outside of the paid economy.[13] But while it has always existed, it has not always been measured. This has been due in part to data constraints, and in part to an institutional, social and economic focus on paid employment. Even today the value of unpaid work is only partially measured by national statistical agencies and there is no legal requirement for them to do so. It is becoming clear that in order to establish a comprehensive picture of the economy, the extent and nature of unpaid work is crucial. This is especially so during times of great social and economic change. The full extent of what people do for themselves is vast. It simply is not practical or desirable to contract out everything. The value of unpaid work needs to be recognized as complementing paid goods and services, rather than seen as activity which could be substituted for by paid goods and services.

In addition, policies designed to support and reward unpaid work should not be considered as extras or luxuries. Rather, they are necessities for our workforce and society. More generous welfare state programmes for families with young children or sick and infirm elderly – including free childcare for children younger than two years old, extended hours of free childcare for working parents, and the provision of adequate housing – represent an important way of recognizing and supporting the many hours of unpaid work that family members devote to performing services and caring for one another.

PART THREE

Leisure and Physical Activity

Family Time Together
—
Giacomo Vagni

Family is one of the most important institutions in contemporary Britain. Family members are still the main providers of care, as well as the main providers of moral and economic support. Everyday life itself is structured around the schedules of household members. Family relations have changed dramatically over the last century. But although a lot has been written about changes in family demographics (marriage, divorce, cohabitation, fertility), much less is known about how time together has changed in the recent past. What exactly *has* changed from a time-use perspective is more difficult to assess than one might think. One of the most interesting findings stemming from such research over the past couple of decades has been the important increases in time that parents are spending in childcare activities (see Chapter 5). However, exactly how much time couples and families spend with each other, and what they do together, remains largely unresearched.

Most of our time when we are not at work is spent, for those in couples, with the partner, and, for those who are parents of young children, with those children. The 2014–15 data tell us that couples in the sample selected from the UK 2014–15 data for this chapter spend about 7 hours together between the hours of 7am and 10am, when averaged over the week. But families with young children spend about 5 to 10 hours together, and parents spend about 5 hours alone with their children. Of course, important differences exist between men and women, as well as between workers, students or retirees. Nonetheless, these simple figures show how important our family members are to us. In this chapter we explore how time together with the partner and the children has changed between 2000 and 2015. This choice of timeframe is significant because it covers the period just before and just after the technological revolution involving personal computers and other devices. The jury is still out on the impact of this revolution on our family time. Many people are familiar with kids escaping early from family meals to get back on to social media with their friends, or to that computer game they had to abandon when dinner was announced. Do parents and children spend less time together because the kids are in their bedrooms using their devices? Do family meals get cut short because of the call of our electronic devices (and who's to say that parents are not guilty of this too?)? Certainly the popular media is full of gloomy pronouncements about the impact of this revolution on our family time.

The common-sense definition of what constitutes a 'family' still revolves around the presence of children. The subject of this chapter is couples with children aged under 8 living together in a single household. One of the most important changes in contemporary families is that there is less pressure on couples nowadays to have children, and couples can choose more freely to stay childless. Nevertheless, most couples do have children, and the common-sense definition of what constitutes a 'family' still revolves around the presence of children.[1]

The context

Tracing family change is not an easy task, because family relations are constantly transforming. For example, the very idea of 'family time' only fully crystallized during the course of the 20th century.[2] In order for such an idea to emerge, the relationships involved in what we commonly think of as the nuclear family had to first become increasingly privatized. Through the Industrial Revolution of the 19th century, the family often served as the active unit of production. The separation between workplace and 'home' was much less concretely delineated, and children were considered as a source of labour, often working long hours in dangerous factories and mines. In a striking contrast, parenting is nowadays commonly regarded as a process of long-term 'investment', with parents focusing on giving greater attention to fewer children.[3] It took a long and slow transformation for 'family time' to emerge as a social category, and many factors contributed to its emergence. For example, work had to become physically separated from home, and work time separated from personal and free time in order for the nuclear family to become demarcated as a distinct entity within its own private space.

It is of course impossible to define precisely when a social category starts to exist, but it is generally considered that the 1950s was the 'golden age' of the *idea* of family time. The idea of family time is still a very important one in contemporary Britain. However, the meaning has certainly changed between the 1950s and today. For instance, attitudes towards gender have changed dramatically. In the 21st century, the great majority of people now have a 'progressive' attitude towards what makes a 'good' relationship, involving attributes such as equality between the partners, mutual respect and shared satisfaction. The ideology of marriage is no longer grounded to the same extent in religious beliefs, and is based more upon ideas about mutual affection and personal development.[4] So, *family time* is still highly valued by families, but for rather different reasons. In this chapter, the focus is on the *practices* of family time from the turn of the 21st century, addressing two central questions: 1) How much time are families spending together? 2) What are families doing together today compared to 15 years ago?

Family time from a time-use perspective

Measuring family interactions within a quantitative framework is not easy. Time-use diaries provide three relevant types of information for each time slot: *what* activity was being done during that time, *where* it took place and *with whom*. The *with whom* information (the so-called 'co-presence' information) enables researchers to estimate *family time*. However, the reports of time use contained in time-use diaries are conditioned on individuals' own perception and interpretation of particular situations. These differences in perception are clearly noticeable when comparing the diaries of different family members. One partner may think that he/she is sharing an activity with the other, while the other partner might consider that they are doing separate activities. In this sense, family time is not an 'objective' category but rather a subjective interpretation of time spent together. Think about a situation where you were sitting with your partner and both of you were using your mobile phones to communicate with someone else. Would you report this as being alone, or being with your partner?

To deal with this complexity two different types of 'family time' are estimated. The first measure only considers family time when both partners report being with each other and with the children (when they both 'agree' that they are together). The second estimate is more flexible and counts family time when at least one partner reports being with the partner and the children. One might think of the first estimate as 'mutually engaged' family time, when both partners actively agree on the interpretation of the situation. The second estimate can be interpreted as a more 'passive' kind of togetherness, when partners are present physically but not fully engaged with each other. The combination of the two can be thought of as 'total' family time. Time together in families is therefore divided in four main categories. The first category is 'family time'. It includes the presence of the partner and children, and is divided into *engaged* and *passive* family time, depending on the agreement of the partners' diaries. The second is 'time (alone) with the partner' or 'exclusive partner time' (referred to as *partner exclusive* in the figures below). The final two categories are 'mother (alone) with the children' and 'father (alone) with the children'. All childcare activities are counted as time with children, and time spent sleeping and in employment are excluded from these measures.[5]

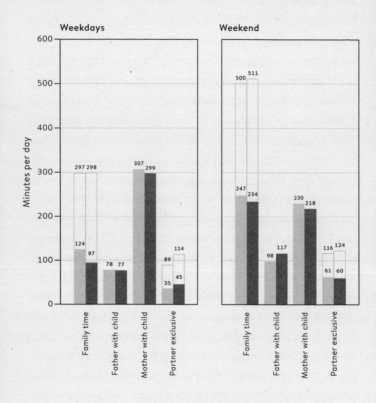

Figure 7.1
Changes in average minutes per day with family members,
UK (2000–2015)

■ Engaged family time (2000)
■ Engaged family time (2015)
□ Passive family time

The general decline in engaged family time (parents and children together)

Figure 7.1 shows the four categories of family time described above, with weekdays and weekends distinguished, for 2000 and 2015. The two measures of family time are presented as filled bars representing 'engaged family time', with unfilled bars stacked on top representing 'passive family time'. We see that *engaged family time* declined by about 30 minutes during weekdays and about 10 minutes during the weekend over the period 2000–2015. However, *total family time* did not show a decline.[6] Mother's time with children also declined, both during weekdays and during the weekend. This is surprising given the general context of documented increases in childcare over recent decades, and we discuss below how this finding might be interpreted. On the other hand, fathers increased their time (alone) with children, but only during the weekend. Finally, time (alone) with the partner ('partner-exclusive time'), increased slightly on weekdays. (Partner-exclusive time is also distinguished into two categories in the same way: the unfilled bars represent the time only one partner reported being with the other, and the filled bars include only the time when both partners reported being together.)

Comparing weekends and weekdays, we find that all types of time together (apart from mother-and-child time) are higher during the weekend, showing the prevailing importance of weekends for family interactions.[7] Despite the fact that most women nowadays are also employed[8] there are still strong gender inequalities. We see that mothers are still the main provider of care in terms of time spent together with their children. During weekdays, mothers spend about 4 times more hours than fathers alone with the children and about twice the time (alone with children) during weekends.

Studying the sequencing of family time, rather than just aggregate average time, reveals that both family time and time alone with the partner is mostly concentrated in the evening, particularly on weekdays. However, comparing across time (not shown) also reveals that family time in 2015 appears more evenly distributed during the day and less concentrated in the evening. It seems that the decline in family time during weekdays is mainly due to a loss of time together in the evening. It is tempting to speculate that this may be due to a substitution of family TV time by individual use of electronic devices in separate rooms (particularly children's bedrooms).

Activities done together: what kind of changes?

In order to better understand what seems to be a small decline in family time over the first 15 years of the 21st century, we investigated the activities done together in families (not shown). Strikingly, the two family-time activities that declined the most between 2000 and 2015 were 'watching TV' and doing 'domestic chores'. We find that 'watching TV' together in families declined both during weekdays and weekends, for both men and women. This is also the case for domestic chores. On the other hand, eating meals together and doing childcare together in a family did not change much. Leisure together in families increased slightly for women at weekends, but decreased slightly on weekdays.

In the case of the time that mothers and fathers spend alone with their children, we find that the activity that most significantly increased for both was childcare, particularly at the weekend. During the weekend, childcare increased by 20 minutes for fathers and 23 minutes for mothers. During weekdays, however, fathers did not increase their childcare time significantly, and their domestic chore time recorded as being together with children stayed approximately the same. In contrast, doing domestic chores accompanied by children dramatically decreased for women. Despite this decrease, however, the overall gender gap in time spent doing domestic chores while accompanied by children remained very large. In 2015, during weekdays, women were doing about 77 minutes of domestic chores accompanied by children, while fathers were doing only 19 minutes accompanied by children.

Sunday family sociability

In the UK, Sunday has traditionally been the day on which families spend time together. To get a more precise sense of how these changes in family time and activities play out across the day, we investigated how time spent with family members during Sundays changed between 2000 and 2015. Figure 7.2 shows the sequencing of the activities of family time across Sundays in 2000 and 2015 separately for women and men.[9] It is important to stress that this graph shows activities performed *only when families are together* (as defined by at least one parent).

These sequence tempograms show that family time spent together on Sundays has become more 'spread out' through the day, resonating with some of the findings discussed in the introductory section of this book. In 2000 it was more

Women's activities

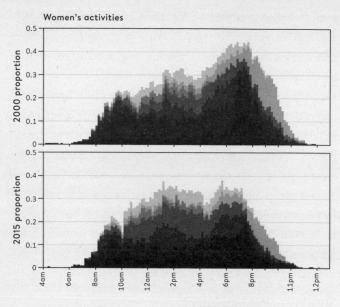

Men's activities

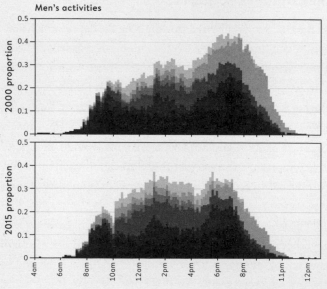

concentrated (it peaked) during the evening, but by 2015 family time was more evenly dispersed through the day. More family time was spent in leisure activities, particularly during the afternoon. Interestingly, though, in 2015 the three clear peaks in family time during the day, representing breakfast, lunch and dinner eaten together, were if anything more pronounced than they were in 2000. This suggests that, in a context where mealtimes in general are more spread throughout the day (as shown in Chapter 1), family meals on Sundays remain, in marked contrast, an important part of family time.

Relatedly, we see a decline in TV watching as a component of family time, and in particular family TV watching during the evening. By 2015 no other alternative family activities really replaced evening family TV watching. It could be that children are either going to bed earlier, or doing separate activities in the evening (using ICT devices?), leaving parents free to spend more evening time together.

Also of interest is the gender difference in the activities that mothers and fathers were doing during their family time on Sundays. Fathers enjoyed more overall leisure and TV viewing during their family time on Sunday. In contrast, mothers did significantly more domestic chores than fathers (i.e. doing domestic chores together with children).[10] This fits with a narrative found in previous research that suggests that men tend to spend more time doing enjoyable activities with their children at weekends than women do.

Childcare
Domestic
Eating
Leisure
Shopping
TV/Radio
Travel

Figure 7.2
Sunday family time tempogram by gender, UK (2000–2015)

The Future of Family Time

In sum, family time has certainly changed over the period since the turn of the 21st century. 'Engaged' family time has declined between 2000 and 2015 while total family time did not change much. This suggests that the technological revolution of personal computers and devices has perhaps reconfigured our family time, but not led to an overall decline in the total time we spend with our children or partners.

In terms of activities, the overall decline in family time between 2000 and 2015 is primarily due to the fact that families spend less time doing domestic chores together, and watch less TV together. One can interpret this change as a type of trade-off from 'quantity' to 'quality' time. Families might be experiencing an increasing shortage of time, so, when they do spend time together, they focus more on leisure and meals together, as opposed to TV watching or chores. The first question, then, is: is the decline in doing domestic chores while accompanied by partners or children necessarily a bad thing? Is there any value for partners, or parents and children, in cleaning the house in each other's company, as there might be, for example, in watching TV together? The decline in domestic chores is part of a historical trend rooted in the transformation of gender relationships over the course of the last 50 years (see Chapter 5). Mothers, as well as fathers, seem to have redistributed their scarce time to childcare rather than chores. The increase in childcare is also part of a more general trend. Children have become, over the course of the last century, the centre of ever-greater attention and scrutiny. The evidence suggests (and time-use studies also seem to point in that direction) that we are still in the throes of this long historical process and that the time spent in childcare will continue to increase. Interestingly, mothers (alone) spend less time with children today than they did at the turn of the 21st century. However, the time that they do spend with their children at the later historical point is devoted more to childcare, and less to domestic chores, than previously. Similarly for fathers, with the difference that fathers have not made this trade-off with domestic chores, but rather with TV watching!

A second question is whether the decline in TV-watching as part of family time should be regarded positively. TV is often regarded as a 'passive' activity with little cultural benefit.[11] Nonetheless, one can make the case that watching TV together in families might have a range of positive outcomes for family life. First of all, watching TV at certain specific hours on a routine basis can serve as a family *ritual*. Rituals are important because they foster solidarity and a sense of identity for families.[12] Watching the same TV programme according to a regular schedule can contribute ultimately to a shared family culture. Moreover, we shouldn't underestimate what is going on when watching television together. Family discussion and debate often sparkle in front of the TV.[13] In this sense, TV *is* a social activity when others are present. Furthermore, watching emotionally 'intense' TV programmes (such as movies, or nature programmes) in the company of others touches the realm of collective emotions. An intimate bond is created when individuals share joint stimulation and excitement.[14] Solidarity is fostered when individuals experience intimate emotions in a collective fashion, and TV as a medium can channel these emotions into a shared experience.

Unlike domestic chores, the decline in TV-watching is not explained by a long-term historical trend related to wider changes in gender ideologies, but rather it is the consequence of an 'exogenous' factor: smartphones and other related ICT devices. It was hard 20 years ago to imagine what would replace traditional TV watching in the future. Nowadays, household members don't need to watch TV programmes at the same time. In principle, everyone can watch what he/she wants to watch when they want to watch it. In this sense, devices have fostered greater 'individualization' in media use. Temporalities have become more tailored to the individual, rather than the collective. Parents' schedules are difficult to organize, and leisure time is often scarce. So devices can enable more leisure for parents because the kind of leisure that devices provide does not need to be synchronized with other family members. In the 1950s, if you wanted to play you had to organize and synchronize your schedule with a playing partner. Now, you can use your device to play with a *virtual* partner, who might, or might not, be a real person, possibly living in a completely different time zone and according to a different time schedule.[15] The impact of such devices on children's and adults' time is discussed more fully in Chapters 10 and 11.

These devices can connect individuals not only beyond physical space but also beyond temporalities and synchronicities. This may be viewed as a positive outcome. But then, as we indicated at the start of this chapter, the question becomes: 'What happens to sociability with the people we *physically* live with?' This can mean our family members, or our friends and neighbours. Some authors make the argument that TV has had a negative impact on our relationship with the community.[16]

We showed that the decline of TV watching is an important factor in the reduction in family interaction. In this sense, more TV time together can foster more family time. While the results suggest that the 'device revolution' has had little impact on overall leisure time together and family meals, the 'device revolution' has impacted family TV watching, particularly in the evening Moreover, the time lost by TV watching together hasn't been replaced by another social activity. It has just been lost in terms of family time. So, what families now have to figure out is how to (re)connect the 'global', to which they can now be constantly connected, with their 'local' *physical* family interactions.

Unequal Eating
The Context of Daily Meals
—

Ewa Jarosz

Eating, in common understanding, is associated with what is on the plate, and is usually considered from the perspective of diet. The 50-year decline in the significance of set mealtimes that we showed in Chapter 1 is generally assumed to reflect a move in the direction of snacking and grazing, a trend that is regarded as deleterious from the perspective of diet and nutrition. The effect that our food, and the way we consume it, has on individual health and weight merits all the attention it receives from academic researchers as well as from popular media. The British case is of particular interest. The NHS website leaves no space for doubt: 'Britain: "the fat man of Europe"', the headline goes, introducing gloomy statistics about soaring obesity rates in the UK. The population's weight problems are blamed on 'lifestyles, including our reliance on the car, TVs, computers, desk-bound jobs and high-calorie food'. This discourse, predominantly associated with calorie intake, the nutritional value of food and the particular health outcomes of different kinds of diet, dominates the way we think about eating. It is framed in terms of healthy or unhealthy eating, and typically equated only with what is being consumed. What is missing from these narratives is, paradoxically, the act of eating itself – an act that carries much social information and meaning, regardless of the type of food consumed.

Thinking outside the plate

What, then, *is* eating? First of all, eating is a purposeful activity performed by individuals. It requires that a given amount of time be allocated to it. How much time is allocated to eating depends both on individual preferences and time constraints. Eating has a spatial and temporal location, and is usually done several times during a day, in various circumstances. Eating breakfast in the morning at home and having lunch in a work canteen accompanied by other co-workers imply different social and environmental experiences, even if in both cases the person eats a sandwich and coffee. Of course, different eating occasions are usually associated with different foods as well, but it is the meal content that is determined by the 'when', 'where' and 'with whom' it happens, and not the other way around. This simple fact is easy to forget when we focus primarily on what is on the plate.

Secondly, eating practices are shaped by cultural and social norms, reflecting the values and priorities of a given society. They therefore provide us with a barometer of social change and an indicator of lifestyle differences. For example, the role and meaning of food for the French is clearly reflected in their eating patterns, which are substantially different from how Americans eat. The USA is generally considered the cradle of fast eating: Americans eat more quickly, and are more likely both to replace meals with snacks and to have higher levels of anxiety related to food. Eating is designed to be functional, quick and efficient,[1,2] and they spend on average only around 60 minutes per day on this activity. The opposite seems to be true for countries such as France[3] or Armenia,[4] where eating takes roughly twice as long as in the US, is regarded as a pleasurable activity, and is also associated with national identity. Great Britain is positioned somewhere between continental Europe and the US. Eating in Britain takes longer than in the US (at 88 minutes per day), but slightly less time than in most of the other European countries. Eating behaviours reflect social inequalities within a single society, too. The eating behaviours of individuals with higher social status tend to be healthier, and include a more diverse diet. One of the main focuses of this chapter is on social-class differences in eating time and behaviour in the contemporary UK.

Thirdly, eating is predominantly a social activity. In the majority of cases, food is consumed in the company of others, and this often taken-for-granted fact has tremendous social significance. Having a meal together brings people closer, creates a sense of belonging, and also affects what is eaten. Eating is ultimately a bonding activity, and this is especially important in the case of families. Family meals have been shown to contribute substantially to the health and wellbeing of family members, particularly children. Healthy or unhealthy eating practices in later life are known to be strongly associated with what was on the family table in childhood.

Last but not least, eating is an important source of daily enjoyment – or, in other words, it imparts small daily pleasures. It acts as an immediate mood enhancer, and it is on average one of the most enjoyed activities in the 2015 UK time-use survey.

Despite the cross-national differences in eating times and behaviours referred to above, some common trends have also been identified. One of the more important is the recent decline in the amount of time people spend in the preparation and consumption of meals, and the increase in the frequency of eating out. These tendencies are associated with modern lifestyles, which have been described as busier and more challenging in terms of coordinating different social relationships and activities. Establishing regular eating routines is certainly more difficult now than several decades ago, when full-time female employment was less common and working hours were more predictable. Feeling pressed for time due to busy work schedules and the associated challenges in maintaining work-life balance encourages people to move eating to a secondary role; that is, to replace meals with snacks. Those under greater time pressure are more likely to cut down on their mealtime or even skip some meals entirely. So what exactly can eating patterns tell us about modern British lives? Perhaps more than one might expect.

The focus in this chapter is on meals considered as any episode of eating recorded in the diary as a primary activity (i.e. the main activity at a given point in time), as opposed to snacking (defined in this chapter as eating recorded as a secondary activity). The reason for focusing on meals rather than snacking is that regular meals are strongly affected by social norms and interaction, while snacking does not play such an important social role and, in fact, might be considered as a way to skip a meal while still satisfying hunger.

Social-class differences in eating in the UK

Social class has been associated with eating behaviours in many ways. Firstly, individuals from different classes have been shown to display preferences for different types of food. Furthermore, individual social status has been associated with both attitudes and behaviour in relation to food and eating. For example, some very insightful qualitative studies report reduced expectations for family and individual meals among respondents with lower social status.[5] Eating may be experienced as a way to satisfy basic bodily needs, without providing adequate nutrition, but also without meeting social needs or boosting personal enjoyment. In addition, lower-status occupational groups have less freedom in choosing when to work. Inflexibility of work schedules and greater work–family conflict have been shown to negatively affect the number of meals eaten and prepared at home, as well as their nutritional quality. For example, fast food might be used to alleviate time pressure and act as a compensation for everyday stresses in poorer families. Similar behaviour is less common among middle-class individuals, who seem on average to attach greater importance to eating. They are more likely to make the effort to eat together and have regular meals, including breakfast. They also pay greater attention to what is consumed in terms of its nutritional value.[6] Furthermore, in middle-class families, meals are more likely to be treated as valuable times to interact with children and instil in them particular eating habits. Taking all of these factors into consideration, it is no surprise that there is an association between socio-economic status and healthy eating practices, as well as between socio-economic status and obesity risks,[7] with those lowest in the social hierarchy being more likely to struggle with weight issues.

Analysis of the UK 2014–15 time-use data shows that working-class respondents allocate least time to eating compared to managers and professionals, or people in intermediate occupations.[8] They report around 83 minutes per day; nearly 12 minutes less than those in the highest class category. These class disparities in the average duration of meals might reflect either a shorter time spent in each meal, or having fewer meals over the day. In fact, in the case of the UK data, it is both. Working-class individuals spend, on average, less time on each meal occasion and also eat significantly fewer meals per day. It is a fact that the number of meals per day has been linked with individual weight status: more frequent eating, whether it is meals or snacks, has been found to be positively related to lower BMI values.[9] Sometimes snacks are consumed in place of meals, but in the case of the UK working-class, that is not the case. Working class respondents do not report more episodes of snacking than individuals from the other two social classes. Overall, taking both meals and snacks into account, they report significantly fewer episodes of eating over a day.

However, crude measures such as the average duration of eating episodes and the number of meals do not reflect all the factors that might contribute to class differentiation in eating patterns. Various socio-demographic and work-associated characteristics, such as different working arrangements, might contribute to time shortages or difficulties with schedule coordination while planning a meal. Figure 8.1 shows the mean predicted number of meals per day from a multivariate

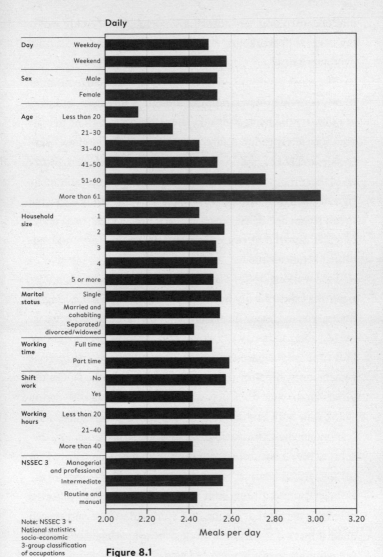

Figure 8.1
Number of meals per day: predicted averages for various socio-economic and demographic indicators, UK (2015)

model controlling for individuals' social class, weekly working time, shift work, and basic demographic and household characteristics.

The most pronounced differences in the average number of meals per day, when holding the other variables constant, are differences by age group. These show that older people are more likely to have three regular meals a day (less likely to skip breakfast!), and younger people to have fewer. Nearly all of these differences between age categories are statistically significant. These differences by age are most likely to be due to life-stage specificity; however there may also be some effect of generational differences in normative values around traditional set mealtimes.

Paid working hours matter too, but differences are statistically significant only between those who work the longest hours, who eat fewer meals per day, compared to those working less than 20 hours per week, who eat more meals per day. Full-time versus part-time work does not make a difference (when controlling for the number of hours worked). On the other hand, what does play an important role is shift work. Those who work in shifts report significantly fewer meals than respondents with more traditional working patterns. The disruption of the natural circadian rhythm has been blamed for the higher incidence of certain health issues, including cardiovascular disease, among shift workers.[10] The findings reported here also suggest that having non-standard working hours can make it more difficult to arrange time for eating. Needless to say, skipping meals is regarded as a health risk, and research shows it is associated with heavier body weights.

Even when working characteristics are controlled for, the

effect of social class remains significant. Working-class individuals have significantly fewer meals than managers and professionals, and working arrangements do not explain these class differences in eating patterns. Previous research cited here has cast much light on the topic; class differences are likely to be due to the combination of lifestyle factors, values and priorities, as well as attitudes towards food.

Finally, more frequent meals eaten over the days of the weekend might reflect fewer temporal constraints on those days (mostly due to much less paid work being performed over the weekend) as well as the existence of certain family-related weekend rituals, such as Sunday family dinners.

Getting round the table: social context and location

Duration and frequency of meals reflect, respectively, the amount of time allocated to eating overall, and how often one is able to arrange time for meals. However, what is probably more important from the perspective of an individual is not for how long or how frequently they eat, but rather where and with whom they do it. Even with regard to the purely nutritional aspects of eating, meal location and social setting make a difference. Eating at home means consuming less fat and salt than eating out, and portions tend to be smaller than those served in restaurants.

The social context of eating has also been shown to affect dietary intake. Interestingly, although people tend to eat more in the company of family or friends, research suggests that countries where social meals are more common have lower obesity rates. Social eating can be used to refer either to eating in the company of people from outside of the household (referred to below as social meals), or to having a meal with one's family (referred to as family meals). Though different, both convey important social meaning and are significant building blocks of the interpersonal relations within an individual's closest social milieu. Social eating in general seems to be beneficial. It can improve one's mood, and fosters a sense of belonging and connectedness. Taking these multiple benefits into account, it is interesting to know how social eating is differentiated by social status.

It turns out that there are significant differences in the frequency of social meals by social class. When we consider meals eaten with non-household members, differences between weekdays and weekends are clear. This difference is even more pronounced when we analyse social meals eaten out of home (shown in Figure 8.2). On weekdays, managers and professionals eat out with non-household members significantly more often than others. It is likely that weekday meals reflect differences in the type of work and working environment. Higher-status occupations might involve institutionalized eating occasions (e.g. business lunches). On the other hand, social meals may not be convenient or even possible in some types of jobs, in particular when one works in shifts, which is more common among the working class. Tellingly, when all social meals (i.e. those eaten at home as well as out of home) are considered, class differences are virtually non-existent at weekends (not shown). It is likely that, while the character of paid employment and occupational characteristics shapes eating patterns on weekdays, the nature of out-of-work relationships with family and friends determines

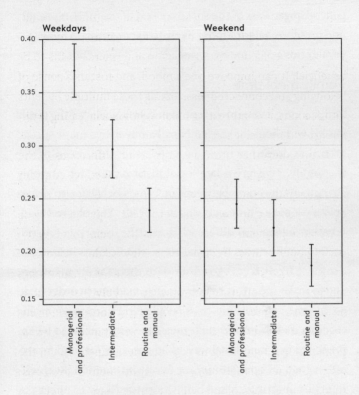

Figure 8.2
Average number of social meals eaten out-of-home per day
by social class, UK (2015)

the frequency of social meals at the weekend. On the other hand, class differences again become visible at the weekend when only meals eaten out of home are considered (8.2). In general, regardless of the social context of the meal, managers and professionals are more likely to eat out than other classes, and this holds for both weekdays and weekends.

Family meal time

Perhaps even more important than social meals are the meals shared with household members. Family meals merit special attention due to their social importance and meaning for the family. They are a key social institution which not only strengthens the bonds between family members but also shapes young people's eating patterns in later life. Sociological studies show substantial differentiation in the importance attributed to family meals by social class. Middle-class individuals are more likely to eat together with their family members, and to make the effort to coordinate schedules in order to do so. In contrast, working-class people tend to consider eating together as less important – meals are more likely to be approached in a functional way, as an occasion for food intake, rather than an opportunity for family interaction. Such differences in attitudes and behaviours are likely to affect the functioning of individual family members as well as the family as a whole. Research shows a positive relationship between the frequency of a family getting together around the table to eat and the cognitive performance of the children. At the same time a negative relationship has been found between the frequency of eating with family members and the risk of child obesity, which points to social context being important for individual health outcomes too.

As we have shown, the frequency of eating at home with household members is clearly associated with social class. However, unlike in the case of social meals, class differences in family meals are significant for weekends only (shown in Figure 8.3). At weekends, working-class individuals have significantly fewer family meals than professionals and managers or people in intermediary occupations. Relatedly, due to the lower number of family meals, working-class families spend less time together around the table (not shown). Differences in the frequency of at-home family meals are not balanced out by differences in eating out with family members. As mentioned earlier, eating out is generally more common among managers and professionals, and eating out with the family is no exception.

So far, only descriptive statistics about family meals have been presented. However, the number of family meals is likely to be related to household composition (the more people there are, the less easy it is to coordinate with all of them) as well as individual working patterns and working time, all of which might be differentiated by class. In a multivariate model controlling for the effects of those variables, as well as for basic demographics, class differences remained significant – those in the intermediary and working classes have significantly fewer meals with their household members than is the case for managers and professionals. So what consequences might these class disparities have? A lower frequency of family meals might have an effect on the way a family functions, as well as on

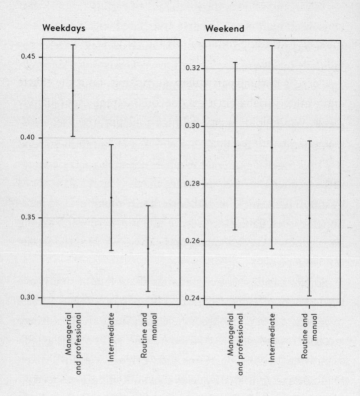

Figure 8.3
Average number of family meals eaten at home, weekdays and weekends, by social class, UK (2015)

individual social capital and relations within an individual's closest social milieu. Fewer family meals implies less time for family interaction around the table, and may mean that children get less supervision in regard of what they eat over the day – a finding reported in qualitative studies on class differences in eating.

There is nothing particularly surprising about the effects of the other variables in the model on the frequency of family meals. While holding other things constant, this frequency is negatively related to shift working. Shift work is likely to make it more difficult for family members to coordinate their schedules and, as a result, to sit together around the table. Individuals are also more likely to eat with other household members in slightly bigger households – in this case there are more potential partners to have a meal with. Weekends also see more episodes of family meals.

One consequence of the fact that working-class individuals are less likely to eat together with their families as well as less likely to eat with people from outside the household (as discussed in the previous section) is that they are also more likely to eat their meals alone. On average, 28 out of every 100 meals working-class people consume are solitary. In the case of managers and professionals, it is 23 per 100, and respondents in intermediary positions have around one fifth of their meals alone.

Breakfast of champions?

The fact that working-class respondents report having fewer meals per day, as shown earlier in this chapter, suggests that some of the routine daily meals must be being skipped. It turns out that fewer working-class individuals record eating any of the regular daytime meals (breakfast, lunch or dinner) compared to the other two classes (Figure 8.4). At the same time, they are more likely to eat food late at night ('supper'). Interestingly, it does not matter whether we consider weekdays or weekends; class differences in this respect are stable across the week. This suggests that this difference is not an effect of paid work schedules, but is, rather, related to class-related lifestyle characteristics.

While skipping meals in general is thought to have an impact on individual health and wellbeing, the importance of one meal in particular has been emphasized in academic research and healthy eating guidelines. Breakfast seems to be associated with certain lifestyle choices as well as important health outcomes. First of all, having breakfast has been linked with lower BMI values.[11] Secondly, giving up on the first meal of the day has been associated with numerous unhealthy lifestyle factors such as lack of exercise, smoking, or substance abuse, both in adults and adolescents.[12] It seems that, while having lunch is more likely to reflect work schedules and conventions, breakfast is more related to personal choices and the home environment. Interestingly, sociological studies have also reported class differences in the importance attributed to having breakfast. Middle-class respondents put greater emphasis on the first meal of the day, as well as on having it together with their families, suggesting greater emphasis on adherence to healthy eating guidelines and to the social importance of breakfast.

These effects of class on the eating of breakfast are supported in multivariate analysis. Holding all other factors

Weekdays

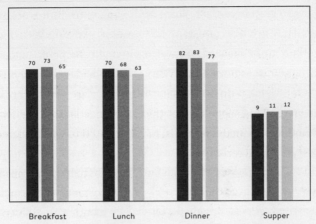

Weekend

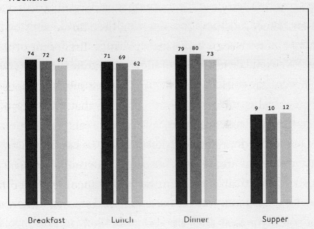

Figure 8.4

Meal types eaten, by social class, UK (2015)

- ■ Managerial and professional occupation
- ■ Intermediate occupation
- ■ Routine and manual occupation

constant, people in routine and manual occupations are more likely to skip breakfast. Since both shift work and working part-time are held constant, this tendency to skip breakfast is likely to be related to non-employment factors, such as the lesser perceived importance of regular meals, or lower levels of preoccupation with healthy eating, or with eating in general – all of which have been reported in earlier studies. Other factors associated with a higher probability of reporting having eaten breakfast are older age, working part-time, and a weekend diary day. The fact that older people are less likely to skip breakfast had been reported in earlier research. Part-time work is mostly performed by adults with children, who might make more effort to maintain healthier eating patterns; in their case the morning meal is likely to involve other family members too. On the other hand, working in shifts was associated with a higher chance of skipping breakfast. Weekend days in general allow more time for eating due to fewer time constraints related to paid employment, so the average higher incidence of eating breakfast at the weekends is not particularly surprising.

In sum, working-class individuals in the UK have less healthy eating patterns – both from the point of view of physical and of social health. They tend to eat less frequently, including having fewer family and social meals, and are more likely to eat solitary meals. They are also more likely to skip regular daytime meals, among them breakfast. On the other hand, they report eating late at night more frequently than others. Over the week, working-class respondents dedicate less overall time to eating than either intermediate or managerial/professional classes. On average, they spend around 12 minutes less eating per day than managers and professionals, amounting to nearly 1 hour 30 minutes per week. Considering that this time is taken out mainly from social and family meals, that means almost 1 hour 30 minutes less interaction with friends, colleagues or family members around the table per week.

Happy meals

While health and obesity risks certainly justify all the research attention they receive, they do not exhaust the list of important outcomes of particular food choices and eating behaviours. Much less attention has been focused, for example, on the effect of meals on individual mood – especially when it comes to meal settings, rather than their nutritional content. Eating is usually enjoyable, and this is reflected in the UK data in which eating is, on average, the most enjoyable of all daily activities (see Chapter 14). However, not every meal brings equal enjoyment. To investigate what factors are associated with meal enjoyment we used a multivariate model to analyse the enjoyment of specific meal occasions. The basic activity settings (when, where, and with whom a meal happens) were included in order to show the net effect of each of these characteristics on mean enjoyment levels.

It seems, perhaps not surprisingly, that what brings the greatest immediate enjoyment is having meals in the company of others. Family meals, and meals with others from outside of the household (presumably friends), are enjoyed the most. By contrast, solitary eating is enjoyed the least. Eating out ranks with eating in company in terms of enjoyment. Compared to eating at home, eating in a restaurant leads to significantly higher levels of enjoyment. Unfortunately, given the higher levels of sugar, salt and additives included in restaurant food, health and enjoyment do not always come together! This contradiction is reversed for the first meal of the day; despite the fact that breakfast is considered an important meal from a nutritional point of view, it is not considered a very enjoyable meal on average. All other meals receive significantly higher enjoyment scores than breakfast. The reason might be that, on the whole, mornings are more hurried and stressful due to the upcoming events of the day – primarily preparation of children for school and paid work. Perhaps for similar reasons meals eaten at work or school are also among the least enjoyed.

Since we have already seen that social classes differ in respect of the timing, social context and frequency of meals, it is intuitively likely that they would also experience different overall levels of meal enjoyment. This is certainly the case, but the direction of the effect might seem puzzling – managers and professionals who have, on average, more social and family meals, and who eat out more often, report the lowest average levels of meal enjoyment. Moreover, when other variables relating to meal activity (such as location, type of meal, weekend or weekday meal, and the social context of the meal) are held constant, these class differences remain. That is, managers and professionals enjoy their meals the least compared to the intermediate and working classes, and the reasons for this class differentiation seem not to be related to meal patterns – that is, the where, when, or with whom they eat.

We might speculate, therefore, that these differences may be due to different attitudes towards eating in general. Middle-class individuals are more likely to have healthier eating patterns and make more effort to eat healthy foods.[13] This might conceivably contribute to higher expectations of meal quality, which might lead to higher stress and feelings of pressure. On the other hand, comfort eating, such as eating out in fast-food outlets, has been described as one of the strategies employed by poorer families to help them cope with everyday stresses. Such behaviours might have a negative effect on physical health in the long run, but they are likely to trigger immediate mood improvement – even if only in the short term.

People's attitudes towards food consumption and their association with class-specific daily eating patterns is an issue that underlies all the analyses presented in this chapter. The results have supported the finding of previous authors that social classes in the UK differ in their food preferences. But, as we have shown, eating behaviours clearly matter not only for individual nutritional health, but also for the quality of social and, in particular, family relations. By using the time-use diary data, we are also able to show *how* the different classes eat – that is for how long, how often, and in what social and spatial settings they eat. All of these dimensions are likely to be linked to the role that food plays in particular social structural locations and in specific lifestyle choices. Class-related values and priorities regarding home and family life have been shown to either promote healthy eating patterns or the opposite – that is, to demotivate individuals from eating regular meals, especially in a situation of time shortage. It may be that the middle classes are more influenced by considerations of social desirability in their attitudes towards food, focusing more on health and what is seen as 'proper' in their social milieu with regard to meal preparation, food consumption and its role in child upbringing. On the other hand, working-class people might be more likely to seek pleasure in eating, or resort to comfort food when faced with stress or other life challenges that they are likely to encounter more often than their middle-class counterparts. Whatever lies behind class differences in eating behaviours, it is worth more research attention, and might prove useful in the understanding of why obesity rates are higher among particular social groups.

CHAPTER 9

Time and Physical Activity

—

Jonathan Gershuny
Teresa Harms

We know that the way we spend our time contributes substantially to our health. The previous chapter looked at the timing and context of eating; in this chapter we look at the physiological value of the physical activity involved in our daily lives. Everything we do has some potential physiological impact, positive or negative. Health authorities tell us that moderate to vigorous levels of physical activity have beneficial effects, and the 'couch-potato' lifestyle has negative ones. However, while *some* physical activity is evidently a good thing, the exact effect of different levels of activity is hard to establish. Public health advice in this area is predominantly based on measures constructed from answers to survey questions about participation in physical exercise that are not always easy to answer.

Time-use evidence can play an important role here, by providing us with accurate estimates of individual – and population – daily activities. By combining this information with estimates derived from medical research on metabolic processes (so-called metabolic equivalence scores, or METs), we are able to show how different totals of daily activity are associated with different personal energy expenditures. We show in this chapter how these daily totals of energy expenditure vary with demographic characteristics such as age and sex, employment status and educational level. Then we assess the extent to which physical activity (and the resulting energy expenditure) is related to health and wellbeing. And finally, we estimate the exercise-related balance of activities through the day and across the population. Emerging from this discussion is a challenge to the science that underlies much of the current public health advice on physical activity.

Comparing time-use diary measures of activity with conventional measures

The conventional approach to establishing the extent of an individual's engagement in physical activity for the purposes of health assessment involves the use of survey questionnaires. The physical activity questions fall generally into three categories. They ask either whether the respondent 'usually' participates in particular specified activities, or (better) whether the respondent has *in fact* participated in the activities over a specified time period (normally last week or last month). They ask, in the 'usual' case, about the frequency ('every day?', 'two or three times per week?', and so on), and in the 'actual' past participation case, how many times the respondent has undertaken the activity during the specified period. Finally, they ask about the duration of the activity, either usually, or on the last occasion it was done. These questions certainly can be asked. But do the people we interview *know the correct answers*? The 'usual' version of these questions, though apparently easy to answer, offers respondents the opportunity to dismiss *actual* experience of activity frequency in favour of preferred or aspirational levels! We may go swimming only irregularly, but we know we should do more exercise, and this becomes translated into an assertion that we 'usually' go swimming. In fact, findings from general reviews of the evidence on the reliability of questionnaire-type self-reporting conclude that the results from the standard Physical Activity Questionnaires (PAQs) may be twice the real rate of physical activity.[1]

The UK 2014–15 time-use diary study did not collect the same questions in the questionnaire accompanying the diaries as those asked on the standard PAQ questionnaires. However, it did include some similar items: asking, for example, about the number of times in the last month that respondents engaged in various cultural and sporting activities. We know that people have regular and predicable habits of physical activity, so it is not unreasonable to assume that last month's pattern of activity is likely to be a good predictor of this month's. So, if our respondent answers that she went to the gym on just one day last month, we might assume that there is something like a one day in 30, or 3.3 per cent, chance that she will go to the gym on the random diary day, while an answer of two days last month implies a 6.6 per cent chance, and so on. This allows us to compare the predicted daily activity probability, calculated from the responses to the question about how many times in the past month the respondent did the activity, with the actual rate of occurrence of the activity on the randomly selected diary day.

For the most part, we find that the predicted rate of occurrence for the exercise-related activities substantially exceeds the actual occurrence rate on the randomly chosen diary day. In the cases of those who claimed the most swimming, running, cycling and walking, the predicted level is indeed two or even three times higher than the actual level recorded in the diaries.[2] So, one of these two estimators, either the last-month participation frequency or the randomly selected diary-day participation rate, must be wrong, either systematically overestimating (upwardly biased) in the questionnaire case or underestimating (downwardly biased) in the diary case. Which is it?

We can choose between the two alternative estimators by making assumptions about their likely relative reliability. This argument returns to the discussion in the introduction to this book about the *unreliability* of survey estimators of time use. The answers to the PAQ-type questions are more difficult to arrive at than they may initially seem. How many times *did* you do a particular activity involving physical exercise in the last month? Maybe you remember the last time you did it, but was it *really* within the last 28 days? Certainly you intend to go to the gym every week, but does that *really* mean you went four times in the last month? Can you actually remember each occasion you did it, or are you *estimating* on the basis of what you intend to do? And so on. Secondly, imagine that you are being interviewed by someone announcing themselves as conducting a health survey. You know that running and cycling and playing sport are all healthy activities and you cannot *quite* remember how many times you went swimming last month . . . twice, or was it perhaps three times? All these factors lead to what is known in the survey business as 'social-desirability bias' (i.e. self-deception, to ourselves as much as to others, about our rates of participation in activities we know we should engage in more, or the simple representation of ourselves to others as in some respect *better* than we actually are!). The time-use diary, by contrast, involves an easier task of recollection. The actual instance of the gym visit is perhaps cued by the memory of the route taken yesterday returning from work. In addition, time-use diaries are usually general-purpose instruments, designed not to alert respondents about why and in what ways researchers are interested in how they spend their time. The lack of an apparent subject focus in our recent time-use survey means that *diarists do not know which activities to over- or under-report*.

New technological advances such as motion and heart-rate sensors (that capture body movement and physiological processes automatically), as well as 'passive' data-collection devices such as smartphones, wearable cameras and smart watches offer us 'objective' methodologies for testing the diary against questionnaire accounts not just against each other, but also more directly. Comparing self-report diaries with wearable cameras that provide a continuous visual record of our activities strongly validates the diary approach.[3] These arguments have been sufficient to convince many researchers that the questionnaire recall (PAQ) approach produces seriously upwardly biased estimates, and that self-report 'yesterday' diary samples are a more appropriate basis for estimating population physical activity.[4]

Assigning metabolic equivalents (METs) to activities: mean daily MET scores

We can calculate whole-day metabolic activity for an individual diary respondent by multiplying the time spent in various activities over their diary day by the appropriate 'metabolic equivalent' (or MET) score. The most widely consulted source for this equivalency between activities and MET scores is the Ainsworth Compendium (2011). The Compendium lists over 750 categories of activities constructed on the basis of clinical measurements of METs as well as some expert estimates. From 2000 onwards, various researchers recognized the potential of time-diary studies for this work and started to construct appropriate assignment tables. For example, Tudor-Locke and colleagues, who assigned METs to all of the activities listed in the coding lexicon of the American Time Use Study (ATUS).[5]

MET scores are scaled against a physiological fixed point (corresponding to the amount of oxygen consumed while sitting at rest, calculated as 3.5 millilitres per kilogramme of body weight per minute).[6] METs are calculated relative to this physical constant, with 'resting' set as the fixed point, and rated as 1 MET. Double the METs means double the metabolic load of that activity. Each category of activity of the day is allocated a MET score, so multiplying the total daily minutes devoted to each activity by an individual respondent by the appropriate MET score and summing the results gives a measure of that individual's total daily metabolic activity.[7] Dividing this total by the 1,440 minutes of the day gives the mean daily MET score for that individual.

Table 9.1 shows the assigned MET scores for illustrative diary activities, ranked according to the different levels of exertion required. In addition, we assigned specific MET scores to various occupational groups when engaging in their paid work, and to various transport modes while travelling.

HETUS activities	METs
Sleeping	0.92
Watching TV and videos	1.33
Eating	1.50
Shopping mainly for food	2.33
Physical care and supervision of a child	2.67
Gardening	3.66
Walking and hiking	3.80
Make, repair, maintain equipment	4.49
Cycling	8.00
Outdoor pairs or doubles games	8.50

Modes of transport	METs
Bus	1.30
Foot	3.50
Bicycle	6.00

Paid-work occupations	METs
Managers (not professional)	1.73
Secretarial workers	1.83
Teachers	2.50
Construction trades	4.29

Table 9.1
Examples of activities from the Harmonized European Time Use Survey (HETUS) and METs assignments (ascending degree of exertion)

Looking at the different diary activities, sleeping, at 0.92 METs, is pretty close to the fixed point of 1 MET. Just above the exertion required in sleeping comes sedentary activities like watching TV and eating. Then moderately active unpaid work activities like shopping and childcare. Gardening, rated at 3.66 METs, involves very nearly as much exertion as walking. Above that, active repairs/DIY is followed, way up the scale, by physical exercise activities such as cycling and sports (at 8 METs and above). In respect of modes of travel, it is no surprise that taking the bus involves far less exertion than walking or, especially, cycling to work. When we look at different occupations, sedentary desk jobs (managerial, secretarial) rate slightly above watching TV and eating, but below moderately active unpaid work tasks such as shopping or childcare. The exertions of teachers, at 2.5 METs, are more or less equivalent to these tasks. Construction trades involve much more exertion, equivalent to active unpaid work tasks such as maintenance/repair/DIY.

Using this metric, we can multiply the MET scores for all the different activities by the time that diary respondents spend in these different activities, to arrive at a mean daily MET score for every respondent.

Mean daily METs and demographics

A question that might reasonably be asked is, 'Do these METs calculations make sense in terms of our common understanding about people's physical activity patterns?' One way of answering this is to look at the way that mean daily METs vary with demographic characteristics. We assume, for example, that people do progressively less exercise as they age. Do we find an age gradient in our METs calculations? Perhaps women are less active than men, or better educated people differ in their activity patterns from those with lower levels of education? Figure 9.1 shows some of these socio-demographic differences from the UK 2014–15 TUS.[8]

Figure 9.1 shows the female diarists. A reasonably clear age pattern is evident: physical activity increasing gently through the first part of adulthood, but declining in middle age (starting in the forties for the less well educated, and in the fifties for those with higher education). Women in paid employment engage in higher levels of physical activity than do those out of paid employment – the reason for this association may be *either* the physical activity that comes as part of the employment, or the fact that it is more difficult for less physically able people to find paid employment. The growing difference between the physical activity levels of older employed women with and without higher education relates mostly, we suspect, to lifestyle choices: it is likely that more highly educated women are intentionally engaging in higher levels of physical activity specifically to improve and maintain their health.

Figure 9.1 provides equivalent estimates for men's physical activities. Across all educational, employment and age groups, men do more physical exercise than women. The shapes of the curves are in two cases rather similar, with the exception being that for younger employed men with lower levels of education. Their estimated level of physical activity is much higher than for other men of the same age. The explanation is straightforward: this group is disproportionally likely to be

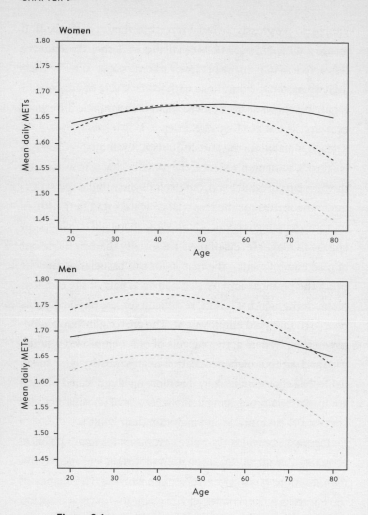

Figure 9.1

Average daily METs by age, education and employment status: women and men, UK (2015)

——— In work, with some higher education
- - - - In work, no higher education
- - - - Not in work, no higher education

employed in manual occupations, with higher levels of physical activity entailed by job tasks, while those employed men with higher education are much more likely to find themselves in jobs which entail long hours of sedentary activity.

However, the relatively high levels of physical activity for this group of men starts to reduce relatively early in life, at around age 40 (in parallel with that for unemployed men with lower levels of education). This is likely to reflect some combination of two processes: some members of this group will be promoted to managerial or supervisory tasks, which have lower physical demands and involve more sedentary activity; others will simply find, as they age, increasing difficulty accomplishing the heavier physical labour required in manual work.

METs and wellbeing

Do these differences in mean daily activity levels ultimately matter in terms of wellbeing? The UK 2015 TUS asked the question, 'How dissatisfied or satisfied would you say you are with your health?' (reported on a 1 to 7 scale, with 4 as the neutral point 'neither satisfied nor dissatisfied', 5 representing 'somewhat satisfied', and 6 representing 'mostly satisfied'). Figure 9.2 has as its vertical axis respondents' mean response scores to this question.[9] This is shown plotted against the individual's mean daily MET score (on the horizontal axis).

The association is clear and unambiguous. People with the lowest levels of physical activity also report the lowest assessment of their state of health. People with higher levels of physical activity have substantially and statistically significantly higher levels of positive self-assessment of their health. Of course, there is a two-way relationship between physical

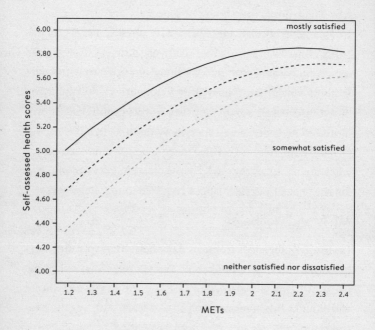

Figure 9.2
Self-assessed health by age and average daily METs,
UK (2015)

——— Age 30
- - - - Age 50
- - - - Age 70

activity and wellbeing. On the one hand, it is evident that engaging in moderate to vigorous physical activity has positive consequences for health and wellbeing. On the other hand, it is equally obvious that less healthy people, and those who feel less satisfied with their health status, are *less able* to participate in such activities. So we can note that these two measures are strongly *associated*, but the direction of causality cannot be determined from this figure. There are evidently causes and effects, but they go in both directions: physical activity promoting health, and good health encouraging physical activity.

METs and the population's Great Day

Health guidelines for desirable levels of physical activity provided by public health agencies tend to take the form of recommended minimum durations in activities. Current World Health Organization guidelines define moderate-intensity physical activity as 3–6 METs, and vigorous-intensity physical activity as greater than 6 METs.[10] They recommend for adults at least 150 minutes of moderate-intensity physical activity throughout the week, or at least 75 minutes of vigorous-intensity physical activity. UK guidelines on the NHS website follow these recommendations, suggesting 'at least 150 minutes per week of moderate aerobic activity such as cycling or brisk walking'.[11]

However, such guidelines tend to overlook (or at least underplay) the physical activity energy expenditure for ongoing everyday activities such as housework, child- and elder care, and paid work. For example, from Table 9.1 we saw that, while gardening exceeds the 3 MET boundary for 'moderate physical activity', and construction work by far exceeds it, most other forms of paid and unpaid work fall below this boundary. Time-use diary data, uniquely, enable us to estimate the contributions of *all* these activities to the population's overall daily metabolic expenditure.

Figure 9.3 shows how the population's Great Day of 1,440 minutes is made up in terms of different activity categories and their associated metabolic load. The horizontal axis shows the minutes of the day from 0 to 1,440 minutes, and the average daily time devoted to each of the various categories of daily activity, while the vertical axis shows the average MET score for those activity categories.

We can see that large percentages of the population's Great Day are made up of sleeping and resting in bed (37 per cent), home leisure (15 per cent), followed by paid and unpaid work (13 per cent each), and eating/personal care (10 per cent). However, only a very small percentage of time is made up of activities that would be classified by most people as 'physical exercise': walking/cycling and intentional exercise (sports, gym, swimming, etc.), at only 1 per cent of time each. (There will of course be some avid devotees of exercise who spend considerably more of their daily lives than this jogging around the streets, at the gym, or in the pool. Others – less inclined to exercise – will spend more of their time in front of the TV, or in various kinds of home leisure. But on average, what this graph shows is how the nation's Great Day is divided.)

These two physical exercise categories (walking/cycling and intentional exercise) are clearly rated far more highly in terms of MET scores than others. While several of the activity categories lie somewhere around the average MET score of 1.6, these two are rated as 3.91 METs (walking/cycling) and

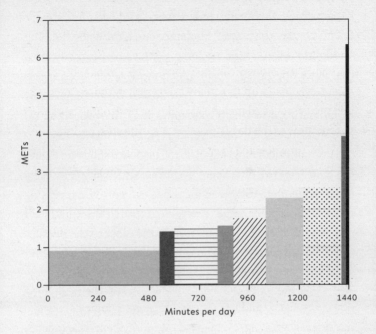

Figure 9.3
Average daily METs by activity type: population
aged 8 and over, UK (2015)

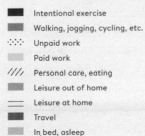

- Intentional exercise
- Walking, jogging, cycling, etc.
- Unpaid work
- Paid work
- Personal care, eating
- Leisure out of home
- Leisure at home
- Travel
- In bed, asleep

6.3 METs (intentional exercise). Sleeping, as we have seen, has a very low MET score (0.92), while paid and unpaid work fall just below the 3-MET boundary conventionally defining 'moderate' exercise, at 2.3 and 2.5 METs respectively. As a nation we do, though, spend much more of our lives asleep and working than exercising! How do we take account of this in estimating how much contribution *all* the various activities make to the nation's overall average metabolic load?

A simple calculation, based on the evidence shown in Figure 9.3, multiplies the time spent in various activity categories by the average metabolic load for those categories, expressing the result as a percentage. This tells us that sleeping and paid and unpaid work actually contribute the most to the population's overall average metabolic load. Although it might seem surprising, as a population we expend 21 per cent of our overall average daily metabolic load while asleep! The reason for this, of course, is that we spend such a large percentage of our time asleep. Conversely, walking/cycling and intentional exercise, each taking up only 1 per cent of our time, contribute just 3 per cent and 4 per cent respectively of the population's overall metabolic energy expenditure. The point of interest is how much of our average overall load is contributed by activity categories that are only relatively moderately rated in terms of METs. Doing paid and unpaid work are, in fact, the activities that contribute the next largest amounts to our overall energy expenditure after sleeping, at 18 per cent and 20 per cent of overall metabolic load respectively. This is so because they both rate moderately highly in terms of METs (significantly above the average), and we spend considerable amounts of time doing them.

To sum up, it is evident that activity durations, derived from time-use diaries which comprehensively cover all the activities of a representative sample of the population, are, potentially, an important public health research tool. The answers given to survey questionnaires on physical activity (PAQs) are still the main evidence base for the estimation of the relationship between physical activity and health outcomes. Yet we know that people exaggerate the amount of physical exercise they engage in – the public health literature shows that this evidence is systematically biased in an upwards direction. Our own comparison from the UK TUS of 2015 of monthly claimed frequency of exercise with actual exercise patterns on randomly chosen diary days suggests that PAQs may be estimating as much as double the actual exercise rate.

What are the consequences of this overestimation?

Paradoxically, it may have a negative impact on public compliance with public health guidelines. The research evidence that underlies the guidelines is the association between the PAQ evidence and identified health outcomes. Assuming that the health outcomes are correctly measured, using the PAQ approach may substantially exaggerate the actual effort required to achieve the health benefit. You might say, '30 minutes five times per week? – simply impossible given the other constraints on my time.' But the PAQ may actually be exaggerating the exercise necessary to achieve the same health benefit, by a factor of two: '30 minutes moderate exercise two or three times a week? – I may just be able to fit that in!'

In short, reducing estimates of current recommended levels of physical activity may actually have the effect of *increasing* future physical activity! Moreover, some people may already be getting healthy levels of exercise in ways that are unrecognized by conventional measures. For example, those who do a significant amount of gardening or other more physically active forms of paid or unpaid work. This potentially very important application of time-diary surveys lies at quite a distance from the original national accounting and gender relations issues in the minds of the economists and sociologists who began collecting these sorts of data in the early decades of the 20th century.

PART FOUR

Technology and Wellbeing through the Life-course

CHAPTER 10

Technology in the Daily Lives of Children and Teenagers

—

Killian Mullan

From the turn of the millennium, arguably one of the biggest and most rapid transformations in our daily lives relates to the use of technology and the internet. The development and rapid diffusion of powerful mobile devices has been one of the most dramatic changes in society over the past decade or so. The impact of this on children's wellbeing and development continues to be a source of concern in some quarters. These concerns primarily relate to questions about the amount of time children spend using technology and the internet, and the impact of this on their time in other activities and social interactions. Parents naturally worry about the time their children spend using computers and mobile devices. They want to make sure their children are spending enough time doing homework, engaging in sports and creative activities, and interacting sociably with their family and friends. Concerns about the time that children spend using computers and mobile devices stem from the potential negative impact of how this affects time spent in other activities, such as sport, and social interaction. The generally accepted opinion is that excessive time using mobile devices has a negative effect on children's social skills and wellbeing.[1] Yet parents also recognize that children benefit from using technology for learning essential new skills, interacting with friends and family, and, importantly, for fun. National media routinely echo the concern that children spend too much time on their mobile devices[2] (even while on holiday![3]). Media reports sometimes centre on mobile devices, but often they focus on screen time in general, including time watching TV or gaming using computers. This is not surprising as children today can access media content, including video and music, as well as games and reading material, seamlessly across a range of devices (such as smartphones and tablets, but also 'old' desktop computers and new 'smart' TVs). Concerns about use of mobile devices and screen time therefore intersect with debates and concerns about children's access to and use of the internet.

As children's exposure to these technologies is relatively recent, our understanding of its consequences remains limited, and this opens up the potential for unfounded claims about its impacts. There is an urgent need for more evidence about how children are actually using computers and mobile devices, and how they have incorporated these devices into their daily lives. The UK 2014–15 TUS asked children to report on the time they spent using computers and mobile devices (smartphones and tablets), allowing us to consider a number of critical questions that relate directly to current debates about children's use of technology and the internet, and its impact on their lives and development. Here we examine how children incorporate computers and mobile devices into their daily activities, and the social context within which they are using these technologies.

Children's access to and use of computers, mobile devices and the internet

Over the past decade, children's access to and use of the internet and mobile devices has increased dramatically. Ofcom reports that around two-thirds of children aged 8–15 had access to the internet at home in 2005, which rose to nine in every ten children by 2015.[4] Smartphone ownership among children aged 8–11 rose from 13 per cent in 2010 to 24 per cent in 2015. Comparable figures for children aged 12–15 are 35 per cent and 69 per cent respectively, and research shows that children in the UK have a relatively high rate of smartphone ownership compared with children in other European countries.[5] In addition, there have been markedly steep increases in children's access to and ownership of tablet computers in the past five years. Ofcom report that around 5 per cent of children aged 5–15 had access to a tablet computer in 2010, which increased to 80 per cent in 2015, and ownership rose from 2 per cent to 40 per cent over the same period.

Sonia Livingstone and colleagues have studied in detail children's (aged 9–16) use of mobile devices and computers to access the internet in the *Net Children Go Mobile* study.[6] They found that the most common device children use to access the internet was a smartphone, with 56 per cent of children using them to go online. Perhaps surprisingly, girls and boys differed little in terms of accessing the internet with other mobile devices and computers.[7] There were, however, very strong differences in the propensity to access the internet related to children's ages, with older children being more likely to use mobile devices and computers to access the internet than younger children. For example, only 37 per cent of children aged 9–10 used mobile devices and computers to access the internet versus 97 per cent of teenagers aged 15–16. These differences are likely to reflect age differences in children's ownership of devices, including smartphones, as noted above.

Debates on children's time using technology and the internet

The proliferation of computers and mobile devices has given rise to much public debate and controversy about their impact on the lives and development of children. Some argue that children's use of computers and mobile devices engenders a sedentary screen-based lifestyle that is harmful to their physical and mental health.[8] They argue that computers and mobile devices expose children to new online risks, and that excessive amounts of time in sedentary screen-based activities come at the expense of time children could be spending in physical activity including outdoor play. Others counter that evidence that children's use of technology and the internet has a negative impact is not conclusive, and that guidelines for children's use of technology must rest on a strong evidence base that is still lacking.[9]

At the core of these debates is an unease, experienced by many parents, that children are spending excessive amounts of time using computers and mobile devices. It doesn't help, though, that exactly what constitutes excessive is far from clear. There are no clear guidelines in the UK, and little evidence that anyone follows such guidelines internationally, or that they are even useful.[10] A more basic question, however, has to do with how good we think our measures of children's time using technology and the internet actually are. Many stories in the media about children's time using technology report on measures of time use that are unreliable.[11] For example, Ofcom's measure of the time children spend using the internet,[12] routinely cited in negative media reports, uses a question asking children to recall how many hours they spend using the internet on a typical day.[13] Unfortunately, in general, we do not have a great ability to recall accurately how much time we spend in many of our routine daily activities.[14] In addition, there is no reason why we should restrict measures of children's time using the internet to a 'typical' day. In contrast, all-purpose time-use surveys provide reliable measures of how we spend our time in various activities. Therefore, the first major contribution of this chapter is simply to provide a reliable measure of the time children spend using devices.

A second related aspect of debates on children's use of technology stems from its potential negative impact on the time they have available for other activities. However, there is no consistent evidence that screen time displaces time in other activities such as sport. Against a backdrop where children's use of technology is continuing to evolve rapidly, we need to know more than we do currently about how children have integrated technology into their daily lives. Along with information about the time spent using devices, the UK TUS provides information on the main activities they are engaging in while using these devices. By studying what children are doing when they report using devices we explore the different ways in which the use of technology and the internet have become embedded in the daily lives of children.

A third issue in debates about children's use of technology

highlights its potential influence on the nature and quality of children's social interactions. At the extreme, worries here centre on the image of a socially isolated, and perhaps introverted, child whose social interactions are mediated largely through technology, via social media or internet forums. In fact, research suggests that rather than replacing face-to-face social interactions, children and teenagers use technology in ways that facilitate and sustain interpersonal relationships.[15] The important point perhaps is that technology is changing the nature of social interactions for children, in both positive and negative ways.[16] The third focus of this chapter is therefore on the wider social context within which children use technology and the internet. Based on the information that children provide about the people they are spending time with throughout the day, we analyse how much time they spend alone, with family, and with others they know, when they are using devices. The chapter uses data from 1,171 children and young people aged 8–18, living with their parents and in education, and who each provided time-use data for up to two diary days.[17]

An overview of children's time using computer devices

Table 10.1 shows that the vast majority of children (82.2 per cent) report using computers and mobile devices at some point during the day. On average, children aged 8–18 spend 2 hours 46 minutes per day using devices (around 20 hours per week[18]). There is very little difference between boys and girls aged 8–18 in their overall use of computers and mobile

		Per cent using device daily	Average time per day (hrs:mins)
	All (n=2,285)	82.2	2:46
Gender	Boys (n=1,092)	82.5	2:50
	Girls (n=1,193)	82.0	2:42
Age	8–11 (n=889)	71.2	1:30
	12–15 (n=857)	86.3	3:11
	16–18 (n=539)	91.7	3:55

Table 10.1
Children's use of computers and mobile devices, UK (2015)

devices. Boys spent only slightly more time using devices than girls, but the difference is not significant.

In contrast to gender, there are pronounced age differences in children's device use. Just over 70 per cent of children aged 8–11 report using a device at least once per day, which increases to 86.3 per cent of children aged 12–15, and increases further to 91.7 per cent of children aged 16–18. Reflecting this, the average time children spend using devices increases substantially with age, rising from 1 hour 30 minutes for children aged 8–11 (around 11 hours per week) to just under 4 hours for teenagers aged 16–18 (close to 28 hours per week). There were no significant gender differences within specific age groups. These results for gender and age are consistent with the findings of Livingstone and her colleagues in showing that girls and boys differ little, but that there are large age differences in children's use of computers and mobile devices.

The distribution of time using computers and mobile devices

Averages can mask considerable variation in the quantity of time children spend using computers and mobile devices on a given day. To gain a better understanding of the full range of time children spend using devices on any given day, we divide children into four groups: those who report 1) no time using a device; 2) up to 2 hours using a device; 3) 2–5 hours using a device; and 4) 5 or more hours using a device. Figure 10.1 shows the distribution of UK children's time using devices on a given day for boys and girls (upper panel), and for children in different age groups (lower panel). It shows that

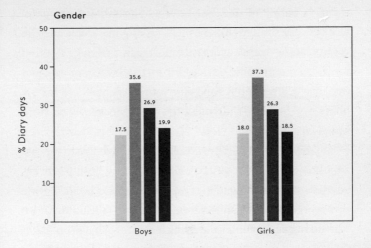

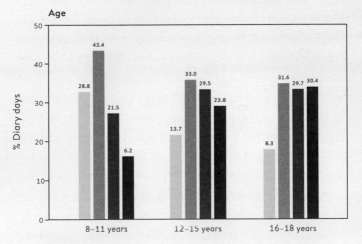

Figure 10.1
Distribution of children's time using devices by gender
and age, UK (2015)

None
Up to 2 hours
2–5 hours
5 hours or more

the distribution of the time boys and girls spend using devices is very similar (Figure 10.1, upper panel), echoing the results for the overall averages reported in Table 10.1. Around one third report using devices for up to 2 hours per day, just over one quarter of boys and girls report using devices for 2–5 hours, and just less than one fifth use devices for 5 or more hours on a given day.

On the other hand, there are clear age differences in the distribution of children's time using devices. Close to three-quarters of children aged 8–11 report, at most, 2 hours of time throughout the day using computer devices (including those who do not report any time using a device). This proportion falls to just under 50 per cent of children aged 12–15, and falls again to around 40 per cent for those aged 16–18. Conversely, the proportion of children reporting more than 2 hours using a device increases with age. The proportion of children who spend 2–5 hours using devices increases from 21.5 per cent for children aged 8–11 to around 30 per cent for children aged 12–15 and 16–18. However, the increase in the proportion of children reporting 5 or more hours is particularly striking, rising from around 6 per cent for children aged 8–11 to 30 per cent for teenagers aged 16–18.

Overall, just over 10 per cent of children report using a device for 5 or more hours on both their diary days (see Figure 10.2). Again, there is no difference between boys and girls, but the proportion of children who report using a device for 5 or more hours on both diary days increases substantially with age. Only 3 per cent of children aged 8–11 report using a device for 5 or more hours on both diary days, rising to 21 per cent for children aged 16–18. It is likely that if we had data for more days

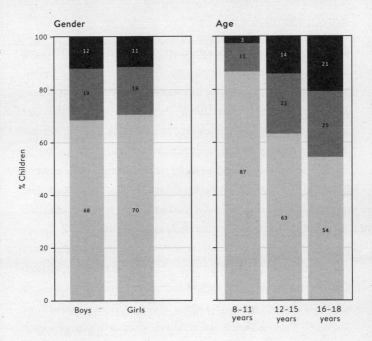

Figure 10.2
Number of days that children report 5 or more hours using a device by gender and age, UK (2015)

■ 5+ hours: 2 days
■ 5+ hours: 1 day
■ 5+ hours: no days

the proportion of children who report large amounts of time using devices every day would be even lower.

Children's activities when using computer devices

Previous research tells us much about what children are doing with the devices, such as playing games, listening to music, streaming video, or using social media.[19] What is missing, however, is an understanding of the extent to which they use devices when engaging in different activities. We see increasingly, for example, that children as well as adults are using mobile devices at the dinner table while eating, in the car while travelling, and when engaging in many other activities. The TUS provides a unique insight into the way in which children incorporate technology into their daily activities.

As noted above, one of the major concerns about children's use of technology and the internet is that it might be crowding out time spent on other important activities. We can examine this in two ways. One way is simply to examine how much of the time reported using devices corresponds with time when children's main activity is using computers, as opposed to when engaging in other activities (e.g. eating or travelling). Another is to look at the total time spent in different activities and examine the amount of time during which children also report using a device.

Firstly, to obtain the overall picture we look at the composition of all time using a device according to whether or not children report using computers as their main activity, or some other main activity. We distinguish between using computers for games and other times using computers such as browsing the internet, sending emails, or other activities. Figure 10.3 provides a breakdown of boys' and girls' total time using a device (left panel) and for children in different age groups (right panel) according to what they report doing as their main activity.

Although there was no difference in boys' and girls' overall time using devices (see Table 10.1), there are clear gender differences in the main activities children report while using devices. Boys spend 46 minutes playing computer games while reporting using a device compared with 8 minutes for girls, and this held across all age groups. Boys also spend a small amount more time than girls using computers as their main activity (28 mins v. 21 mins). Taken together, for around 44 per cent of boys' total time using a device, they report playing video games and using computers as their main activity, compared with 18 per cent for girls. Consequently, girls spend most of their total time using a device, in both absolute and proportionate terms, while they report a main activity other than using computers. These findings echo those from research showing that boys are more likely to use devices for games, whereas girls' spread their device use across a wide range of other activities such as streaming video, listening to music and using social media,[20] which can be more readily combined with time engaging in other activities.

In relation to patterns for children in different age groups, the right panel of Figure 10.3 shows the composition of time in different activities when using a device for children aged 8–11, 12–15 and 16–18. Children aged 8–11 spend 28 minutes playing computer games and 19 minutes using computers for other purposes (including the internet) while reporting using a device. This comprises just over half (52 per cent) of all

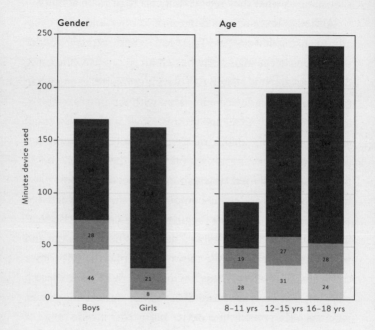

Figure 10.3
Children's time using a device by gender and age, UK (2015)

■ Other time using device
■ Internet (other computer)
■ Computer games

time children aged 8–11 use a device. In absolute terms the average time children spend using computers as their main activity (both for games and for other purposes) when they report using a device is very similar for older children aged 12–15 and 16–18. However, as the total time using a device increases substantially with age, in proportionate terms time using computers as a main activity (both for games and other purposes) when reporting using a device decreases to 30 per cent of all time using a device for children aged 12–15, and to 22 per cent for older teenagers (aged 16–18). Inversely, time in other activities when reporting using a device increases with age.

Figure 10.4 shows that the composition of time using a device is relatively similar for children who report using devices for varying amounts of time during the day. Note particularly that the percentage of time spent using devices (right-hand panel) for those who use devices heavily (5 or more hours per day) is not concentrated in using computers as the main activity. Children's use of devices is, rather, spread across many other activities, which we consider now in more detail.

Incorporating device use into key activities

We illustrate here how children incorporate the use of devices into the time they spend in the following key activities: 1) eating; 2) study; 3) social/entertainment; 4) sport; 5) play/hobbies; 6) TV; and 7) travel. These activities comprise three-quarters of all other time spent using a device when children are not using a computer as a main activity (for games or other purposes). We deconstruct the time children spend in these key activities into time when they are engaging in the

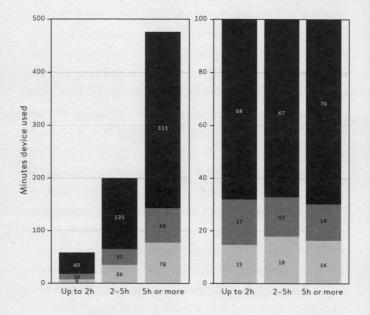

Figure 10.4
Children's time using a device: usage levels, UK (2015)

■ Other time using device
■ Internet (other computer)
■ Computer games

activity with a device, and time when they are engaging in the activity without a device. While previous research has focused on what children are using devices for, the results presented here complement this by shedding light on the proportion of time that children incorporate device use while engaging in a number of key daily activities.

Table 10.2 shows the average time children spend in these activities when reporting using and not using devices, and the proportion of the total time in these activities during which device use is reported. The extent to which children incorporate device use into their daily activities varies from 10 per cent of the total time in sport (3 minutes), to 27 per cent of all time watching TV (29 minutes), and around 30 per cent of all time studying (10 minutes).[21] Children report using devices for on average about one fifth of the total time they spend in social and entertainment activities (16 minutes), and the time they spend travelling (13 minutes).

Figure 10.5 shows that there are differences between boys and girls in how they incorporate device use into these activities. Proportionately (and in absolute terms) slightly more of girls' time studying is carried out when they also report using a device. Girls use a device when studying for an average of 13 minutes, which is about one third of their total time studying (40 minutes). In absolute terms, girls spend twice as much time as boys who average 7 minutes studying while using a device, though girls spend more time studying over- all. Girls also report using a device for a higher proportion of their total time in social/entertainment activities, and time in play/games. Girls and boys are similar in terms of how they incorporate device use into time eating, doing sport, watching

Activities	Using device	Not using device	Total	Per cent total time using device
Eating	0:10	0:59	1:09	14
Study	0:10	0:23	0:33	30
Social/entertainment	0:16	1:00	1:16	21
Sport	0:03	0:28	0:31	10
Play/hobbies	0:07	0:36	0:43	16
TV	0:29	1:20	1:49	27
Travel	0:13	0:49	1:02	21

Table 10.2
Children's time in key activities when using and not using devices, UK (2015)

Note: Excludes time using computers, personal care, paid work, housework, civic activities and non-reported activities

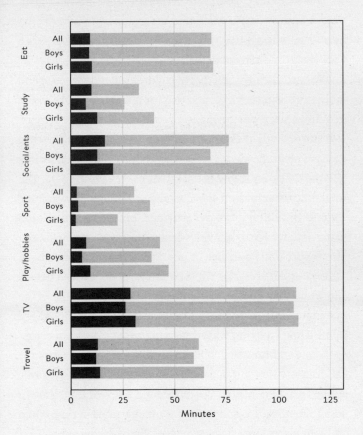

Figure 10.5
Children's time using and not using devices in seven key activities: boys and girls aged 8–18, UK (2015)

■ Using device
■ Not using device

TV and travelling. Therefore, although much more of girls' time using a device is when they are engaging in other activities (Figure 10.3), this time spreads roughly evenly across a wide range of different activities.

We have already seen that as children get older they spend more time using devices, and that for proportionately less of this time they report using computers as their main activity. Not surprisingly therefore, as shown in Figure 10.6, as children get older they increasingly incorporate the use of devices into the time they spend in the activities considered here. The total time that children spend studying, socializing, watching TV and travelling increases with age, but these age-related patterns differ across activities depending on whether children also report using a device or not. Study time increases both for time spent studying while children report using a device and while they do not. Children aged 8–11 spend on average 14 minutes studying compared with 54 minutes for those aged 16–18. Time studying while reporting using a device increases from 2 minutes for children aged 8–11 to 18 minutes for children aged 16–18 (34 per cent of all time studying for this age group). In contrast, age-related increases of total time in social activities, TV and travel are concentrated in time when children also report using a device. Time playing games and engaging in hobbies declines substantially among children in secondary school (aged 12 and over) compared with children aged 8–11, but time using a device during these activities is relatively similar across age groups. The nature of this activity likely varies widely across age groups. Proportionally, more of older children's time eating is reported with a device, as a result of both spending more time reporting using a device

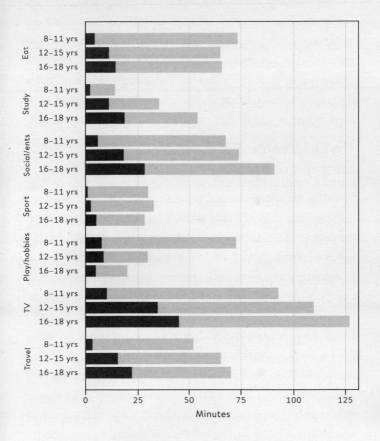

Figure 10.6
Children's time using and not using devices in seven key
activities by age group, UK (2015)

- Not using device
- Using device

when eating, combined with slightly less time eating over all. Lastly, children's average time in sport is very similar across age groups, being slightly lower among those aged 16–18 (28 minutes) compared with children aged 12–15 (32 minutes) and children aged 8–11 (30 minutes). Older children spend more time using a device when engaging in sport than younger children, however.

The social context of children's computer device use

The time we spend using computers and mobile devices can often appear to be solitary, with all our attention focused on the device screen. Increasingly, we seem to spend time 'together but not together', with each one absorbed in her/his device. For children, the concern is that increasing amounts of time using devices is associated with less time in face-to-face social interactions with others, leading to diminished social and emotional wellbeing. Research suggests that this is not the case, but we know very little about the social context of children's device use. To redress this, we examined who children reported being co-present with when they are using a device. Figure 10.7 shows the composition of children's time using devices when alone, with family and with others who are known to them. The left panel compares boys and girls, and the right panel compares children in different age groups.

For around one hour of both boys' and girls' time using a device they report being alone, and for a further hour they report being with their family. They spend about 30 minutes with others they know when using a device, while co-presence data is not reported for just under 10 minutes of time using

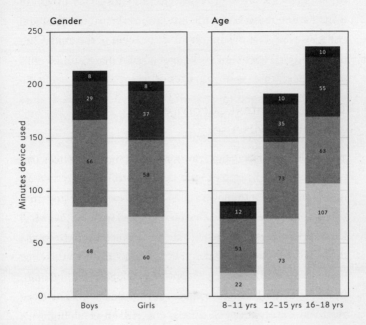

Figure 10.7
The social context of time using computer devices by gender and age, UK (2015)

- ■ Not reported
- ■ Family
- ■ Others you know
- ■ Alone

a device. Therefore, for the majority of time children report using devices, they are in the company of others (either family or others they know). Nevertheless, they are on their own for a substantial minority of the amount of the time they spend using a device, comprising about 40 per cent of the total. Children aged 8–11 spend an average of 20 minutes using a device while alone, which is one quarter of their total time using devices. Children aged 12–15 spend over an hour using devices alone (73 minutes), while teenagers aged 16–18 spend almost 2 hours using devices while alone (107 minutes). The proportion of all time using a device when children report being alone increases also, rising to 38 per cent for children aged 12–15, and 45 per cent for teenagers aged 16–18. This means that even though time alone with a device increases with age, it is still the case that most time using a device is when children report being in the presence of others. For younger children this time is skewed towards being with parents and other family members. For older teenagers aged 16–18 this time is balanced relatively evenly between time spent with co-resident family members, and time with friends and others they know outside the household.

Lastly, Figure 10.8 shows the same analysis across different levels of device usage time. Here we ask whether those who use their devices more spend more or less time alone than others. It turns out that, although time alone when using a device increases across different levels of device usage, time alone as a proportion of all time using a device is relatively stable across different levels of device usage. Those who report up to 2 hours of device use spend on average one third of all time using a device alone (20 minutes). This increases

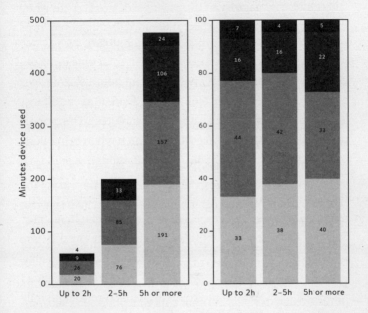

Figure 10.8
The social context of time using computer devices by usage
levels, UK (2015)

■ Not reported
■ Family
■ Others you know
■ Alone

to 38 per cent for children who use devices for 2–5 hours (76 minutes) and 40 per cent of all time using a device for children using devices for 5 or more hours (191 minutes). Therefore, the majority of time using a device is spent when co-present with others across the entire distribution of time that children spend using computers and mobile devices.

To sum up, there is no doubt that many children spend a substantial amount of time using computers and mobile devices on a daily basis. However, our results show that previous estimates of younger children's time using technology and the internet are overstated. Children aged 8–11 spent 1 hour and 30 minutes on average per day, almost half the amount cited in some media reports about children's time using the internet.[22] Only around 6 per cent of younger children's diaries contained reports of 5 or more hours per day using devices, and less still (3 per cent) reported spending this amount of time using devices on two diary days. We found, in line with previous research, that boys and girls spent similar amounts of time using devices, but that this time increased substantially with the age of children. Teenagers aged 16–18 spent close to 30 hours per week using devices, and one in five older teenagers reported using 5 or more hours using devices on both diary days.

This level of usage begs the question about the impact of time using devices on time in other activities. We show here for the first time how children are incorporating their use of computers and mobile devices into their time across a broad range of different activities. The first key point is that the majority of time spent using devices is time when children do not report 'using computers' as their main activity. This is especially so for girls, and for older children. Looking closer at different types of activities, we found that children incorporated device use into a range of activities including eating, studying, social activities, watching TV and travelling. Girls spent more time using devices while studying and in social activities, though they spent more time in these activities overall. Although we are not able to explore this distinction in detail, devices might well be used in conjunction with the main activity (e.g. to watch TV, or for study purposes), or they could be facilitating a secondary activity (e.g. watching TV on a device while travelling, using a device to listen to music while studying).

With respect to the social context of children's time using devices, we found that children reported being alone for a sizeable minority of their total time using a device. However, time spent using a device with family and with others outweighed time alone with a device, most notably for younger children. Although this doesn't give us direct information on the nature of children's social interactions (they could report being with family though not interacting with them, for example), these findings do provide something of a bulwark against exaggerated claims about social isolation arising from children's time using computers and mobile devices. It's also important to bear in mind that technology and the internet are altering the nature of our social interactions, and consequently our understanding of the character of time alone, and time spent 'with' others.

What is emerging from research on the relationship between technology and its potential impacts on children does not in general suggest that there is a straightforward direct negative link. Increasingly, the debate is shifting towards trying to get a clearer picture of the substance and context of children's time using technology and the internet. This chapter has revealed that younger children are not spending as much time using computers and mobile devices as previous reports suggest, and highlights the fact that children's time using devices varies from day to day. In addition, while children do indeed spend substantial amounts of time using computers and mobile devices, it is not confined to time that they are alone, and is spread across their engagement in many different activities.

CHAPTER 11

Technology in the Daily Lives of Adults

—

Killian Mullan

At the turn of the millennium, 44 per cent of households in the UK owned a computer, and 32 per cent were connected to the internet at home.[1] Smartphones and tablet computers were not yet invented. A decade later, ownership of computers and home internet connection had increased to 77 per cent and 73 per cent respectively.[2] At this point smartphones were relatively new, with just over one quarter of adults in the UK owning one,[3] while the iPad tablet had just been released on the market. By 2014, 85 per cent of households in the UK owned a computer, and 82 per cent were connected to the internet.[4] Moreover, smartphone ownership among adults had increased to 61 per cent, and there was a tablet computer in 44 per cent of UK households.[5] Along with these changes in hardware, our use of the internet has also changed dramatically. Internet speeds and capacities have increased steadily over the past couple of decades, and our ability to use the internet for a wide variety of purposes on powerful mobile devices has firmly embedded technology and the internet into our daily lives.

The combination of changes in the available hardware, along with changes in the facilities afforded by the internet, has affcctcd many aspects of our daily lives. These changes affect the way we interact with others, the way in which we consume media, the way in which we purchase goods and services, and the way in which we manage our personal finances. Firstly, they have expanded the ways in which we can do things. Today, for example, we can stream and watch TV on multiple devices, at times and places that suit us. Secondly, and relatedly, it enables multi-tasking, or task-shifting, in an entirely new way, and at unprecedented levels.[6]

Consider a simple situation where you are watching TV and the telephone rings. Prior to smartphones, and smart on-demand TV, the ringing telephone would have definitely constituted an interruption, presenting you with a stark choice: answer and forego watching TV, or ignore the telephone and forego talking to friends or family (for example). Modern technology lessens the starkness of this choice, perhaps even effectively removing it. It is now possible to pause TV (even including 'live' TV). While there would still be an interruption, taking the call would merely displace time watching TV to a slightly later time. Alternatively, communication with friends and family on mobile devices is now more likely to occur in tandem with watching TV (via social media or instant messaging), perhaps making the phone call less likely in the first place. For example, you might see that your friend is calling and not take the call, but text that you are 'busy' and will call them back later. In this regard, technology makes it easier to integrate communication with other activities.

This simple scenario demonstrates some of the ways in which technological change might influence basic choices and options in daily life – what to do and when to do it – but is it actually changing how we spend our time in general? There are a number of ways in which technological change might affect time use. Firstly, in a very direct way, there is little doubt that we are spending more time using computers and mobile devices today than we were a decade ago. Yet we know surprisingly little about the amount of time we spend using these devices on a daily basis. Secondly, the capacity for mobile devices to enable multi-tasking means that we can use them to accomplish various tasks, while engaging primarily in a wide range of different activities. For example, checking work email while eating, interacting with friends on social media while watching TV, watching TV while travelling, and so on. On this issue, we know next to nothing about the different types of activities we engage in when using computers and mobile devices. Thirdly, there is a question about whether the use of digital devices influences the amount of time we spend in particular activities. For example, as technology has become increasingly embedded in our daily lives, are we watching more or less TV, or spending more or less time interacting with others, either in person or 'online'?

As well as potentially affecting how we spend our time, computers and mobile devices may impact upon our subjective experience of time. Rapid technological change, such as we have experienced in the past couple of decades, is often implicated in debates about the 'speed-up society', and feelings of time pressure and stress. The picture that is often presented in the media is of time-squeezed adults seeking to juggle the many different aspects of their lives, and finding it increasingly difficult as technology blurs traditional boundaries between home and work. In the face of this, there are recurring calls for a 'digital detox'.[7] Surprisingly, although technology can clearly influence how we use our time and how pressured it seems in myriad and sometimes contradictory ways,[8] there is little actual evidence from time-use diary data that our daily lives have become increasingly congested or pressured over this period (see Chapter 13).

Much of the ongoing debate and controversy around the impact of technology focuses attention on children, young people and the general working-age population. However, older adults' use of technology is also increasingly of interest in the context of an ageing population. While for children the concern is that they are spending too much time using technology (see Chapter 10), for older adults the reverse is the case. Here, interest centres on the fact that older adults are much less likely to access and use technology, with negative implications for their health and wellbeing.[9] Access to technology and the internet provides a critical means of maintaining social contact with family and others for those who are less mobile,[10] and is increasingly a primary source of information on vital government services.[11] Bearing this in mind, there is concern that older adults are excluded from accessing many of the benefits of technological change enjoyed by the wider population. This chapter provides a first insight into the time older adults spend using computers and mobile devices today, and the different activities they engage in when using digital devices. So while the first part of this chapter focuses on adults aged 19–59, the second part focuses on the time older adults (aged 60 and over) spend using computers and mobile devices. For both we examine patterns relating to gender (as previous data show that a higher proportion of men report using the internet than women[12]) and social class, exploring associations between device use, time pressure and subjective wellbeing.

Adults' time using computers and other digital devices: 2000 and 2015

In line with national trends reported above, the proportion of respondent households in the UK 2014–2015 Time Use Survey with home computers, and internet connections at home, increased substantially between 2000 and 2015.[13] Not surprisingly therefore, as shown in Table 11.1, adults' time using computers as a main activity increased almost three-fold, from 10 minutes in 2000 to 28 minutes in 2015. These increases were found for both men and women, and in all age groups. Looking at patterns relating to gender and age in each year, men spent more time using computers than women in both 2000 and 2015. This gender difference in time using computers as a main activity was found within all age groups analysed at both time points, though the difference is largest among young adults aged 19–29. With respect to age, younger adults (aged 19–29) averaged more time using computers than adults aged 30 and over, in both 2000 and 2015. Note, however, that adults aged 19–29 spend a half hour less on average using devices than teenagers aged 16–18 (see Chapter 10). At 16–18 years old, teenagers therefore represent the peak age for time spent using devices.

Table 11.1 also shows, for 2015 only, the average time men and women aged 19–59 spend using digital devices (smartphones, tablets, or computers) when they do not report using computers as their main activity ('other time using

	Using computers (main activity)		Other time using devices
	2000	2015	2015
All	0:10	0:28	2:54
Men	0:15	0:35	3:10
Women	0:05	0:21	2:38
19–29 years	0:14	0:37	3:24
30–49 years	0:09	0:25	2:55
50–59 years	0:07	0:27	2:27

Table 11.1
Average time per day spent using computers as a primary activity (2000 and 2015), and using devices (2015), UK

Note: Time using computers includes playing computer games and internet shopping; device use includes time using computers, smartphones, and tablets.

devices'). We can see that today, using computers as a main activity comprises only a fraction of all the time we spend using technology, and that for the vast majority of the total time adults are using digital devices they do not report using a computer as their main activity (2 hours 54 minutes, compared with 28 minutes in 2015). Men average more time using digital devices when doing a main activity other than using a computer than women, and time spent using such devices decreases with age. In further analysis cross-tabulating age by gender (not shown), we found that while there is a gender difference among the older age groups, among young adults (aged 19–29) there was no difference in the time that men and women spent using digital devices. Also, there were no age differences in the time spent using such devices between men aged 19–29 and 30–49. Only 50–59 year-old men spent less time using digital devices than other men.

These results show that the widespread use of smartphones and tablets, as well as laptops and 'traditional' desktops, has greatly expanded the amount of time we spend using technology. They also suggest that we incorporate these devices extensively into different activities. For the remainder of this chapter we dig further into the time adults spend using devices when they are not using computers as their main activity ('other time using devices'). In particular, we want to learn more about the ways in which they incorporate digital technology into their daily lives by looking at the different types of activities that adults do when they are using digital devices. Figure 11.1 shows the broad distribution of time that adults spend using devices (net of time using computers as a main activity), for men and women (upper panel),

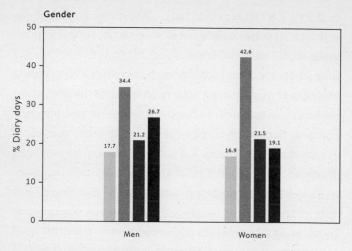

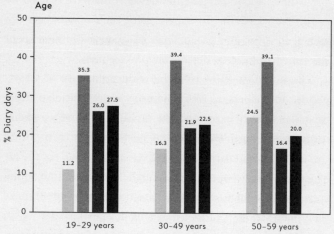

Figure 11.1
Distribution of adults' time using devices by gender and age,
UK (2015)

- ■ 5 hours or more
- ■ 2–5 hours
- ■ Up to 2 hours
- ■ None

and adults in different age groups (lower panel). This shows that the most frequent amount of time adults spend using devices is between 10 minutes and 2 hours per day ('up to 2 hours' column). This holds for both men and women, though this peak is more marked for women (at 42.6 per cent v. 34.4 per cent). It also holds for adults in all age groups, although the peak is higher for adults aged 30 and over (around 40 per cent) than for younger adults aged 19–29 (35.3 per cent). Just over one quarter of men, and adults aged 19–29, spend 5 or more hours using a device. In contrast, only around one fifth of women, and adults aged 30 and over, spend 5 or more hours using a device.

What are adults doing when using devices?

Mobile devices offer unprecedented capacity to incorporate the use of technology across a wide range of daily activities. Here we examine the amount of time adults spend in four major activity groups, differentiating between time in these activities when using a device and when not using a device. These activities are: 1) paid work; 2) domestic work; 3) leisure and personal activities (excluding sleep); and 4) travel. Figure 11.2 shows time using devices (dark shading) and not using devices (light shading) during these four activities for men and women, and Figure 11.3 shows patterns for adults in different age groups.

In Figure 11.2 we see that the gender difference in total time using devices in 2015 is most pronounced in respect of time using them while doing paid work. Men report using devices in paid work for 95 minutes, compared to 71 minutes for women. Women also spend less time using devices

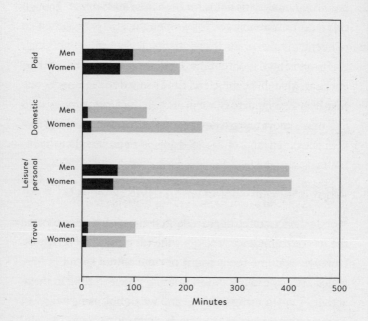

Figure 11.2
Time using and not using devices in four major
activity groups: men and women aged 19–59,
UK (2015)

Not using device
Using device

during leisure and personal activities, and travel, but the differences are much smaller than those shown for paid work. Lastly, women spend slightly more time using devices when engaging in domestic work, but this pales in comparison with gender differences in total time in domestic work activities (Chapter 5).

Patterns across different age groups, shown in Figure 11.3, are somewhat different. Here, time using devices at work was relatively similar across age groups. In fact, workers aged 30 and over report more time using a device at work than their younger counterparts. Further analysis showed that the increased time working with a device among high device users (5+ hours) was especially pronounced for older workers, highlighting that the use of technology at work is far from the preserve of the young. The age differences in total time using a device in 2015 seen in Table 11.1 is shown in Figure 11.3 to be concentrated in the time adults spend using devices while engaging in leisure and personal activities, and while travelling. Younger adults averaged most time using devices in these activities. Adults aged 19–29 averaged 85 minutes using a device while engaging in leisure and personal activities compared with 45 minutes for adults aged 50–59. Interestingly, the latter averaged more time in these activities overall, which is partly a reflection of age-related differences in paid work. A closer examination of device use during different leisure activities is the focus of the next section.

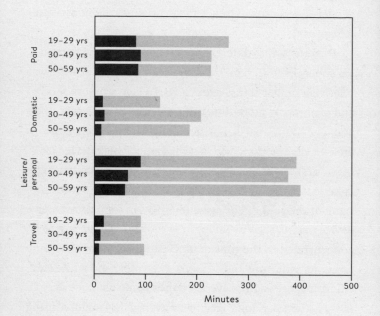

Figure 11.3
Time using and not using devices in four major
activity groups by age group, UK (2015)

■ Not using device
■ Using device

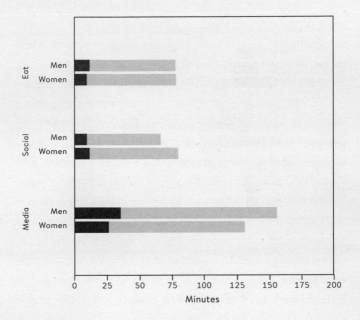

Figure 11.4
Time using and not using devices in selected
leisure/personal activities by gender: men and
women aged 19–59, UK (2015)

Not using device
Using device

What leisure and personal activities are adults doing when using devices?

Leaving paid work aside, for the majority of time they spend using digital devices, adults are engaging in leisure and personal activities. Most device use during this time is spent while eating, in social activities, and in media activities (primarily watching TV).[14] In this section we examine time when adults report using a digital device when engaging in these three central personal and leisure activities. Figure 11.4 shows time using devices (dark shading) and not using devices (light shading) during these three activities for men and women, and Figure 11.5 shows patterns for adults in different age groups.

Overall, gender difference in leisure time using a device is concentrated in media activities (Figure 11.4). Men average 35 minutes using a device while engaging in media activities compared with 26 minutes for women. Women average very slightly more time than men using devices in social activities (11 mins v. 9 mins). With respect to age, Figure 11.5 showed that older adults spent less time using devices during leisure and personal activities in general than their younger counterparts. We can see from Figure 11.5 that this applies across each of the three separate leisure activities considered here. That is, younger adults spend more time using a device when eating, during social activities, and media activities than adults aged 30 years and over. For example, adults in their 20s averaged close to 40 minutes using devices during time in media activities, which decreases to 23 minutes for adults in their 50s.

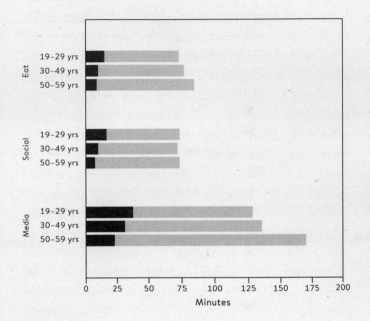

Figure 11.5
Time using and not using devices in selected
leisure/personal activities by age group, UK (2015)

Not using device
Using device

Device use and social class

We have seen that both gender and age are strongly associated with certain elements of adults' time spent using devices. Previous data suggest that there might also be a digital divide by class, with a positive association between socio-economic status and adults' use of technology and the internet (see above). To investigate this, we compared the time adults in different occupational social classes spend using devices in paid work, and in leisure and personal activities. The results, shown in Figure 11.6, reveal that time using a device while working varies substantially across workers in different social classes. Professionals and managers average the most time using a device during work (133 minutes), followed by those in intermediate occupations (83 minutes), while workers in routine and manual occupations spend the least time using a device while working (36 minutes). This result most likely reflects differences in the types of jobs workers in different occupations perform. But it is not just about the attributes of the job. It is also likely to reflect differences in the extent to which workers are able to incorporate the use of technology (in particular mobile devices) for other activities while working (listening to music, for example). In striking contrast, there are no differences related to social class in the time adults spend using devices during their leisure and personal activities. This overall picture is replicated across different age groups, and for both men and women (results not shown).[15]

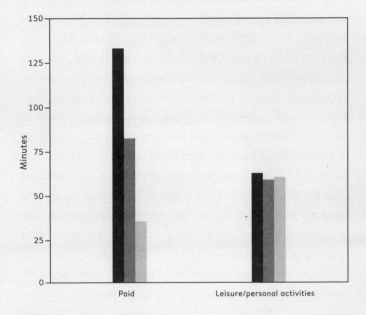

Figure 11.6
Time using devices during paid work and leisure/personal
activities by social class, UK (2015)

- Professional/manager
- Intermediate
- Routine/manual

Device use, time pressure and subjective wellbeing

Many of the arguments made about the way in which technology has impacted our lives contend that technology has made our lives more stressful and time-pressured than in the past. We know little, though, about how technology influences our experience of time and general wellbeing. Here we explore associations between adults' use of technology, time pressure and subjective wellbeing. Specifically, we look at whether there are significant differences in time using digital devices between those who report always feeling rushed (as an indicator of time pressure), or stressed, or dissatisfied with life in general, and those who do not. Table 11.2 reports the average time men and women spend using devices, differentiating between those who report feeling rushed, stressed or dissatisfied with life, and those who do not.

The main finding here is that those who state they have relatively high degrees of time pressure, stress or dissatisfaction with life do not spend significantly more (or less) time using devices than those who do not. While men who report dissatisfaction with life spend on average 20 minutes more using a device, and equivalent women report close to 30 minutes more, these differences are not statistically significant.[16] Further analysis (not shown) considered links between these factors and different levels of time using devices, and likewise found no significant association. For example, those who reported 5 hours or more using a device on the diary day were not more likely to report being rushed, stressed or dissatisfied with life overall than those who did

	Men		Women		All	
	No	Yes	No	Yes	No	Yes
Always or often rushed	3:48	3:49	2:50	3:03	3:18	3:20
Always or often stressed	3:47	4:01	2:50	3:12	3:17	3:30
Dissatisfied with life in general	3:53	4:14	2:48	3:15	3:18	3:42

Table 11.2
Time pressure, subjective wellbeing and average time (hrs:mins) using a device: men and women, UK (2015)

not report using a digital device at all during the day. These findings resonate with the conclusions of Chapter 13, where the implications of this – perhaps surprising – result are discussed further.

Device use among older adults

Because of the association between paid work and technology, and the emphasis on new and emerging forms of social media, relatively little is known about the time spent on computing and the detail of how digital devices are incorporated into other activities among the elderly population. In this final part of the chapter we look at computer and device use among older adults (aged 60 and over) in 2015, and the different types of activities they engage in when using these digital devices.[17] Throughout this section we distinguish between those who are retired and those who are not. Most non-retired adults are in their 60s, with close to 95 per cent of adults aged 70 and over being retired.

Table 11.3 reports the average time retired and non-retired men and women aged 60 and over spend using computers as their main activity, together with the average time spent using devices when engaging in other activities ('other time using devices'). Irrespective of retirement status, men of this age group average 34 minutes using computers as their main activity, and women of this age group average around 20 minutes using computers. For both men and women, these averages are comparable with those for adults in their 50s reported in Table 11.1. Apparently, the gender difference in computer and digital device usage among adults extends to older adults aged 60 and over.

	Computers (main activity)		Other time using devices	
	Non-retired	Retired	Non-retired	Retired
Men aged 60+	0:34	0:34	1:39	0:39
Women aged 60+	0:18	0:20	1:35	0:33

Table 11.3
Average time per day spent using computers as the main activity and using devices: retired and non-retired men and women aged 60 and over, UK (2015)

Although retirement status is not linked to time spent using computers as a main activity, there are pronounced differences between retired and non-retired adults in the average time they spend using devices when engaging in other activities. Specifically, compared with retirees, non-retired men and women average one hour more using devices when engaging in other activities. We have already seen that, unlike time using computers as a main activity, there is a substantial decrease in time spent using devices while doing other main activities, of around one hour, for adults aged 60 and over compared with those in their 50s (see Table 11.1). In fact, looking across the entire population aged 8 and over, we can discern that time using devices reaches a high point among teenagers aged 16–18, and a minimum for retirees aged 60 and over (predominantly those in their 70s).

Interestingly, irrespective of retirement status, men do not spend more time using devices when doing other activities than women. Data from the Office for National Statistics (ONS) reports that older men are more likely to use the internet than older women.[18] Our results confirm that, but only in relation to time spent using computers as a main activity. It is likely that other devices, particularly mobile devices, are being used to access the internet when engaging in other activities, and our results suggest that there are no gender differences here.

We have already seen that much device use occurs during paid work. Figure 11.7 shows that non-retired adults aged 60 and over report doing paid work for the majority of the time they spend using devices (at just under one hour), and this applies equally to men and women. Older adults report using

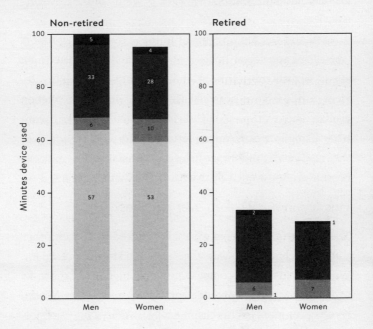

Figure 11.7

Major activities when using a device by gender and retirement status: adults aged 60 and over, UK (2015)

■ Travel
■ Leisure/personal
■ Domestic
■ Paid

a device while doing leisure and personal activities for around a half an hour on average. For retired adults aged 60 and over, this accounts for almost the whole of their total time using a device.

Men and women are similar in the activities they report when using a device, although both retired and non-retired men spend slightly more time than equivalent women using devices during leisure/personal activities. Non-retired women aged 60 and over spend slightly more time in domestic work while using a device. Among retired adults aged 60 and over the small gender difference in total time using a device is concentrated almost entirely in leisure time with a device.

Has technology taken over our lives?

There is little doubt that we are connected with each other through technology in ways that have no historical precedent. We are increasingly accomplishing more and more of the tasks of daily life using computers, smartphones and tablets. Yet the results presented in this chapter suggest that, while technology has infused into our daily lives to a considerable extent, it is far from saturating our time completely.

We find that a substantial amount of time using devices occurs during paid work, especially among those workers who use devices for a large part of the day. Moreover, device use at work was especially high among professional and managerial occupations. While not diminishing the importance of this, the use of technology at work for these occupations is hardly new. If the UK 2000 Time Use Survey had asked individuals to report times during the day when they were using a computer, regardless of whether using a computer was their main activity, it is reasonable to suppose that these same occupational groups would have reported substantial amounts of time using computers when at work. While it is likely that smartphones and tablets have increased the use of technology at work (though not necessarily *for* work) in jobs where the use of computer technology is long established, this increase is perhaps not as great as we might have thought.

Our results also highlight that gender differences in device use stem, to a great extent, from the strong link between device use and paid work. In short, women and men are much more similar in their use of devices outside of paid work than in it. In contrast, the strong age differences in time spent using digital devices were concentrated outside rather than in paid work, primarily in media activities. Beyond the confines of paid work, most other time using digital devices was combined with leisure and personal activities. This no doubt reflects substantial changes in the way we experience and engage in these activities. It is important, however, not to overstate the extent to which we combine the use of digital devices with leisure and personal activities. Even among those who reported using devices for much of the day, the use of devices never exceeded more than half of their total time in these activities. Overall, about one fifth of all time in these activities was combined with the use of a digital device. Within the broad group of leisure and personal activities, we found that device use was most typically combined with media activities such as watching TV, followed by time combining device use with eating and social activities. Unfortunately, we cannot tell exactly what people are using their devices *for* when engaging in these different leisure and personal activities, so we do not know whether the devices are being used in conjunction with the activity, or whether their use indicates that they are multi-tasking. Sometimes this becomes clear from the nature of the primary activity. For example, we can safely assume that we are not using devices for eating or travelling (though we can use them to facilitate both activities). In these cases, device use certainly indicates a secondary activity, and although we cannot tell exactly what this is, our results are nonetheless revealing in terms of giving us some much-needed perspective on the magnitude of the time spent in secondary device use.

For other activities the picture is less clear. When reporting doing media activities with a device, a person could be using the device for the activity (e.g. watching TV on a tablet), or could be using the device for some other activity while also watching TV (e.g. interacting with friends on social media with their smartphone). This ambiguity is interesting in the light of the overall decrease we found in time spent in media activities as the main activity, especially among younger adults. It could well be that there has been an increase in reporting media activities as secondary activities, facilitated by the capacities of digital devices. For example, watching TV on a tablet while travelling.[19]

Although it is widely thought that technology lies at the root of a supposed time-pressure epidemic, we found no evidence for this (see also Chapter 13). While our analysis here is descriptive, these results largely hold when controlling for a number of other factors associated with device use.[20] In trying to understand this it is worth noting that the past decade or so has witnessed remarkable technological change and we, as a society, have been on something of a steep learning curve. It may be that as we become more comfortable, and competent, in using new technology, and mobile devices in particular, they become less tied to feelings of time pressure. It could also be the case, however, that there are aspects of the use of digital devices that are linked to time pressure, which we have not succeeded in capturing in time-use diaries. Mobile devices enable instant checking and responding to notifications and communications, which might take only moments. While not registering in a time diary, these moments could well be tied to feelings of time pressure and stress. This notwithstanding, our results show no direct link between overall time using digital devices, time pressure and subjective wellbeing.

Echoing previous research, we found that the reach of technology into daily life falls off dramatically for older adults, especially for those who have retired. Broadly, the way in which older adults incorporate technology into their daily activities was very similar to the wider population, but the amount of time that older adults spend using digital devices is considerably lower. These results underscore concerns that older adults may be excluded from some of the benefits of these devices, and of technology more generally. The pattern of increasing time using technology in the teenage years shown in the previous chapter lessens through the twenties, and our time using devices appears to continue to decline as we get older. As we move forward, however, it is likely that the crest of this technological wave will push on for longer across an individual's lifespan. Today's young people will enter retirement with perspectives and technological competencies very different from contemporary retirees. Of course, they themselves may not keep up with seemingly relentless technological change as they age.

Time Use and Wellbeing in Later Life

—

Jiweon Jun
Jooyeoun Suh

'They said I was no longer useful to them. They thanked me for my service, as if that was all it was. I found a flat in the end. My problem was what to do with all the time I had. I mean, the flat – it's so small, I can have it spotless in half an hour. And then, you know, what am I supposed to do, for the rest of the day?'

— *The Best Exotic Marigold Hotel,* 2011

In the film *The Best Exotic Marigold Hotel,* a retired British housekeeper, Muriel, talks bitterly about her retirement to a young girl she met in India, where she travelled for a hip-replacement surgery. Muriel's problem of 'what to do for the rest of the day' is a commonly discussed problem in relation to retirement, especially in advanced societies, where older people can at least be free from the burden of paid work. What do older British adults actually do 'for the rest of the day', and how is it related to health and wellbeing in later life?

With the population ageing, the average age in the UK exceeded 40 for the first time in mid-2014, and nearly one in seven people are expected to be aged over 75 by 2040.[1] While many aspects of ageing, such as the relationship between labour supply and retirement age and the importance of wealth in later life have been extensively studied, how British older people spend their time has not received nearly as much attention. However, understanding how the patterns of time use change as people grow older is important as it is strongly linked to health and wellbeing in later life. Time spent on meal preparation, for example, plays an important role in older people's health. It is of course more time-consuming to prepare healthy meals than heating up microwavable packaged meals or purchasing fast food. Yet the additional investment of time yields other benefits, as demonstrated in research that shows women who spend more time preparing home-cooked meals have lower body mass index (BMI) than those who spend less time on such activity.[2] In terms of leisure activities, watching television has been shown to undermine older people's health and wellbeing due to its sedentary nature.[3] Research has also documented the importance of staying connected with others and maintaining socially supportive relationships, both of which can improve the mental and physical health of older populations.[4] In this chapter we compare the time-use patterns of people aged 65 and older in relation to health and wellbeing measures.

Overall trends in daily time use

As Britons move into retirement, the demands on their days change. Figure 12.1 shows the distribution of average time spent in eight broad categories of activity, comparing three age groups: those aged between 25 and 64 (the bulk of the working population), those aged between 65 and 74, and those aged 75 and older.

Currently in the UK the majority of people begin to disengage from paid work in their early sixties. Figure 12.1 shows that overall average hours of paid work across the population in 2015 decreased from an average of 4.1 hours per day for those aged 25–64, to 40 minutes for those aged 65–74. As time spent on paid work declines for those aged 65–74, the amount of time spent on unpaid work increases, to 4.8 hours per day. For people aged 75 years and older the amount of time spent on unpaid work decreases. Clearly, disengagement in some tasks is associated with increased engagement in other activities. People aged 75 and older spend more time on personal care, especially sleeping or resting (an increase from 8.2 hours per day, for both 25–64-year-olds and 65–74-year-olds, to 8.9 hours for those aged over 75). They also increased the amount of time spent in leisure activities. Leisure makes up an important part of older Britons' lives both in terms of the amount of time they spend in leisure activities and in terms of how engagement in specific activities can contribute to their wellbeing. Leisure activities include activities such as exercising, attending sporting events, going to the pub, knitting, doing crafts, reading, listening to music, walking, going to parties, and so on. Watching TV and listening to the radio comprise a separate category from the general leisure category. As Britons grow older, they increase the amount of time they spend both on leisure activities in general, and in watching TV and listening to radio.

Figure 12.2, a daygraph (similar to the tempograms presented in Chapter 1), provides an aggregate overview of activities done in sequence through an average weekday for these different age groups. It shows the proportions of

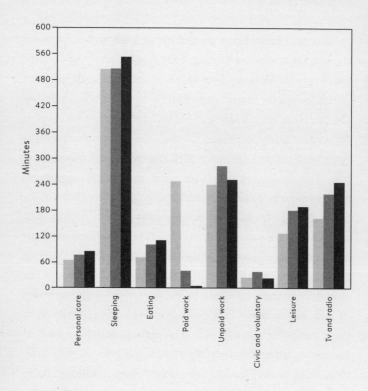

Figure 12.1
What do older Britons do?: average hours per day in different activities by age group, UK (2015)

- 25–64
- 65–74
- 75 and over

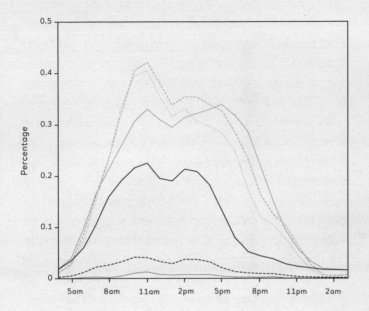

Figure 12.2
Paid and unpaid work tempogram by age group, UK (2015)

.... Unpaid work 75 and older
▪▪▪▪▪▪▪▪▪ Paid work 75 and older

––––––– Unpaid work 65–74
- - - - - Paid work 65–74

––––––– Unpaid work 25–64
––––––– Paid work 25–64

people in the UK in 2014 engaged in paid work (in darker lines) and unpaid work (lighter lines) for each age group throughout the day. An M-shaped structure of the weekday for both paid and unpaid work is evident. Over all age groups, more people in the population are engaged in unpaid work compared to paid work throughout the waking hours, and this unpaid work extends into the evenings. The 25–64 age group (the bulk of the working-age population) does more paid work during standard working hours, but catches up on unpaid work after 5pm. For older age groups, however (both the 65–74 and 74 and older groups), the peak time for unpaid work is mid-morning.

As we saw from Figure 12.1, people past retirement age spend more time on leisure activities than younger people. Reduction in paid work time allows people during later life to allocate their time to a variety of different activities. However, not all leisure time is the same from the point of view of health. We split leisure time here into active and passive activities (largely corresponding to the out-of-home/in-home distinction used in previous chapters). Active leisure activities include attending entertainment (going to the cinema or a pub) or sporting events, and participating in any type of physical exercise. On the other hand, passive leisure consists of such activities as watching TV, listening to the radio, doing crafts, reading, writing letters, playing cards, and so on. Figure 12.3 shows the day-graph of active and passive leisure activities through the day by age group. Unlike paid work, it is difficult to clearly assign leisure activities to specific periods, as they are engaged in throughout the waking hours – although there is a clear peak in the evening for passive leisure activities.

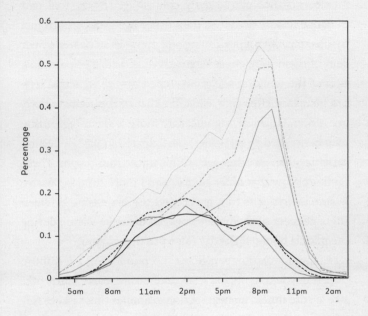

Figure 12.3
Passive leisure activities tempogram by age group, UK (2015)

.... Passive 75 and older
------------ Active 75 and older

– – – Passive 65–74
- - - - - Active 65–74

——— Passive 25–64
——— Active 25–64

Nonetheless, two clear patterns in how time is allocated to active and passive leisure activities are apparent. More members of the 'young-elderly' cohort (aged 65–74) took part in active leisure activities than other age groups until just before 5pm, with a peak at around 2pm, when nearly 20 per cent of them were engaging in active leisure. The participation of the working-age group (aged 25–64) in active leisure increased after 5pm, equalling that of the young-elderly age group. However, significantly more 'elderly' age group members (aged 75 and older) participated in passive leisure activities than all other age groups until around 9pm. These findings show that older adults spend more time in passive leisure activities as they age, but at the same time between 10–15 per cent of them were engaged in active leisure during the middle hours of the day (also peaking at 2pm).

In summary, on average, as the population ages, more time is devoted to unpaid work and leisure, particularly passive leisure time. The next section examines these issues further in relation to health and wellbeing, applying the concept of 'life balance' in time use among the elderly.

The life balance of British older adults

The life-balance model described here was developed to illustrate older people's daily life in terms of time use.[5] The method of using a triangle to display the distribution of the three domains is based on the 'life-balance triangle', which comprehensively displays how the balance between paid work, unpaid work and leisure has changed historically and cross-culturally (as illustrated in Chapter 2).[6] The life-balance model used here is based on the balance between three domains of time use that are identified specifically in relation to the wellbeing of older people: 'discretionary' time, 'constrained' time, and 're-generative' time.[7] Discretionary time, as described previously in Chapters 2 and 3, refers to free time – time spent on activities that are self-chosen and have a high level of flexibility in terms of the schedule and amount of the activity, such as hobbies, leisure and socialization. Constrained time refers to time spent on activities that people are constrained or committed to do, such as paid work, household management and compulsory education. This is the dimension that provides time structure for the day, as activities in this domain offer less flexibility in scheduling. Regenerative time ('necessary' time in the original Ås model) refers to time spent on activities that are necessary to maintain our body biologically, such as sleep, eating and personal care. The main assumption of the model is that, for health and wellbeing among the elderly population, it is important to maintain balance between discretionary and constrained time, provided that there is sufficient time for meeting biological needs. A lack of discretionary time leads to stress, while too much of it (as among the unemployed and the retired) can lead to the loss of time structure, which is often associated with boredom and a feeling of 'role-lessness'. These factors are also known to be detrimental to wellbeing, and are frequently associated with retirement. Time spent on sleep, eating and personal care (regenerative time) may also have greater implications in later life, especially for the very elderly group for whom time spent on this dimension can be a significant source of constraint in daily life (we will see that poor health is associated with increased regenerative time).

The life-balance triangle is an intuitive tool developed to

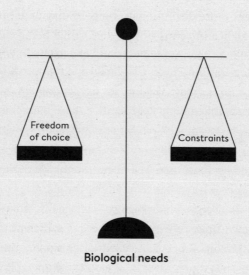

Figure 12.4
The life-balance model

examine the issue of balance in later life, enabling us to easily visualize how the 24 hours of the Great Day are distributed between the three domains among different age groups.[8] The horizontal axis of the life-balance triangle represents the balance between constrained time and discretionary time. Being closer to the right side of the triangle indicates that the day consists of more discretionary time, i.e. having more freedom of choice in terms of time use, while being closer to the left side of the triangle indicates the day involves more constrained time, i.e. having less time flexibility. The vertical axis indicates the balance between regenerative time and the other two domains. The higher the data points on the vertical axis, the greater proportion of time is spent on regenerative activities such as sleep.

Figure 12.5 presents the life-balance triangle for British adults (aged 18 and over) by age group and gender from the 2015 UK TUS. Women and men are represented by a triangle symbol and a circle ('balance points') respectively, while age groups are indicated by the letters A–E. The graph shows how balance in time use changes across different age groups for men and women. In general, as age increases, the balance points for each gender shift towards the right side of the triangle, indicating that people have greater discretionary and less constrained time. There is also a slight upward shift by age group, indicating an increase in regenerative time. The rightward shift towards greater discretionary time in later life may be understood in two, contradictory, ways. The first is a conception of later life as a period of freedom and self-fulfilment, as described, for example, by Peter Laslett in his book *A Fresh Map of Life: The Emergence of the Third Age.*[9]

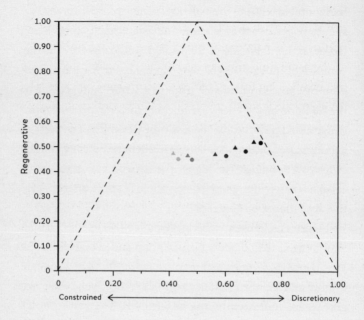

Figure 12.5
The life-balance triangle by age group and gender, UK (2015)

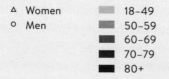

Freed from responsibilities of work and family care, later life is regarded as offering 'the time to reflect and create which is so scarce in the Second Age [working age]'.[10] The location of the balance points for the elderly in Figure 12.5 shows that older British people certainly have a lot of such discretion over their time, beginning on average from their 60s. At the same time, the increase in discretionary time points to a challenging feature of later life for many older people: having too little to occupy them. As is frequently found in the literature on retirement and its outcomes, having too much free time and a lack of a definite time structure often leads to negative outcomes such as ill-health and depression.[11] The gender difference in life balance in later life observed in Figure 12.5 suggests that men after retirement ages have more discretionary time than elderly women, and may therefore be most likely to suffer from these problems after retirement. Unlike in the working–age groups aged 18–49 and 50–59, where relatively little difference is found by gender, larger gender gaps in the balance points are observed in later life (until they converge again in the oldest elderly group, aged 80 and above). Men also experience a greater jump in their discretionary time between their 50s and 60s, around the ages of retirement, than women.

These issues may be explored further by dividing the life-balance points of older men and women according to their economic activity status (not shown). Jiweon Jun argued that it is life stage, rather than biological age, that is the primary factor in determining balance in time use, and analysis from the 2015 UK data supports this argument.[12] The life-balance point for people still in paid work at ages 65 and over is near to the centre of the triangle (similar to the position of people in their 50s or younger). This means that the shift in life balance towards having more discretionary and regenerative time in later life occurs not as a factor of age itself, but rather due to social position, in this case, retirement. Both the direction and the degree of the gender gap in life balance are associated with retirement. For people aged 65 and over not in paid work, the balance points of men and women show that men have more discretionary time, while women have greater amounts of constrained time. There are two contrasting dimensions of gender inequality to be considered here, each of which may affect wellbeing. Firstly, gender inequality in time use persists into retirement – even when both men and women are freed from the responsibility of paid work, the greater constrained time of women indicates that the responsibility of household management still falls largely on women. On the other hand, the greater distance between the balance points of men who are in paid work and those who are not means that men, on retirement, are forced to readjust their time structure to a greater extent than women, which can itself be a challenging demand.

Life balance and wellbeing in later life

How is the balance in time use in later life associated with health and wellbeing? Can we discern a link between the amount of discretionary or regenerative time and how healthy people feel? Figure 12.6 shows an enlargement of a life-balance triangle, demonstrating how life balance among those aged 65 and over varies according to self-assessed health status. This health status measure is taken from the questionnaire accompanying the time-use diary, in which people are asked to report their own assessment of their general health. This kind of subjective assessment is known to be a good predictor of mortality and overall health among older people. Figure 12.6 shows that there is a linear relationship between life balance and health status. Compared to people with good or very good self-reported health status, the balance points of people with poor health status are located much further towards the upper right side of the triangle, indicating higher levels of both regenerative and discretionary time. It seems that poorer health is actually associated with larger amounts of discretionary time, and smaller amounts of constrained time. This is consistent with the assumption of the life-balance model that both too many time constraints and too much discretionary time are detrimental to health in later life. Of course, we cannot identify the direction of the causal relationship between patterns of time use and self-assessed health status. Healthier older people may be more likely to be engaged in constrained-time sorts of activities such as paid work or household work, simply because their health allows them to be. However, this result at least shows a consistent association between the health of older people and life balance in time use. Considering that it is usually not mandatory to do paid work or to have other commitments in later life, especially in advanced societies, it is possible that maintaining a certain level of constrained time and not having too much discretionary time may contribute to the better health of older people.[13] The evident gender differences in Figure 12.6 also suggest that this conclusion may apply even more so for women than men. While

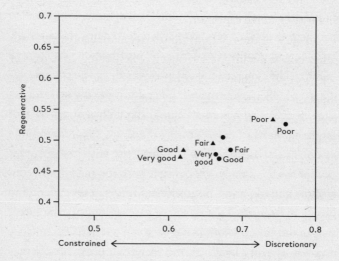

Figure 12.6
The life-balance triangle (enlarged) by self-assesed
health status: men and women aged 65 and over,
UK (2015)

▲ Women
● Men

the balance points of women for each self-assessed level of health are further to the left than those of men (indicating greater amounts of constrained time), the greatest gender gap occurs for those who report their health to be 'good' or 'very good' (although, of course, we cannot dismiss the possibility of reverse causation).

Analysis of the relationship between life balance and another questionnaire item relating to wellbeing – feelings of self-worth (not shown) – further supports the argument that life balance matters. People's feelings of self-worth were recorded on a 1 to 10 scale, 1 being the lowest score and 10 being the highest score.[14] We divided our sample of older people into three groups based on their scores: low (below the median), median (score 8), and high (above the median). If maintaining certain levels of constrained time, and not having too much discretionary time, matters for wellbeing in later life, we would expect to see the balance points to shift towards the right side of the triangle (i.e. more discretionary time) for older people with the lowest sense of self-worth. This is indeed what we observe. Older people reporting low self-worth have greater proportions of discretionary time and lower proportions of constrained time, compared to older people with median or high self-worth. Considering the importance of maintaining positive feelings of self-worth in later life, this finding implies that time allocation can be one of the main factors influencing the wellbeing of older people.

Health and wellbeing-related activities of older people: 1985–2015

Although we do not know all the secrets for remaining healthy and happy into older age, several specific activities have been shown to promote health and wellbeing in later life. Based on longitudinal data accumulated from following a sample of 2,500 people across 35 years, the Caerphilly Cohort Study, for instance, found that following health recommendations about eating well, exercising, drinking moderately, not smoking, and keeping to the appropriate body mass index had preventive power against common diseases in old age.[15] In terms of time use, Jun suggested focusing on five dimensions of activities that have been found to be important for older people's health and wellbeing: physical, social, cognitive-related, productive and out-and-about activities.[16] We investigated whether there have been any changes in these activities between 1985 and 2015, assessing the argument that older people are now healthier and enjoy more active lifestyles than in previous periods (along the lines that '70 is the new 50'!).

The health benefits of being physically active in old age are well established. Maintaining a sufficient level of physical activity in later life is known to reduce the risk of illnesses such as cancer and heart disease, and delay the onset of disability.[17] According to the physical activity guideline for older adults published by the NHS,[18] older people should do 'at least 150 minutes of moderate aerobic activity such as cycling or walking every week', or 'at least 75 minutes of vigorous aerobic activity such as running or a game of singles tennis every week'. As time diaries record activities done over the course of single days, we can only look at how much sports or exercise-related activities older people do on their actual diary days. On average, men spent about 21 minutes per day on sports or exercise-related activities (such as walking and cycling) in 2015, while women spent about 11 minutes per day. If we assume rather simplistically that people continue the same pattern throughout the week, this means that men aged 65 and over did 147 minutes per week on average, and older women did 77 minutes of sports activities weekly – remarkably close to the NHS guidelines.

It is important to remember, though, that these figures are averaged across the elderly population. That is, many older people may be exercising for 10 minutes or less per day, while others are doing 2 hours of exercise or more. The important thing is to assess what percentage of older people are meeting daily recommended guidelines. The American Heart Association (AHA) and the American College of Sports Medicine (ACSM) recommend more detailed guidelines than the NHS: a daily minimum of 30 minutes moderate-intensity physical activity, on five days every week.[19] According to this criterion, only 17 per cent of older men and 12 per cent of older women in the UK 2014–2015 Time Use Survey met the recommended daily guidelines, taking into account only sports and exercise-related activities. Indeed, the NHS guidelines explicitly exclude 'daily chores such as shopping, cooking, or housework'. However, it is known that such activities *are* effective in reducing many health risks for older people (even more effective than vigorous levels of activity, according to some studies).[20] Including household chores in the calculations, older adults in 2015 were much more active in terms of moderate to vigorous activities than older adults in 1985. Men participated in such activities for about 2 hours per day in 1985, while by 2015 this had increased to almost 3 hours (a 52-minute increase). The same trend is evident for women, although women appeared to spend rather more time in moderate to vigorous activities than men in 1985, and rather less in 2015, so that the historical change is not so great as in the case of men.

What of productive activity? Participating in productive activity, such as unpaid work, but also including paid and voluntary work, has been found to be positively associated with health and wellbeing in later life.[21] Arguments have been made that older people today are more likely to be engaged in productive activities (and to be engaged in them for much longer) than in the past. In 2011, the compulsory retirement age (at the time, 65) was abolished in the UK. Do British older people in 2015 spend more time on productive activity compared to their counterparts in 1985? The answer seems to be yes. Compared with 1985, older men spend 45 more minutes on productive activities per day (5.14 hours in 2015), and older women spend 13 minutes more (5.47 hours). If we examine these results more closely, we can see that the increase is mainly associated with an increase in time spent on unpaid, rather than on paid, work. The percentage of older men in paid work reduced by 5.8 percentage points (from 17.6 per cent to 11.8 per cent) compared with 1985, although that of women slightly increased, by 2.4 percentage points (from 2.6 per cent to 5 per cent). On the other hand, the average time spent on unpaid work increased by 40 minutes in the case of older men, and 8 minutes in the case of older women. Older people in 2015 were certainly more engaged in productive activities than older people in the past, but this increase occurred more in the sphere of unpaid, as opposed to paid, work.

Older people in 2015 were also more engaged in cognitive-related activities than in 1985 (although the difference is not large), and they were less sedentary (down by 22 minutes for men, and 10 minutes for women). Considering the importance of these dimensions in maintaining health and wellbeing in later life, our findings suggest that there have been some positive changes over time in older people's daily lives. An interesting exception, however, is participation in social activity. The average time spent on social activities decreased considerably for both older men and women between 1985 and 2015. This change may reflect technological developments such as increasing access to home media and internet shopping, rather than indicating that older people today are inherently less social. Although this topic deserves further exploration beyond the scope of this chapter,[22] the main reduction seems to be coming from a decline in out-of-home leisure, including attending sporting events as a spectator, and going to the cinema, theatre or concerts. Older people's time spent in volunteer work, for instance, actually increased over the period 1985–2015, and receiving or visiting friends is still ranked seventh in the top 20 activity list for older people.

At the end of the film *The Best Exotic Marigold Hotel*, Muriel not only recovers her health and mobility, but also starts a new life as a manager in the Marigold Hotel, helping the inexperienced young owner. If Muriel's bitterness is one stereotypical image of an older person who has withdrawn from the labour market and no longer contributes to society,[23] her comeback represents another popular image of the contemporary older person, who is socially active, busy volunteering and helping others.[24] The results from the 2015 UK time-use data imply that, as in Muriel's case, the balance in time use changes considerably with retirement, and the abundance of time associated with this transition can pose a challenge for older people. An abundance of discretionary time was found to be associated with poor health and a lower level of self-worth. At the same time, however, our findings show that older people are certainly more active and engaged in social activities and volunteering than they were 30 years ago. We may not yet have reached the point of '70 is the new 50', but that day may not be too far off.

PART FIVE

Speed-up Society and National Wellbeing

CHAPTER 13

Feeling Rushed
Is Our Daily Life Really Speeding Up?
—

Oriel Sullivan
Jonathan Gershuny

There has been huge interest generated by the idea of an increasing pressure of time in modern societies, as indicated by a large and still-growing volume of both academic and popular literature. Many accounts of the relationship between modern living and wellbeing, both academic and popular, refer to a speed-up in the tempo of our daily lives as an increasing source of stress. Arguments such as: we live in an ever more pervasive 24/7 environment; we increasingly find ourselves multi-tasking throughout the day; we rush from one activity to another with less and less 'down-time'. Concepts relating to accelerating-time pressure, or hurriedness in daily life, receive widespread attention in the media.[1] Many of these accounts are directly related to the impact of information and communication technologies (ICT) on our daily lives. As the previous chapters showed, we know that there have been big changes in the use of digital technologies since the turn of the 21st century. There is also a growing volume of literature focusing on the acceleration of the pace of life and increased pressure of time caused by constant connectivity, digitalization and gaming technologies.[2] Time-use diary data is perhaps the closest we can get to finding objective measures for this speed-up in our time (or in our *perceptions* of that time) over the 21st century – the period during which digital technologies have really taken off.

The experience of time pressure can be measured and tested from time-use diary data in a number of different ways. For example, has there been an increase over time in the number of activities we engage in simultaneously (multi-tasking)? The combination of activities might have the effect of producing a feeling of greater time pressure. The multi-tasking literature based on time-use data has focused particularly on the way in which women's greater levels of multi-tasking mean that their time is more pressured than that of men.[3]

Secondly, is our time more fragmented than in the past? That is, do we spend more and more time rushing from one activity to another, doing each less and less well. This change would be manifested in diary data by shorter durations of activities; meaning a speed-up in the pace at which our activities change. As a consequence, time might seem more fragmented, and thus more pressured.

Thirdly, is there a connection between exponentially increasing connectivity/ICT use and increasing pressure of time? In her book *Pressed for Time*[4] Judy Wajcman, for example, refers to an acceleration of life in 'digital capitalism' where ICT provides the potential to speed up work, and to permit work at any time. Mobile phone technology creates the possibility of constant connectivity across time and location, blurring the distinctions between work time and other time. We become constantly available to our work places through e-mail and messaging. While there is an assumption that this blurring leads to increasingly harried time both in work and in leisure, others have questioned whether these fears may be exaggerated.[5] A question about how rushed respondents are feeling appears in the questionnaire accompanying the UK TUS data, both in 2000 and 2015. This measure of 'rushedness' allows us to compare indicators of time intensity derived from the diary data with the same individual's perception about how rushed they normally feel. We are also able to examine changes in people's reported use of a computer as a main or secondary activity from the turn of the 21st century, and assess the relationship to feelings of 'rushedness'. Are people's perceptions of rushedness related to objective measures of the intensity of their time? And is there a relationship between their reports of feeling rushed and the growth in time spent using the computer, and screen time more generally?

Fragmentation and multi-tasking: indicators of speed-up in pace and time intensity?

Figure 13.1 shows the number of events per day according to gender and socio-economic class[6] in 2000 and 2015. From the existing literature on time pressure, we would expect to see an occupational class difference, with those in professional and managerial occupations increasingly splitting their time between a myriad of conflicting demands from their work and family lives. In fact, we see little change. There is some indication of a gradient from higher to lower socio-economic status for men, with those with higher occupational status

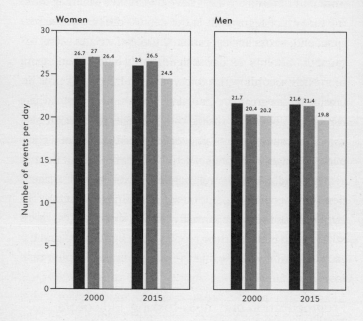

Figure 13.1
Number of events per day by socio-economic class (SEC) and gender: men and women aged 16–64, UK (2000–2015)

■ Professional/Managerial
■ Intermediate
□ Routine

doing slightly more activities per day than those in routine occupations.[7] And at a more detailed level of activity, only paid work and personal care activities show increases in the number of events per day (not shown). But the most striking feature of Figure 13.1 is the gender differential: across time, and across socio-economic groups, women's average number of events per day is significantly higher than that of men. This accords with what we know already from the literature on the greater fragmentation of women's time, where it has been shown that women's leisure time is more fragmented; i.e. more likely to be interrupted by other activities, and shorter in duration than men's leisure time.

Figure 13.2 is the equivalent figure for our measure of time density: the percentage of waking time spent multi-tasking by gender and socio-economic class for 2000 and 2015. Most strikingly, it is clear that women spend a significantly greater proportion of their time multi-tasking than men. Interestingly, though, men spent more of their time multi-tasking in 2015 than in 2000, while women's multi-tasking didn't change, so that the gender gap in multi-tasking became less pronounced by 2015. The fact that there is no evidence for an increase in multi-tasking by women over time is perhaps surprising given the general assumption of the literature on the gender division of labour: that women are doing more multi-tasking as a way of managing the increasing burden of employment and continuing responsibility for domestic work.[8]

There is a socio-economic gradient evident for men and women in both surveys; women of a higher socio-economic status, in particular, spend more of their time multi-tasking than their lower-status counterparts. This at least accords

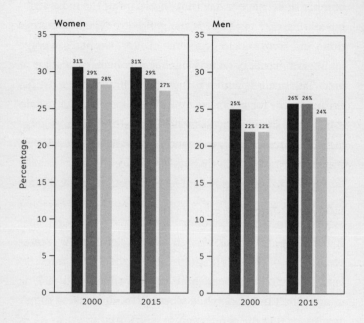

Figure 13.2
Percentage of waking activities multitasked by SEC and
gender: men and women aged 16–64, UK (2000–2015)

■ Professional/Managerial
■ Intermediate
■ Routine

with the idea that multi-tasking is one of the things that may help account for a greater feeling of time pressure among higher socio-economic groups. At the more detailed level of activities (not shown), only personal care activities and out-of-home leisure (for women only) are more likely to be multi-tasked over time.

To summarize, we find evidence for the expected socio-economic gradients in these indicators of time intensity, but little evidence for any speed-up in the tempo of daily activities over time. The single most noticeable feature of these figures is that women's time is both more fragmented and involves more multi-tasking than that of men's. So why do we experience the general impression of the speed-up of our time?

Who is feeling rushed?

Figure 13.3 shows that, overall, higher-status respondents were more likely to claim to 'always' or 'often' feel rushed than respondents of a lower socio-economic status. Yet over the 2000–2015 period there was a substantial reduction in the proportion of those who reported 'always' feeling rushed. This is particularly the case for higher-status men and women – an effect that results by 2015 in the elimination of the strong socio-economic gradient for men that was evident in 2000. The decline in reporting of feeling 'always rushed' is similar in magnitude for women (from a higher baseline), although for women the socio-economic gradient is still not completely eliminated by 2015. Again, what is most striking is the much higher reporting of 'always' feeling rushed among women than men.

Do those who experience greater time fragmentation and/

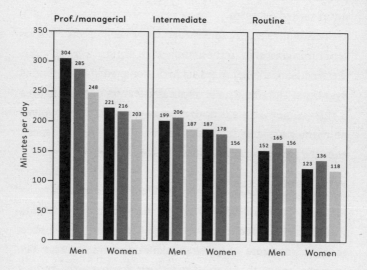

Figure 13.3
Percentage feeling 'always rushed' by SEC and gender:
men and women aged 16–64, UK (2000 and 2015)

■ Professional/Managerial
■ Intermediate
■ Routine

or multi-tasking also feel more rushed? We found no clear relationship with time fragmentation. As we have seen, women both experience more time fragmentation and are more likely to feel rushed in general, but there is no evidence for a general relationship between time fragmentation and feelings of being rushed. In contrast, we found a surprising, although rather weak, relationship between always feeling rushed and a *lower* proportion of time spent multi-tasking. Again, this gradient is the reverse of what would be expected if multi-tasking contributed to a sense of time pressure.

Once again, overall gender differentials are the most notable feature of these results. Women are more likely to feel always rushed than men. These differentials are hardly consistent with the 'speed-up' hypothesis of late modernity – but they are much more consistent with what is known from the feminist literature about women's problems in combining employment with family responsibilities. However, it seems that we cannot draw the simple conclusion – i.e. that multi-tasking is one of the reasons for women's greater sense of feeling rushed – since there is no obvious overall relationship between multi-tasking and feelings of rushedness.

Computing, screen time and rushedness

The UK 2014–15 TUS allows us to calculate not only the amount of time spent using computers as a main or secondary activity, but also the amount of time spent using any kind of digital device. Chapters 10 and 11 document the very large increase in time spent using ICT over the 2000–2015 period. We ask here whether this increase is associated with an increase in feelings of time pressure.

Figure 13.4 shows total daily screen time (time spent using any ICT device) in 2015 cross-classified by feelings of rushedness, gender and socio-economic status. This figure suggests that there is a reasonably strong relationship between ICT use and feeling 'always rushed' for men in professional/managerial occupations. Within this group greater ICT use does seem to be associated with a greater probability of feeling 'always rushed'. There is some indication, too, of a similar relationship for women in both the professional/managerial and intermediate class. However, there does not seem to be a consistent pattern for men in other socio-economic classes, or for women in the routine category.

Finally, in a multivariate analysis that tested the relationship between feeling 'always rushed' in the 2015 data and the other variables that we postulated might lead to feelings of rushedness (i.e. time fragmentation, multi-tasking, gender, socio-economic class and ICT use), we found no association between feeling 'always rushed' and either of the time intensity variables (fragmentation and multi-tasking). Nor was there any significant association between always feeling rushed and the total time spent using ICT. Instead, the strongest association, again, was with gender. In particular, being a woman increased the likelihood of feeling 'always rushed' by almost 70 per cent compared to being a man. The other main influences on feeling 'always rushed' were: 1) being employed rather than non-employed; 2) the time spent in unpaid work; and 3) age. When all of these other factors are taken into account there was no effect of socio-economic class on feelings of rushedness.

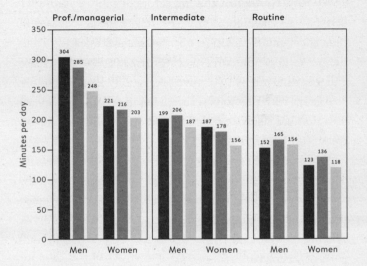

Figure 13.4
ICT time 'feeling rushed' by gender and SEC, men and women aged 16–64, UK (2015)

- ⬛ Always feel rushed
- ⬛ Sometimes feel rushed
- ⬛ Never feel rushed

Why do we think things are speeding up?

We find little evidence in our data for the idea of a generalized speed-up in the experience of daily life over the period 2000–2015. Neither of the indicators of time pressure we derived (the fragmentation measure and the percentage of time spent multi-tasking), nor the 'rushed' question from the survey questionnaire, indicates any substantial increase either in time intensity or time pressure. These findings are consistent with previous research based on time-use measures that has likewise failed to find much evidence for increases in time pressure.

What we pose here is, therefore, a challenge for theories of speed-up – if the world is indeed 'speeding up' we need to find ways to explain it that are not related at the average population level to the fragmentation of daily activities, or whether they are multi-tasked or not, or even to people's reports of feeling rushed.

We believe that one of the answers to this question lies in distinguishing the experiences of different socio-demographic groups.[9] Different subgroups of the population have different experiences, which are not necessarily reflected in overall trends. In particular, the substantial increases in overall workloads over the last 50 years have been in the main a feature affecting those who are more highly educated, in higher-status jobs and in dual-career households with small children. These groups are not only over-represented among long-hours workers, but they are among those who are 'likely to shape the terms of public discussion and debate'.[10] In other words, the idea of the speed-up as an objective empirical phenomenon may partly reflect the social status of those groups who were studied, or those who wrote about them. It *is* an objective phenomenon, but only among specific groups, and these are exactly the people who are over-represented among both the researched and the researchers.

Another, related, explanation relates to individual life-course trajectories. As we become older our commitments tend to increase (our paid work time, our family responsibilities, etc.), with the result that, when we think about our own lack of time, we are actually making a comparison with earlier stages of our own lives, while the true comparison would be with comparable stages of the life-course of older generations. This comparison, again, is likely to be particularly pertinent for those from higher socio-economic classes, whose professional careers progress steeply into middle age.

As a third consideration, the nature of activities, and the feelings associated with them, may be changing over time. For example, leisure activities may be becoming more intensive, involving higher amounts of effort and expenditure.[11] It could therefore be that, even if leisure time has remained the same (or indeed increased slightly), the time that is spent in leisure has come to feel more intensive in character, and consequently more pressured. In a previous paper we presented the concept of 'cultural voraciousness' as a dimension of leisure consumption based upon both the range and the frequency of leisure participation.[12] When we investigated the socio-economic correlates of 'voracious' leisure participation, it was clear that those with high social status are more voracious in their leisure participation.

Relatedly, in response to the general conclusion that time

pressure is a phenomenon experienced primarily by specific groups of the population (in particular those with high educational qualifications and high-status jobs), we have previously advanced the 'busyness as the badge of honour' hypothesis.[13] This states that busyness may have more to do with higher socio-economic classes' *self-representation* as busy, rather than any objective reality. The words 'I'm terribly busy at work' act as a means of status enhancement, signalling importance and indispensability. The most privileged now spend more time at work than the less so, and busyness therefore becomes a symbolic marker of social status.

As we showed in the first section of this book, and entirely in keeping with these findings, neither paid nor unpaid work times in the UK show substantial change from the turn of the 21st century, contrary to the idea that we're all working much harder. What has increased dramatically, however, is time spent using computing technologies. Of all the activity categories, computing time is the only one that shows a very large increase over the period 2000–2015. That increasing connectivity creates greater feelings of pressure on time is certainly the overall conclusion of the writings on speedup. However, despite this dramatic increase, we don't find a strong relationship between the experience of feelings of rushedness and ICT use.

So what are the underlying social inequalities of time?

Instead of evidence for generalized speed-up, we find consistent differentials by gender, socio-economic class and educational level.[14] Our main conclusions, therefore, support the idea of relative stasis in the underlying social inequalities of time. The professional/managerial class is more likely to be under pressure of time according to measures of time fragmentation and multi-tasking. Similarly, among both women and men, those in higher-status occupations and those with higher levels of education report feeling more rushed than those with lower levels of education or occupational status. What is really striking, however, is the overall much higher reporting of 'always' feeling rushed, and of multi-tasking among women. Women's higher levels of reported rushedness deserve much more attention than they are currently accorded in theoretical descriptions of speed-up in late modernity. The relative strength of the differential by gender as compared to either changes over time or occupational-status differentials would be completely unexpected if one were relying exclusively on theories of late modernity to understand changes in our experience of time pressure.

How can we understand this gender differential? Much previous research has referred to higher levels of time pressure among women, related to greater work–family conflict.[15] A growing number of women face onerous multiple obligations (i.e. paid work and domestic work) – and this is mainly an effect of more women entering the labour force, together with the growing percentage of single households. Clearly, time pressure will be particularly acute for those with exceptionally stressful schedules, such as mothers with young children who also have their own career, or those who are single parents. It is likely that in a situation where women are both increasingly moving into the labour force and still largely responsible for domestic work, the conflicts involved in managing work and family lead to heightened feelings of time pressure, irrespective of socio-economic class or education.

The socio-economic gradients we identify in both time fragmentation and multi-tasking are consistent with the theory of voracious consumption. Those from higher socio-economic groups and with higher educational attainment experience more fragmentation of their time, do more multi-tasking, and (in the case of men) use more ICT. However, while there are class and educational gradients in reported rushedness, these gradients do not seem to be growing. In fact, reported 'rushedness' has decreased over time, especially for men.

With respect to ICT use, there is evidence for a very large general increase in time spent using computers, tablets and smartphones over the period 2000–2015. Our multivariate analysis did not indicate that total screen time is significantly associated with 'feeling always rushed', when controlling for other variables. Interestingly, it is the measure of the total time spent in unpaid work that proved to be much more important. It appears that these rather simple measures of time spent in 'constrained' activities (employment and family care) are more strongly associated with feelings of rushedness than the measures of time intensity that we defined specifically in order to address the speed-up hypothesis (activity fragmentation and multi-tasking). The implication of this is entirely in keeping with our other conclusions regarding changes in time use. Since we know that, overall, time spent in paid work did not change much over the period, and time spent in unpaid work was relatively stable for men but decreased for women, there is nothing here to suggest that there is any significant speed-up in the experience of rushedness for either women or men associated with increases in paid or unpaid work. These conclusions leave us with the question whether the idea of a generalized speed-up in our time may actually be more of a 'folk narrative' about rapid changes in society than a real reflection of our daily lives.[16]

Time and Enjoyment
Measuring National Happiness

—

Jonathan Gershuny

Moments of time are directly linked in our UK time diaries to respondents' assessments of their *enjoyment* of that time, reflecting their instantaneous experience of time. And our enjoyment of time can be expected to feed directly into our feelings of happiness, or wellbeing, which, aggregated up, is in the end perhaps the most important measuring standard we have. There has been a growing interest over the 21st century from national and international policy agencies in the measurement of national happiness, or wellbeing. Aggregate population measures of wellbeing can act as alternatives to the standard economic money-based measures (such as Gross Domestic Product, or its extensions to include unpaid work as in Chapter 6) for assessing the success of societies' policies. The influential 'Stiglitz Report',[1] commissioned by the OECD Commission on the Measurement of Economic Performance and Social Progress, concluded that 'the time was right to shift emphasis from measuring economic production to measuring people's wellbeing'.[2]

We measure diary respondents' enjoyment of their time from the column we included for this purpose in the 2014–15

UK TUS (column on the far right-hand side of the diary illustrated in Figure 1 of the Introduction).[3] The enjoyment of time measured in this way is sometimes referred to as a measure of 'objective happiness'[4] (though this can be confusing given that enjoyment, and its accumulation as a feeling of happiness, is so obviously a *subjective* phenomenon!).

This method of measuring the instantaneous enjoyment associated with particular episodes of time provides an alternative to more conventional methods of measuring the enjoyment of time. The most straightforward of these is simply to ask the general questionnaire survey-type question: 'How much do you enjoy . . . cooking? . . . shopping? . . . doing DIY? . . . going to the gym? . . . caring for children?' But do we really know how much we enjoy the different categories of things we do, in the abstract? Perhaps we may be more aware of how much we generally enjoy some of these things, less aware of others. Or do we simply have some sort of general *expectation* that we will enjoy particular activities? So how do we answer these questions? Do we try recalling and balancing all our past experiences to produce some sort of average estimate? Unlikely – indeed, pretty near impossible. Or do we simply recall the last time we did something? Or again, do we provide some response corresponding to a general principle of self-representation along the lines of 'I'm the sort of person who enjoys . . .'?

In fact, since these feelings are in reality attached to specific *instances* of activity, people are much more likely to respond accurately to a column in a diary asking how much they were enjoying themselves at a specific time.[5] So a measure of enjoyment derived by asking diary respondents to report their enjoyment of each 10-minute interval of time, is just about as close as we could hope to get to a valid and reliable measure of instantaneous enjoyment. And these measurements of the instantaneous enjoyment of individual episodes of time (sometimes referred to as 'experience' measures) can be aggregated, for individuals or for whole populations, into an overall measure of happiness, or wellbeing.

Enjoyment from the UK 2014–15 time-use diary

Figure 14.1 shows what the UK population enjoyed doing most (and least) in 2015. It provides a plot of mean daily enjoyment levels from the UK Time Use Survey for 63 different activities (or groups of closely related activities) that together add up to the 24-hour day. The activities are ranked by their mean daily enjoyment level, from the least enjoyable on the left side of the graph, to the most enjoyable on the right-hand side.[6] Ninety-five per cent confidence bars for the means are shown (the mean is at the exact midpoint of the confidence bar for each activity).[7]

There are interesting and easily interpretable differences in the levels of enjoyment of time spent in different activities. The activities receiving the lowest ratings are predictable: doing school homework (the lowest-rated activity, with a mean of 4.14); job search; and various housework activities. The most enjoyed activities, with mean scores above 6.25, also predictably involve outdoor leisure activities such as eating out, going to sports events or cultural performances, and playing with children.

As we read along the ranked range of activities from left

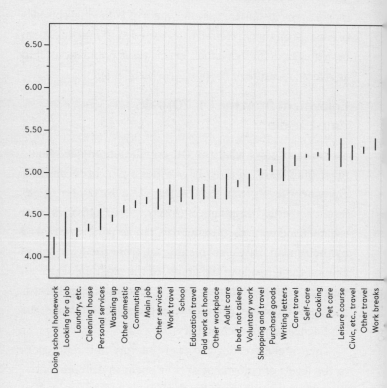

Figure 14.1
Average daily enjoyment levels (95 per cent confidence interval: sample aged 8 and over, UK (2015)

Other outdoor
Email, internet
Work meals
Childcare
Listen to radio
Gardening, etc.
Read, teach child
Walking
Accompany child
Talk person, phone
Relax, do nothing
Watch TV, etc.
Other meals
Reading
Walk dogs
Arts, musical
Listen to music
Cycling
Play sport
Friends visiting
Party, etc.
Hobbies, sew, knit
Religious acts
Out-of-home leisure
Computer games
Games at home
Other events
Sleep, etc.
Restaurant, pub
Play with child
Go to sport
Theatre, concert

to right (least to most enjoyed), we find small clusters of activities with somewhat similar enjoyment levels (main job, school, work and educational travel, for example). As we would hope, these groupings tend to include rather similar sorts of activities. Right at the bottom of the enjoyment scale (at the left-hand side of the figure), we find unpaid work: laundry, house cleaning, and so on. And then, next to the bottom of the enjoyment order, with a mean around 4.75, we find paid work, whether at the workplace or at home (generally and quite significantly preferred to the basic housework activity categories).

Moving on, with mean scores ranging from 5.00 to 5.25, we find other sorts of somewhat more pleasant chores, shopping, and care of others, with their associated travel; then self-care (personal toilet) and cooking, all significantly preferred to the various sorts of paid and unpaid work activities located to their left in the graph. Rising towards a mean enjoyment score of 5.50 we have some of the more entertaining aspects of work including workplace breaks and do-it-yourself decoration and construction. Then, between scores of 5.50 and 5.75, we have activities that combine aspects of work and recreation – gardening and accompanying children – as well as listening to the radio. Approaching an enjoyment score of 6.00, we pass through various leisure activities: television, reading, walking dogs, listening to music. Between 6.00 and 6.25 we find playing sports, cycling, social life, parties, hobbies, computer games and religious activity. And finally, with an enjoyment rating just under 6.25, we have sleep – exceeded in enjoyment only by out-of-home eating and drinking, playing with children, and going to sporting events. Absolutely top-ranked is going to cinemas, theatres and concerts, with a mean score of 6.60.

The enjoyment ranking of the various activities emerging from the diary data is, in short, entirely clear and plausible. It is also historically quite stable. In 1986 a Unilever market research survey in the UK used a similar technique to collect diary enjoyment measures.[8] Despite being nearly 30 years older, and based on a more limited sample (adults in couples), the results that emerged from this survey were really very similar. Figure 14.2 plots the mean enjoyment scores for each activity in the two studies against each other, re-categorizing the 2015 results to correspond to the 30 categories of activity used in the 1986 study. The linear correlation of .886 between the 30 pairs of mean enjoyment levels shows that the two sets of scores are surprisingly close – about three-quarters (0.886^2) of the variation in the 2015 scores is explained by the 1986 scores (or vice versa). This shows that the ranking of levels of enjoyment is broadly consistent throughout the period between the two surveys, with laundry and other housework right at the bottom, and going out to the cinema or concerts, pubs and restaurants and sleep at the top.

Those activities that lie above the diagonal line shown in Figure 14.2 are those that were more enjoyed in 1986 than in 2015. Those below the line were more enjoyed in 2014–15 than in 1986. The most evident changes in enjoyment levels between the surveys are reasonably easily explicable by what we know has changed in the UK during the 30 years between the surveys. Paid-work time, for example, was much more highly rated in 1986 than today: we suspect this is a reflection of the fact that jobs have since become more precarious, pressured and stressful. Voluntary activity, similarly much more highly rated in the earlier survey, may be affected by the deterioration in the level of welfare provision by the state, and the resulting extra burden on people providing care for others on an unpaid, informal or voluntary basis. The enjoyment of rest time may perhaps have been affected by the growth in use of new ICT technologies eating into time that previously was spent in a more relaxing way (see Chapter 13). On the other hand, there are a cluster of activity categories that were more enjoyed in the 2015 survey. In particular, developmental childcare activities such as playing with children are, simply, more highly regarded now than they were previously. This change is clearly reflected in the increase of the amount of time devoted to such activities by parents over this 30-year period (Chapter 5). Sewing also stands out as an activity that is much more enjoyed today than 30 years ago! While the prevalence of sewing has decreased substantially over the 30-year period, its enjoyment rating has markedly increased. This reflects its progressive change in status, over this period, from a domestic responsibility to an elective hobby. Similar arguments may be made in respect of cooking, DIY and shopping – all activities with mid-level enjoyment rankings – which, with the growth of outsourcing and online opportunities as substitutions, have become more elective and enjoyable activities for those who spend time doing them.

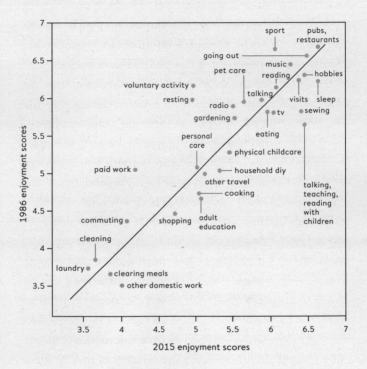

Figure 14.2

Comparing the enjoyment of activities in the UK in 1986 and 2015: men and women aged 16–65

Who enjoys doing what?

Time-diary recording of the enjoyment of activities yields consistent and plausible results at the overall level. However, we might expect these enjoyment rankings to vary according to socio-economic and demographic variables such as by gender, educational level and employment status. And indeed, there are some systematic differences in the extent to which different sorts of people enjoy different activities. But these socio-economic and demographic differences seem to have hardly any systematic effect on the *ranking* of the preferences for these activities. For example, there is an almost constant relationship between educational level and the enjoyment of seven major groups of activities[9]: in almost all cases, the higher the educational level, the lower the mean enjoyment level. The one exception is in the case of sleep: those with the lowest level of education report lower levels of enjoyment of sleep than do those with higher educational levels. This may be related to the stress and depression known to be associated with living in a 'just coping' financial situation. But in the other six major activity groups, the inverse relationship between educational level and enjoyment holds. Of course, we can't know from this data whether the better educated *actually* enjoy their activities less than others, or whether they simply express their enjoyment more moderately. But indubitably they do, on average, report lower levels of enjoyment.

Cross-classifying this data by gender, age or employment status makes essentially no difference to the ranking by education, with only a few exceptions. In particular, employed women with no educational qualifications enjoy both the 'paid work' and 'shopping' groups of activities less than women with some educational qualifications. This may reflect on the one hand the tedious and precarious nature of women's unskilled paid work, and on the other the stress of shopping with little money to spend.

A second regularity also emerges from this cross-classification. Activity group by activity group through these educational and demographic breakdowns, women generally claim higher mean enjoyment levels than do men. We see five exceptions to this (out of 21 groups), all involving the educationally least-well qualified. Apparently, women with no educational qualifications enjoy many activities less than equivalent men, probably for similar reasons as those we discussed above relating to the stress of precarious employment combined with low income.

It is hard to avoid the conclusion that there is a strong consistency in the levels of enjoyableness of the various different activities of the day. At this point in UK history, it seems that this ranking, as set out in Figure 14.2, has, as Daniel Kahneman suggested,[10] something close to the status of an objective social fact.

Enjoying the whole day: overall mean daily enjoyment

We have shown that there are remarkably stable assessments of the enjoyment rankings of activities both over time and between socio-demographic groups. The next question is, how much do people enjoy their time overall? We can assume that people try to maximize as far as possible the most enjoyable ways of spending their time, but we also know that there are constraints (imposed by the need to do various forms of work, for example).

The next step is to put the various activities of the day together to consider *overall* mean enjoyment levels calculated over the whole day's activities. Whole-day mean enjoyment scores are calculated as the average minutes of time devoted to each group of activities multiplied by their level of enjoyability, divided by the total of minutes in the day. Some economists[11] have argued that these estimates of 'national utility' may provide a radical alternative to measures based on national income such as GDP and GNP. They suggested that 'process benefits' – their term for the whole-day mean enjoyment measures[12] – provide important information about the population's wellbeing that is independent of money income measures.

Our method of calculating these process benefits as the product of total time spent in each of an exhaustive set of activities and their reported enjoyment values tells us something entirely different to what we get from income-based calculations. It corresponds quite closely, in fact, to John Stuart Mill's original idea of 'utility': in this case, each member of the population individually decides on the value, to her or him, of each sort of activity.[13]

Returning to the concept of the aggregated Great Day described in Chapter 2, Figure 14.3, a base-proportional histogram, shows the make-up, for the adult UK population in 2015, of the overall mean daily enjoyment (or, in the terms above, the overall population process benefit) of the UK population's Great Day. The vertical axis shows enjoyment

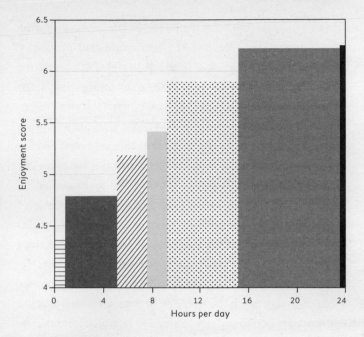

Figure 14.3

Average daily enjoyment of time: men and women aged 15 and over, UK (2015)

Doing homework, looking for job, laundry etc., cleaning house, personal services, washing up

Other domestic work, commuting, main job, other services, work travel, school etc., education travel, paid work at home, paid work at workplace, adult care, in bed but not asleep, voluntary work

Shopping travel, shopping, leisure courses, writing letters, travel to care for others, self-care, cooking and preparing, pet care

Travel for civic and communal duties, other travel, unspecified indoor activities, work breaks, second job, DIY, other outdoor activities, e-mail, internet, work meals, childcare, listening to radio, gardening etc., reading to or teaching child, walking, accompanying child

Talk in person or phone, relax, do nothing, watch TV etc., meals at home, reading, walking dogs, arts and music, listen to music, cycling, playing sport, visit friends, party, celebration, hobbies, sewing knitting crafts, religious activity, unspecified out-of-home leisure

Sleep

Go to restaurant pub or bar, play with child

scores, while the horizontal axis shows the amount of time (in hours per day) spent in the seven different groups of activities, which are ranked from left to right, as previously, according to their mean daily enjoyment ratings. Bar 6, for example, showing sleep, is both rated highly in terms of enjoyment (scoring between 6 and 6.5), and also takes up quite a large chunk of the day across the population (over 8 hours). Putting these two together, we can see that a lot of enjoyment over the Great Day derives from time spent asleep!

Bars 5 and 7 (the 'relaxation' and 'going out' activity groups) show the overall enjoyment derived by the population from that part of the Great Day described in monetary terms by the conventional measure of National Product. Extended National Product, on the other hand, places a money value on pretty much the whole of Groups 5, 6[14] and 7. In the conventional economic view, Extended National Income, the actual and imputed wages and profits of the society, balances this Extended National Product. However, when we consider mean daily enjoyment we can see that the areas enclosed by bars 5, 6 and 7 (broadly, the process benefits of consumption, including sleep) by far exceed those enclosed by bars 1 to 4 (broadly, the enjoyment of work). The final section of this concluding chapter discusses the implications of this evident mismatch between national utility measured as monetary value (through the National Product) and national utility measured as enjoyment.

National income and national happiness: are they the same?

So what can this measure of overall daily enjoyment tell us in terms of 'national happiness'? The University of Michigan researchers who started this discussion more than 30 years ago referred to 'the problem' of the joint dependence of well-being on both money income and enjoyment. An example would be a retired person, living on a state pension, who has the time to spend in the most enjoyable activities (the 'going out' activities), but not necessarily the income to do so.

The beauty of time-use data here is that we can utilize them, over the same 24 hours, to produce exactly matching measures of both money income *and* the process benefits derived from the enjoyment of time. The Extended National Income measure is arrived at by multiplying the diary sample's work time, paid or unpaid, by the appropriate wage rates (and adding the return on the capital used in production). The part of the 24 hours that is not work is defined as consumption time. If we multiply each consumption event within this 24 hours by an appropriate price (or, for the final commodities produced from unpaid work, the 'shadow price'), and add the savings that contribute to the capital stock, we arrive at an Extended National *Product*. The central idea of National Accounts is that the total of National Income is identical to the total of National Product. The two parts of the day represent the same money value from two different perspectives, respectively the money value as produced by the producer and as consumed by the consumer. The 24 hours of the diary day can thereby be used to produce two identical estimates of money income – the time spent producing and the time spent consuming.

However, at the same time, exactly the same 24 hours of the diary day can produce matching estimates of process benefits, equivalent to overall mean daily enjoyment for the population. Just as in the money income/output case, every minute of the day has an enjoyment value (as well as a monetary value). But in the case of enjoyment the value relates to the *direct* subjective experience of each respondent, as opposed to the collective wage or price values imposed on the various sorts of work and non-work time by the market or some other remote mechanism. This allows us to consider the subjective experience of work and non-work time in parallel, using the same units. Consider Figure 14.3. We can use the overall mean daily enjoyment calculations to understand what the effect of particular policy changes might be on national wellbeing, or 'happiness'. The bulk of the society's paid and unpaid work is located in bars 1–4, below the 8.5-hour point on the horizontal axis. Work time is enjoyed less, sometimes much less, than the overall mean daily enjoyment level, while consumption time is enjoyed more. What if, for example, future policy changes were to reduce public support for paid elder care and other social provisions, passing the burden of these relatively non-enjoyable activities to unpaid voluntary agencies and private households. Social care activities, irrespective of whether they are paid or unpaid, are not subject to much technical change, so they will exhibit little productivity growth, but at the same time, as the population ages, these policy changes would mean that more unpaid work emerges in this sector. Meanwhile, assume that a proportion of the paid work associated with social care has been transferred to other sectors of the economy which have higher apparent productivity growth. Under these conditions GNP might show a healthy rising trend – but process benefits, the population's overall mean level of enjoyment of daily life, would simultaneously decline.

This is not to say that we necessarily expect this particular pattern of change to happen (though it does correspond to a central plank of the UK Conservative Party's austerity public policy just a few years ago). It is possible to envisage various scenarios that might produce quite different patterns of association between GNP and national happiness. But the conclusion that emerges is that if we take GNP alone as our guide to economic policy we might inadvertently *damage* national happiness (as measured through overall daily enjoyment). The joint dependence of national product and national happiness on the same 24-hour statistics provides a straightforward means for a properly integrated account of the evolution of these two important dimensions of public policy outcome, allowing us to postulate which courses of policy action might produce gains in both national product *and* happiness simultaneously.

Pressing Questions for Our Time
—
Jonathan Gershuny
Oriel Sullivan

As we have shown throughout this book, time can be valued in many different ways. We are used to hearing that *time is money*, and we have presented ways of accounting for the monetary value of our time. But, crucially, time is also about subjective experience. The previous two chapters have addressed, directly and indirectly, two central and pressing questions of our time, about our time: 1) are we speeding up and feeling increasingly pressed for time?; and 2) how happy are we as we go about our daily lives – and can time-use data provide us with an alternative to standard economic-based accounts of social progress?

Unlike the other chapters of this book, these questions relate primarily to the way in which we *experience* time – the different ways that we are feeling as we move through our daily sequence of activities. We have shown that time-use data provide a challenge to the idea of an inexorable increase in time pressure; simple measures of time fragmentation and multi-tasking do not show any general increase over the years of the 21st century. At the same time, measures of time spent in 'constrained' activities (employment and family care) are more strongly associated with reported feelings of rushedness than anything else, including ICT use. That we are able to provide these, perhaps unexpected, answers to questions about the subjective understandings and experience of our time underlines the future potential for time-use diary studies.

Were the data available, we would be able, for example, to compare the experience of time enjoyed by the Flintstones and the Jetsons. Did the Stone Age Flintstones actually experience a less stressful pace of life than the space-age Jetsons? Did they juggle fewer things simultaneously, enjoying more leisure, and slower cooking? And did the Jetsons spend more time speeding around in their space-age transportation, exposing themselves to greater levels of environmental hazards such as solar radiation? Did more advanced technology contribute in any way to a more gender-equal division of labour? And, crucially, did their space-age way of life make them more or less happy overall than the prehistoric Flintstones? Time-use diary data gives us a means of providing answers to these questions for contemporary societies on a historical, cross-national basis.

The chapters of this book have documented some important consistencies and changes in the way that the UK population has been using its time over the past half-century. Our analyses of general time-use trends in some respects run rather contrary to expectations. True, women's core housework has been reduced, men's and women's unpaid work totals have converged somewhat, and IT use has grown explosively. But the broadest summary result is of a certain consistency in time-use patterns. The totals of (paid and unpaid) work, the amount of sleep, and hence the total of leisure/consumption time – over a 50-year observation window – all changed much less than was expected by the futurologists of the 1960s.

By comprehensively summarizing the information provided by time-use diaries, the minutes of the Great Day provide a time-based metric allowing direct empirical comparison across the full range of human activities, social contexts, locations and feelings of enjoyment, only a very few of which may be accounted for in money terms. This points the way to a new approach to social science, more inclusive than either traditional economics or traditional sociology, capable of integrating accounts of what goes on in 'the economy' with information on the division and balance of the 'extra-economic' activity more usually studied by sociologists.

To conclude, the Great Day, gathering together everything done by everyone in the society, provides the evidential basis for various new sorts of accounting for historical change. It allows us to produce economic accounts, extended to include the product of work that is not undertaken as part of any sort of exchange activity, and the value of the consumption that takes place outside the broadly drawn sphere of work. It provides the raw material that allows us to estimate the extent of time devoted to nutrition and to all the various sorts of exercise and sedentary activity. It allows us to consider feelings of wellbeing and enjoyment, and their relationship to all the things we do during our days and nights. And we can in principle use these historical accounts and descriptions, in turn, as the base material for grounded speculation about the future – in the hope that in doing so we might help to promote better health, more wealth and greater wellbeing. We are now turning our minds to some serious economic and sociological futurology. But in this book, we seek merely to provide the prequel to this future: the most concrete and comprehensive recent description of each of the elements of time use that come together to constitute the society's Great Day.

Notes

INTRODUCTION: THE TIMELINESS OF TIME USE

1. John Maynard Keynes (1970 edn). 'The Economic Prospects for our Grandchildren'. *Collected Works*, vol. 8. Cambridge: Cambridge University Press.

2. See for example Juliet Schor (1991). *The Overworked American: The Unexpected Decline of Leisure*. New York: Basic Books; Brigid Schulte (2014), *Overwhelmed: Work, Love and Play When No One Has the Time*. London, New York: Bloomsbury Publishing.

3. Early 20th-century research into the psycho-social adjustment effects of unemployment, conducted in an Austrian township whose only major employer closed as a result of the 1929 Great Crash, revealed various 'latent functions' of common experiences in paid employment – social contact, feelings of societal contribution, as well as requirements for physical exercise and routine alternation of active and sedentary activities through the week: Marie Jahoda, Paul F. Lazarsfeld and Hans Zeisel [1931] (1972). *Marienthal: The Sociography of an Unemployed Community*. London: Tavistock Publications.

4. Michael Young and Peter Willmott (1975). *The Symmetrical Family: Study of Work and Leisure in the London Region*. London: Penguin Books.

5. Oriel Sullivan (1996). 'The Enjoyment of Activities: Do Couples Affect Each Other's Well-Being?' *Social Indicators Research* 38(1): 81–102; Oriel Sullivan. (2000). 'The Division of Domestic Labour: Twenty Years of Change?' *Sociology* 34(3): 437–56; Alain Chenu and John P. Robinson (2002). 'Synchronicity in the Work Schedules of Working Couples'. *Monthly Labor Review* 125(4): 55–63.

6. W. Keith Bryant and Cathleen D. Zick (1996). 'An Examination of Parent–child Shared Time'. *Journal of Marriage and Family* 58(1): 227–37; Sandra L. Hofferth and John F. Sandberg (2001). 'How American Children

Spend Their Time'. *Journal of Marriage and Family* 63(2): 295–308;
Anne H. Gauthier, Timothy M. Smeeding and Frank F. Furstenberg.
(2004). 'Are Parents Investing Less Time in Children? Trends in
Selected Industrialized Countries'. *Population and Development Review*
30(4): 647–71.

7. UNECE (2013). *Guidelines for Harmonizing Time-Use Surveys.* Geneva,
    Switzerland: United Nations Economic Commission for Europe.

8. As established in, for example, Jonathan Gershuny (2000, 2nd edn 2003).
    Changing Times: Work and Leisure in Postindustrial Society. Oxford and New
    York: Oxford University Press; John P. Robinson and Geoffrey Godbey
    (1999). *Time for Life: The Surprising Ways Americans Use Their Time.*
    University Park, PA: Pennsylvania State University Press.

9. Kimberly Fisher and Richard Layte (2004). 'Measuring Work–life Balance
    Using Time Diary Data'. *Electronic International Journal of Time Use
    Research* 1(1): 1–13.

10. These weekly work grids also have contributed to significant advances
    in sequence analysis using time-use data. See Laurent Lesnard (2014).
    'Using Optimal Matching Analysis in Sociology: Cost Setting and Sociology
    of Time'. In Philippe Blanchard, Felix Bühlmann and Jacques-Antoine
    Gauthier (eds). *Advances in Sequence Analysis: Theory, Method, Applications.*
    Berlin: Springer eBooks.

11. A more detailed account of the UK historical sequence of time-use diary
    surveys and relevant worldwide developments in the collection of time-use
    data can be found in the following chapter.

12. See, for example, Benjamin Cornwell, Jonathan Gershuny, Oriel Sullivan,
    2019. 'The Social Structure of Time: Emerging Trends and New Directions'.
    Annual Review of Sociology 45:1 Online publication 1/5/19 https://doi.
    org/10.1146/annurev-soc-073018-022416.

CHAPTER 1: FIFTY YEARS YEARS OF CHANGE IN UK DAILY LIFE AT A GLANCE

1. E.g. Giacomo Vagni, Benjamin Cornwell (2018). 'Patterns of everyday
    activities across social contexts'. *Proceedings of the National Academy of
    Sciences* 115 (24) 6183-6188; doi: 10.1073/pnas.1718020115

2. Andrew Abbott and Alexandra Hrycak's 'Measuring Resemblance in
    Sequence Data: An Optimal Matching Analysis of Musicians' Careers'

(*American Journal of Sociology* 96(1): 144–85 (July 1990)) introduced the use of the biologists' 'optimal matching' approaches to the analysis of sequence data to sociological research; Laurent Lesnard and Man Yee Kan's 'Investigating Scheduling of Work: A Two-stage Optimal Matching Analysis of Workdays and Workweeks' (*Journal of the Royal Statistical Society* Series A, 174(2): 349–68 (2011)) provides an ingenious application of the technique to daily activity sequence data.

3. We make use both of the 16,500 diary days sampled in the most recent UK time-use survey of 2014–15, and the more than 70,000 days from the earlier UK surveys.

4. Different applications of time-use data require different ways of aggregating the data. In this chapter we use a classification that groups activities by their purposes. In particular, travel time is not considered on its own, but rather in the context of the purpose of each trip: we include relevant travel within each relevant activity category. So, for example, trips involving taking children to school are included in 'childcare', journeys to the supermarket in 'shopping', travel to the gym in 'exercise', and so on.

5. An initial qualification is needed concerning the evidence. The diaries collected from the 1980s onwards cover the entire 24 hours, from 4am on one day to the same time on the following day. But the original 1961 BBC diary did not include information on six and a half hours of the night, between midnight and 6.30am, and the 1974 survey is missing three and a half hours of the night, between 2am and 5.30am. It is nevertheless possible to make reliable population-level estimates about time use during the night-time hours in the 1960s and 1970s on the basis of the 1980s data. To do this, we adapt one of the very oldest statistical techniques: 'Life Table Analysis'. We can use the evidence of what those who were awake at 2am in 1983 were doing at 2.15am as the basis for an estimate of the 2.15am activities of those awake at 2am in 1975, using the real 1985 quarter hours to estimate activities in each successive unobserved quarter hour up to 4am in 1975. We have to make the simple but plausible assumption that sleep is, in the demographers' jargon, an 'absorptive state' – that is, between 2am and 4am, those who go to bed in each quarter hour, stay there! And then, in turn, we use the newly reconstructed mid-1970s data to reconstruct the early 1960s post-midnight and pre-6.30am activities. As we can see from the 1980s data, only a very small proportion (less than 5 per cent) of the population are out of bed after midnight or before 6.30am, so – somnambulists apart – the assumptions involved here are quantitatively rather small. But, in considering the graphs that follow, we

must simply remember, first, that for the 1961 survey, 'asleep' should in fact be understood as meaning 'after going to bed and before getting up in the morning' and second, that this means that pre-1980s sleep time may be slightly over-estimated.

CHAPTER 2: ADDING UP AND FITTING TOGETHER: THE UK'S GREAT DAY ACROSS TIME

1. D. Ås (1978). 'Studies of Time-use: Problems and Prospects'. *Acta Sociologica* 21(2): 125–41.

2. Kathryn Walker (1969). 'Time Spent in Household Work by Homemakers'. *Family Economics Review* 62(5): 5–6; Oli Hawrylyshyn (1976). 'The Value of Household Services: A Survey of Empirical Estimates'. *Review of Income and Wealth* 22 (2): 101–3.

3. Gary S. Becker (1965). 'A Theory of the Allocation of Time'. *Economic Journal* 75(299): 493–517.

4. However, as in Oriel Sullivan and Jonathan Gershuny's 'Inconspicuous Consumption Work-rich, Time-poor in the Liberal Market Economy' (*Journal of Consumer Culture* 4(1): 79–100 (2004)), goods may be purchased, but then simply stored and never used!

5. Jonathan Gershuny (2000, 2nd edn 2003). *Changing Times: Work and Leisure in Postindustrial Society*. Oxford and New York: Oxford University Press. Chapter 8.

6. In this chapter we use a ten-activity classification with separate totals for:

   - **Sleep and resting** (time in bed)
   - **Self-care and eating** (including washing and bathing, personal toilet, dressing, and meals alone or with other household members)
   - **Paid work and full-time education** (together with associated breaks, travel and job-search activity)
   - **Household work** (cooking, cleaning, doing dishes, laundry, house and vehicle maintenance, gardening, voluntary work, and associated travel)
   - **Shopping,** and the use of retail services such as hairdressers, and associated travel
   - **Child- and elder care,** and associated travel.
   - **Out of home leisure** (cinema, theatre, and other spectacles, eating and drinking out, attending sports events, parties, religious worship, and associated travel).

- **Exercise** (walking, cycling, playing physical games, attending gym. dog-walking etc.)
- **Home leisure** (pet care, conversations, visits to/from friends, handy crafts and hobbies, non-computer-based correspondence)
- **Media use** (reading print media, music listening, radio, television, computer use)

These categories are further aggregated to become 'personal care' (sleep + self-care), and 'all work' (paid + household + shopping + caring activities). The ten categories of time use together sum to 1,440 minutes.

7. See, for example, T. Roenneberg (2012). *Internal Time: Chronotypes, Social Jet Lag, and Why You're So Tired*. Cambridge, MA: Harvard University Press.

8. M. Calem, J. Bisla, A. Begum et al. (2012). 'Increased Prevalence of Insomnia and Changes in Hypnotics Use in England over 15 Years: Analysis of the 1993, 2000, and 2007 National Psychiatric Morbidity Surveys'. *Sleep* 35(3): 377–84.

9. Note that the BBC's focus on 'viewer and listener availability' led to what is for our purposes an over simplified classification of out-of-home leisure in the 1974 time-use survey. If we ignore the 1974 data points in Figure 2.6, and instead draw a straight line between the (for this particular purpose) more reliable 1961 and 1985 estimates, we arrive at a reasonably simple picture of change in the two out-of-home leisure categories.

10. The 'trickle-down' principle of emulation, widely used in popular sociological and economic writing, seems to have been first elaborated in Thorstein Veblen's *Theory of the Leisure Class* (1899). It is an essential element in, for example, J. K. Galbraith's T*he New Industrial State* (1967), and it is the driving force behind the growth of time pressure predicted in Staffan Burenstam Linder's *The Harried Leisure Class* (1970) (whose title explicitly identifies the origin of the central idea). In Michael Young and Peter Willmott's *The Symmetrical Family* (1973), it is transformed to become a marching column, with successive ranks representing the social status order, advancing so as to consume tomorrow what the higher ranks consumed yesterday, and described as 'the principle of stratified diffusion'. And in Fred Hirsch's *Social Limits to Growth* (1976), which quotes extensively from *The Symmetrical Family*, it becomes, finally, established as the ultimate explanation for the pervasive phenomenon of growth in national incomes.

11. Michael Burda, Daniel S. Hamermesh and Philippe Weil (2013). 'Total Work and Gender: Facts and Possible Explanations'. *Journal of Population Economics* 26(1): 239–61.

CHAPTER 3: THE UK IN CROSS-NATIONAL CONTEXT

1. Note that the UK data, in this figure, start in the mid-1970s. This reflects the decision by the original data-collection agency, the BBC Audience Research Department, to restrict their 1961 diary to the 6.30am to midnight period during which the BBC was then 'on air'. Though we were sufficiently satisfied with the statistical procedures described in Chapter 2 to make inferences for the hours immediately following and preceding the diary end and start times, and though we know that the great majority of the middle hours of the night are spent in bed by a large majority of the population, we are still reluctant to ascribe the whole of the missing 390 minutes to sleep.

2. This excludes eating out in restaurants and other people's private homes, which we group in the out-of-home leisure category.

CHAPTER 4: OUR WORKING LIVES: PAID WORKING TIME

1. Adriana Mata-Greenwood (1992). 'Integrated Framework for the Measurement of Working Time'. Stat Working Papers 92–2. Geneva: International Labour Office.

2. Benjamin H. Snyder (2016). *The Disrupted Workplace: Time and the Moral Order of Flexible Capitalism*. New York: Oxford University Press.

3. Deborah M. Figart and Lonnie Golden (eds) (2000). 'Introduction and Overview: Understanding Working Time around the World'. In *Working Time: International Trends, Theory and Policy Perspectives*. London: Routledge.

4. Robinson, A. Chenu and A. S. Alvarez (2002). 'Measuring the Complexity of Hours at Work: The Weekly Work Grid'. *Monthly Labor Review* 125(4): 44–54.

5. Mata-Greenwood (1992). 'Integrated Framework for the Measurement of Working Time'.

6. These figures are very close to the current estimates from the Annual Survey of Hours and Earnings conducted by the Office for National Statistics. Office for National Statistics (2016). *Annual Survey of Hours and Earnings, 1997–2015* [data collection]. 8th edn. UK Data Service. SN: 6689.

7. P. Walthery and J. Gershuny (2019). 'Improving Stylised Working Time Estimates with Time Diary Data: A Multi Study Assessment for the UK'. *Social Indicators Research*.

8. R. D. Williams (2004). 'Investigating Hours Worked Measurements'. *Labour Market Trends* (Office for National Statistics) 112(2): 71–9. issn: 13614819.

9. Figart and Golden (2000). 'Understanding Working Time around the World'.

10. The slightly larger total of paid weekly working time in Chapter 2 reflects the inclusion of travel to work.

11. Eurofound (2016). 'Developments in Working Life in Europe 2015: EurWORK Annual Review'. Luxembourg: Publications Office of the European Union.

12. Laurent Lesnard and Man Yee Kan (2011). 'Investigating Scheduling of Work: A Two-stage Optimal Matching Analysis of Workdays and Workweeks'. *Journal of the Royal Statistical Society*: Series A (Statistics in Society), 174(2): 349–68.

13. Jennifer Tomlinson (2006). 'Women's Work–life Balance Trajectories in the UK: Reformulating Choice and Constraint in Transitions through Part-time Work across the Life-course'. *British Journal of Guidance & Counselling* 34(3): 365–82.

CHAPTER 5: DIVIDING DOMESTIC LABOUR AND CARE

1. For instance, Gary Becker (1981). *A Treatise on the Family*. Cambridge, MA: National Bureau of Economic Research; Sarah F. Berk (1985). *The Gender Factory: The Apportionment of Work in American Households*. New York: Plenum.

2. Shannon N. Davis and Theodore N. Greenstein (2013). 'Why Study Housework? Cleaning as a Window into Power in Couples'. *Journal of Family Theory & Review* 5(2): 63–71.

3. Ann Oakley (1974). *The Sociology of Housework*. London: Martin Robinson.

4. Oriel Sullivan (2019). 'Gender inequality in work–family balance'. *Nature Human Behaviour*. http://dx.doi.org/10.1038/s41562-019-0536-3.

5. For the 1990s, see Scott Coltrane (2000). 'Research on Household Labor: Modeling and Measuring the Social Embeddedness of Routine Family Work'. *Journal of Marriage and the Family* 62(4): 1208–33; for the first decade of the 21st century, see Suzanne M. Bianchi , Liana C. Sayer, Melissa A. Milkie and John P. Robinson (2012). 'Housework: Who Did, Does or Will Do It, and How Much Does It Matter?' *Social Forces*, 91(1): 55–63, and Mylene Lachance-Grzela and Genevieve Bouchard (2010). 'Why Do Women Do the Lion's Share of Housework: A Decade of Research'. *Sex Roles* 63(11): 767–80.

6. Beth A. Latshaw and Stephanie I. Hale (2016) '"The Domestic Handoff": Stay-at-home Fathers' Time-use in Female Breadwinner Families'. *Journal of Family Studies* 22(2): 1–24.

7. Shelley Pacholok and Anne Gauthier (2010). 'Non-participant Fathers in Time-Use Studies: Uninvolved or Data Artifact?' *Social Indicators Research* 96(2): 249–66.

8. Annette Lareau (2003, 2nd edn 2011). *Unequal Childhoods: Class, Race, and Family Life*. London: University of California Press; Gary Ramey and Valerie A. Ramey (2010). 'The Rug Rat Race'. *Brookings Papers on Economic Activity* 41(1, Spring): 129–99; Oriel Sullivan (2010). 'Changing Differences by Educational Attainment in Fathers' Domestic Labour and Child Care'. *Sociology* 44: 716–33; Evrim Altintas (2016). 'The Widening Education Gap in Developmental Childcare Activities in the United States, 1963–2013'. *Journal of Marriage and Family* 78(1): 26–42.

9. Lareau (2011). *Unequal Childhoods*.

10. Paula England (2010). 'The Gender Revolution: Uneven and Stalled'. *Gender and Society* (24:2): 149–66; David Cotter, Joan M. Hermsen, and Reeve Vanneman (2011). 'The End of the Gender Revolution? Gender Role Attitudes from 1977 to 2008'. *American Journal of Sociology* 117(1): 259–89; Evrim Altintas and Oriel Sullivan (2016). '50 Years of Change Updated: Cross-national Gender Convergence in Housework'. *Demographic Research* 35(16): 455–70.

11. Lareau (2011). *Unequal Childhoods*; Altintas (2016). 'The Widening Education Gap in Developmental Childcare Activities'.

12. Michael Braun and Jacqueline Scott (2009). 'Changing Public Views of Gender Roles in Seven Nations, 1988–2002'. In Max Haller, Roger Jowell and Tom W. Smith (eds.) *The International Social Survey Programme 1984–2009: Charting the Globe* (pp. 358–77). Oxford: Routledge.

13. Evrim Altintas and Oriel Sullivan (2017). 'Trends in Fathers' Contribution to Housework and Childcare under Different Welfare Policy Regimes'. *Social Politics: International Studies in Gender, State & Society* 24(1): 81–108.

14. E.g. Lareau (2011). *Unequal Childhoods*.

15. As suggested, for example, in Gøsta Esping-Andersen and Francesco C. Billari. (2015). 'Re-theorizing Family Demographics'. *Population and Development Review* 41(1): 1–31.

CHAPTER 6: UNPAID WORK MATTERS: VALUING HOUSEHOLD PRODUCTION TIME

1. Nancy Folbre and Julie Nelson (2000). 'For Love or Money – or Both?' *Journal of Economic Perspectives* 14(4): 123–40; Nancy Folbre (2012). 'Should Women Care Less? Intrinsic Motivation and Gender Inequality'. *British Journal of Industrial Relations* 50(4): 597–619; Gail Hebson, Jill Rubery and Damian Grimshaw (2015). 'Rethinking Job Satisfaction in Care Work: Looking Beyond the Care Debates'. *Work, Employment and Society* 29(2): 314–30.

2. Note that GDP includes some non-market work such as public services, non-profit institutions serving households (NPISH), imputed price of accommodation, production of goods for own use. In this chapter, we define non-market work narrowly as housework, care work for children and adults, and travel related to housework and care work.

3. See the statistics on the following Office for National Statistics websites: <http://www.ons.gov.uk/employmentandlabourmarket/peopleinwork/ employmentandemployeetypes/compendium/participationratesinthe uklabourmarket/2015-03-19/participationratesintheuk2014women>; and <http://www.ons.gov.uk/employmentandlabourmarket/peopleinwork/ employmentandemployeetypes/articles/womeninthelabourmarket/ 2013-09-25>.

4. Even though new childcare benefits took effect from September 2016, providing 30 hours (previously 15 hours) of free childcare for working parents of three- and four-year-olds in the UK, there is no adequate childcare policy for children younger than three (except for some disadvantaged two-year-olds). See more details of the change in childcare policies at <https://www.gov.uk/government/news/ thousands-of-parents-benefit-from-30-hours-free-childcare-early>.

5. It is well recognized that the time devoted to primary childcare activities understates the temporal demands that children can impose. In fact, research has shown that childcare measured in terms of primary activity may capture no more than about 25 per cent of time devoted to children (Duncan Ironmonger (2004). 'Bringing Up Bobby and Betty: The Input and Output Hours of Child Care' in Nancy Folbre and Michael Bittman (eds.) *Family Time: The Social Organization of Care*. New York: Routledge). 'Secondary activity', which is a response to the question 'What else were you doing during the primary activity?', offers one way of accounting for time spent on childcare when it is not the primary activity. A mother might report that her primary activity is cooking dinner, but her secondary

activity is talking with her children while she does so. And even measures of childcare that account for secondary care activity fail to capture supervisory or 'on call' time (for more details, see Nancy Folbre (2008). *Valuing Children: Rethinking the Economics of Family*. Cambridge, MA: Harvard University Press). On the other hand, it is significant in this context that, although supervisory responsibilities make up a significant portion of the effort devoted to childcare, they typically represent spatial constraints – being present in order to keep an 'eye on' or an 'ear open' for dependants – rather than activities in their own right.

6. Margaret Reid (1934). *The Economics of Household Production*. New York: John Riley. p. 11.

7. For the purpose of valuation of unpaid work in this chapter, we did not break the numbers down by gender or age. Men's time devoted to total unpaid work increased between 1975 and 2015, while women's has remained pretty much the same (150 minutes per day for men and 260 minutes per day for women). The difference between age group (18–64 and 65 and over) is more striking. On average, men aged between 16 and 64 in 2015 spent around 100 minutes per day on unpaid work, while men aged 65 and over spent 180 minutes per day. There is also less difference between the time that women and men spend in unpaid work at ages over 65.

8. The needs of adults who require assistance are far more variable than those of young children. Some need only a small amount of assistance, while others suffer extreme illness or infirmity and call for almost constant attention. Therefore, if we only look at those who engaged in adult care on the survey – meaning excluding those who did not spend any time on adult care – the average amount of time devoted to adult care is around 50 minutes per day.

9. The Systems of National Accounts (SNA) report (2008) provides a comprehensive and consistent set of macro-economic accounts for policymaking, analysis and research purposes under the guidance of the United Nations, the European Commission, the Organization for Economic Co-operation and Development, the International Monetary Fund and the World Bank Group. It is available at http://unstats.un.org/unsd/nationalaccount/docs/SNA2008.pdf.

10. Benjamin Bridgman et al. (2012). 'Accounting for Household Production in the National Accounts, 1965–2010'. *Survey of Current Business* 92(5): 23–36; J. Steven Landefeld, Barbara M. Fraumeni and Cindy M. Vojtech (2009). 'Accounting for Household Production: A Prototype Satellite Account Using the American Time Use Survey'. *Review of Income and Wealth* 55(2):

205–25; Joo Yeoun Suh and Nancy Folbre (2016). 'Valuing Unpaid Child Care in the U.S.' *Review of Income and Wealth* 62(4): 668–84.

11. The UK Office for National Statistics offered an estimate in 2014 of the total value of unpaid work using output valuation, including intermediate goods, capital and raw materials, that came to just over £1 trillion. This is the equivalent of 56 per cent of the UK's GDP. See the report by the Office for National Statistics at <https://www.ons.gov.uk/releases/householdsatelliteaccounts2011to2014>.

12. https://onlinelibrary.wiley.com/doi/10.1111/ecca.12289.

13. Jonathan Gershuny (1978). *After Industrial Society? The Emerging Self-Service Economy*. London: Macmillan; New York: Humanities Press.

CHAPTER 7: FAMILY TIME TOGETHER

1. G. Esping-Andersen and F. C. Billari, (2015). 'Re-theorizing Family Demographics'. *Population and Development Review* 41(1): 1–31.

2. E. Shorter (1977). *The Making of the Modern Family*. New York: Basic Books; L. Tilly and J. W. Scott (1988). *Women, Work, and Family*. London: Routledge. J. R. Gillis (1996). 'Making time for family: The invention of family time(s) and the reinvention of family history', *Journal of Family History* 21(1): 4–21.

3. G. Becker (1993). *A Treatise on the Family*. New York: Basic Books. Stephanie Coontz (2005). *Marriage, a History*: From Obedience to Intimacy or How Love Conquered Marriage. New York: Viking.

4. A. J. Cherlin (2009). *The Marriage-Go-Round: The State of Marriage and the Family in America Today*. New York: Alfred A. Knopf.

5. Unfortunately, the 2000 survey did not record time with spouse but only time with other household members. So, in order to compare the two surveys, we had to broaden the definition of the 2015 survey to include time with other household members. We therefore removed from the analysis all 'complex' households, and focused only on households with children less than eight years old. Because of these restrictions, we believe that the 'other household member' reported by a spouse is, in most cases, the partner.

6. Multivariate OLS regression analysis (holding constant marital status, age, number of children, age of children, social class, employment status and day of the week) confirms that, when controlling for these other factors, family time declined during weekdays. However, the 10-minute difference

during weekends is not significant when controlling for these socio-demographic characteristics.

7. Consistent with L. Lesnard (2009). *La famille désarticulée. Les nouvelles contraintes de l'emploi du temps.* Paris: Presses Universitaires de France.

8. Results from OLS regression shows that full-time mothers spend significantly more time (alone) with children than full-time fathers (controlling for other characteristics).

9. For a colour version of this figure, please see: https://giacomoragni.com/publications/2019_VAGNI_Family_Time_Together

10. However, we find domestic chores during family time diminishing for both mothers and fathers between 2000 and 2015.

11. This view is generally held by middle- and upper-class individuals. For a discussion of the issue, see P. Bourdieu (1979). *La distinction.* Paris: Les Editions de Minuit.

12. E. Durkheim (2013). *Les formes élémentaires de la vie religieuse.* Paris: Presses Universitaires de France. (Original work published 1912.) For a contemporary theory of rituals, see R. I. Collins (2014). *Interaction Ritual Chains.* Princeton, NJ: Princeton University Press; for family rituals, see Lesnard (2009). *La famille désarticulée.*

13. One example is the Channel 4 programme *Gogglebox* where we can observe couples, friends and families literally watching TV together. Even though the camera might contribute to forcing the discussion and reactions, we can recognize the extent to which watching TV is a true social activity.

14. Collins (2014). *Interaction Ritual Chains.* Princeton NJ: Princeton University Press.

15. Some authors have made the argument that 'virtual' contacts cannot replace face-to-face contacts ('physical co-presence') in terms of health benefits (see S. Pinker (2014). *The Village Effect: Why Face-to-face Contact Matters.* London: Atlantic Books), but also in terms of solidarity (see Collins, *Interaction Ritual Chains* 2014).

16. See R. D. Putnam (2000). *Bowling Alone. The Collapse and Revival of American Community.* New York: Touchstone Books. Chapter 12.

CHAPTER 8: UNEQUAL EATING: THE CONTEXT OF DAILY MEALS

1. H. Veit (2013). *Modern Food, Moral Food: Self-Control, Science and the Rise of Modern American Eating in the Early Twentieth Century.* Chapel Hill, NC: University of North Carolina Press.

2. J. Mudry (2005). 'Quantifying an American Eater', *Food, Culture & Society*, 9(1): 49–67.

3. A. Warde et al. (2007). 'Changes in the Practice of Eating: A Comparative Analysis of Time-use'. *Acta Sociologica* 50(4): 363–85.

4. E. Jarosz (2016). 'Food for Thought: A Comparative Analysis of Eating Behavior in the U.S., Poland and Armenia'. *Food, Culture and Society* 19(4): 655–79.

5. C. Devine et al. (2006). '"A Lot of Sacrifices": Work–family Spillover and the Food Choice Coping Strategies of Low Wage Employed Parents'. *Social Science and Medicine* 63(10): 2591–603.

6. K. Backett-Milburn, W. Wills, S. Gregory, J. Lawton (2006). 'Making Sense of Eating, Weight and Risk in the Early Teenage Years: Views and Concerns of Parents in Poorer Socio-economic Circumstances'. *Social Science and Medicine* 63(3): 624–35.

7. J. Armstrong and J. Reilly (2003). 'The Prevalence of Obesity and Undernutrition in Scottish Children: Growth Monitoring within the Child Health Surveillance Programme'. *Scottish Medical Journal* 48(2): 32–7.

8. The social class categories used in this chapter are from the National Statistics Socio-Economic Classification (NSSEC), based on occupational 'employment relations'.

9. D. Hamermesh (2010). 'Incentives, Time Use, and BMI: The Roles of Eating, Grazing, and Goods'. *Economics and Human Biology* 8(1): 2–15.

10. A. Knutsson. (2003), 'Health Disorders of Shift Workers'. *Occupational Medicine* 53(2): 103–8.

11. S. Cho, M. Dietrich, C. Brown, C. Clark and G. Block (2013). 'The Effect of Breakfast Type on Total Daily Energy Intake and Body Mass Index: Results from the Third National Health and Nutrition Examination Survey' (NHANES III). *Journal of the American College of Nutrition* 2(4): 296–302.

12. G. Rampersaud, M. Pereira, B. Girard, J. Adams and J. Metzl (2005). 'Breakfast Habits, Nutritional Status, Body Weight, and Academic Performance in Children and Adolescents'. *Journal of the American Dietetic Association* 105(5): 743–60.

13. W. Wills, K. Backett-Milburn, E. Roberts and J. Lawton (2011). 'The Framing of Social Class Distinctions through Family Food and Eating Practices'. *Sociological Review* 59(4): 725–40.

CHAPTER 9: TIME AND PHYSICAL ACTIVITY

1. Philip S. Brenner and John DeLamater (2014). 'Social Desirability Bias in Self-Reports of Physical Activity: Is an Exercise Identity the Culprit?' *Social Indicators Research* 117(2): 489–504. See also Philip S. Brenner and John DeLamater (2016). 'Lies, Damned Lies and Survey Self-reports? Identity as a Cause of Measurement Bias'. *Social Psychology Quarterly* 79(4): 333–54.

2. This result is not, as some have claimed, simply an effect of 'regression to the mean', in which single extreme values last month will on average be associated with less extreme values this month. We are comparing two very different measures here: an estimate of a mean for each individual respondent across an entire month, with a mean probability of participating on a single day, calculated for the entire group with a particular last-month mean estimate. In general, we find that the mean rate of participation in the particular activity on the randomly chosen diary day is substantially lower than what we expect when we calculate the expected participation rate from the questionnaire responses.

3. Jonathan Gershuny, Teresa Harms, Aiden Doherty, Emma Thomas, Karen Milton, Paul Kelly and Charlie Foster (October 2017). 'CAPTURE24: Testing Self-report Time-use Diaries against Objective Instruments in Real Time'. CTUR Working Paper.

4. J. Y. Chau, D. Merom, A. Grunseit, C. Rissel, A. E. Bauman and H. P. van der Ploeg (June 2012). 'Temporal Trends in Non-occupational Sedentary Behaviours from Australian Time Use Surveys 1992, 1997 and 2006'. *International Journal of Behavioral Nutrition and Physical Activity* 19(9): 76; H. Millward, J. E. Spinney and D. Scott (2014). 'Durations and Domains of Daily Aerobic Activity: Evidence from the 2010 Canadian Time-use Survey'. *Journal of Physical Activity and Health* 11(5): 895–902; L. P. Smith, S. W. Ng and B. M. Popkin (2014). 'No Time for the Gym? Housework and Other Non-labor Market Time Use Patterns are Associated with Meeting Physical Activity Recommendations among Adults in Full-time, Sedentary Jobs'. *Social Science Medicine* 120(C): 126–34; C. Tudor-Locke, C. Leonardi, W. D. Johnson and P. T. Katzmarzyk (2011). 'Time Spent in Physical Activity and Sedentary Behaviors on the Working Day: The American Time Use Survey'. *Journal of Occupational and Environmental Medicine* 53(12): 1382–7.

5. Catrine Tudor-Locke, Tracy L. Washington, Barbara E. Ainsworth and Richard P. Troiano (2009). 'Linking the American Time Use Survey (ATUS) and the Compendium of Physical Activities: Methods and Rationale',

Journal of Physical Activity and Health 6(3): 347–53; Hidde P. van der Ploeg, Dafna Merom, Josephine Y. Chau, Michael Bittman, Stewart G. Trost and Adrian E. Bauman (2010) 'Advances in Population Surveillance for Physical Activity and Sedentary Behavior: Reliability and Validity of Time Use Surveys'. *American Journal of Epidemiology* 172(10): 1199–206.

6. M. Jette, K. Sydney and G. Blumchen (1990). 'Metabolic Equivalents (METS) in Exercise Testing, Exercise Prescription, and Evaluation of Functional Capacity'. *Clinical Cardiology* 13(8): 555–65.

7. We should note that although this approach of assigning METs to the detailed activity categories of time-use diary studies is emerging as a standard procedure for estimating physical activity at the population level, it is not without its problems. Each individual MET/activity assignment in the Compendium is based, ultimately, on results from laboratory studies or estimates. The laboratory studies are conducted by recruiting experimental subjects to engage in carefully specified activities – swinging a pick-axe of a measured weight, running on a treadmill at a particular rate per minute, working at a desk, or whatever, each for a specified period – while wearing a mask to measure oxygen uptake.

8. Figure 9.1 is in fact generated by a statistical model that relates the diarists' age, sex, educational level and employment status, in various combinations, to the level of metabolic activity.

9. Figure 9.2 is generated by a similar multivariate statistical model as that used for Figure 9.1.

10. See <http://www.who.int/dietphysicalactivity/physical_activity_intensity/en/>.

11. See <https://www.nhs.uk/live-well/exercise/#guidelines-for-adults-aged-19-to-64>.

CHAPTER 10: TECHNOLOGY IN THE DAILY LIVES OF CHILDREN AND TEENAGERS

1. See <https://www.theguardian.com/commentisfree/2016/jan/07/british-kids-unhappy-screen-time-children>.

2. See <http://www.bbc.co.uk/news/technology-32067158>.

3. See <http://www.telegraph.co.uk/technology/mobile-phones/11511337/Parents-children-spend-too-much-time-playing-with-gadgets-on-holiday.html>.

4. Ofcom (2015). *Children and Parents: Media Use and Attitudes Report 2015*.

5. G. Mascheroni and K. Olafsson (2016). 'The Mobile Internet: Access, Use, Opportunities and Divides among European children'. *New Media and Society* 18(8): 1657–79.

6. S. Livingstone, L. Haddon, J. Vincent, G. Mascheroni and K. Olafsson (2014). *Net Children Go Mobile: The UK Report*. London: London School of Economics and Political Science.

7. A higher proportion of boys had access to the internet on their mobile / smartphone.

8. See <https://www.theguardian.com/education/2016/dec/25/screen-based-lifestyle-harms-health-of-children>.

9. See <https://www.theguardian.com/science/head-quarters/2017/jan/06/screen-time-guidelines-need-to-be-built-on-evidence-not-hype>.

10. A. Blum-Ross and S. Livingstone (2016). 'Families and Screen Time: Current Advice and Emerging Research'. *Media Policy Brief* 17. London: Media Policy Project, London School of Economics and Political Science.

11. J. P. Robinson (1985). 'The Validity and Reliability of Diaries versus Alternative Time Use Measures'. In F. T. Juster, and F. P. Stafford (eds.). *Time, Goods and Wellbeing* (pp. 33–62). Ann Arbor, MI: University of Michigan.

12. Ofcom (2015). *Children and Parents: Media Use and Attitudes*.

13. Academic studies also commonly use recall-type measures of children's use of technology and the internet. See for example, A. R. Lauricella, E. Wartella and V. J. Rideout (2015). 'Young Children's Screen Time: The Complex Role of Parent and Child Factors'. *Journal of Applied Developmental Psychology* 36: 11–17; K. Corder, A. J. Atkin, D. J. Bamber et al. (2015). 'Revising on the Run or Studying on the Sofa: Positive Associations between Physical Activity, Sedentary Behaviour and Exam Results in British Adolescents'. *Behavioral Nutrition and Physical Activity* 12: 106.

14. J. Gershuny (2003). *Changing Times*.

15. See, for example, A. Lenhart, A. Smith, M. Anderson, M. Duggan and A. Perrin (2015). 'Teens, Technology and Friendships'. Pew Research Center, August 2015. M. Orleans and M. C. Laney (2000). 'Children's Computer Use in the Home: Isolation or Sociation?' *Social Science Computer Review* 18(1): 56–72.

16. K. Subrahmanyam, P. Greenfield, R. Kraut and E. Gross (2001). 'The Impact of Computer Use on Children's and Adolescents' Development'. *Applied Developmental Psychology* 22(1): 7–30.

17. We excluded 79 diaries with more than 4 hours of time not reported.

18. As weights were applied weekly estimates can be derived simply by multiplying daily estimates by 7.

19. Livingstone et al. (2014). *Net Children Go Mobile*.

20. Ibid.

21. Based on averages across school and non-school days. Study time is higher on school days.

22. See, for example: <https://www.theguardian.com/media/2016/jan/26/children-time-online-watching-tv>.

CHAPTER 11: TECHNOLOGY IN THE DAILY LIVES OF ADULTS

1. Office for National Statistics (2002). *Family Spending*. <http://webarchive.nationalarchives.gov.uk/20160105160709/http://ons.gov.uk/ons/rel/family-spending/family-spending/index.html>

2. Office for National Statistics (2012). *Family Spending*. See <http://webarchive.nationalarchives.gov.uk/20160105160709/http://ons.gov.uk/ons/rel/family-spending/family-spending/family-spending-2011-edition/index.html.>

3. Ofcom (2011). See <https://www.ofcom.org.uk/research-and-data/cmr/cmr11>.

4. Office for National Statistics (2014a). *Family Spending*. See <http://webarchive.nationalarchives.gov.uk/20160105160709/http://ons.gov.uk/ons/rel/family-spending/family-spending/index.html>. Note also that the *Internet Access – Households and Individuals* survey reports that 84 per cent of households in the UK had access to the internet in 2014. See <https://www.ons.gov.uk/peoplepopulationandcommunity/householdcharacteristics/homeinternetandsocialmediausage/bulletins/internetaccesshouseholdsandindividuals/2014-08-07>.

5. Ofcom (2014). See <https://www.ofcom.org.uk/research-and-data/cmr/cmr14>.

6. S. Turkle (2012). *Alone Together: Why We Expect More from Technology and Less from Each Other*. New York: Basic Books.

7. For example, see <http://www.telegraph.co.uk/technology/10540261/screen-time-ipad-tablet-digital-detox-digital-addiction.html> and also <http://www.bbc.co.uk/news/technology-36964081>.

8. J. Wajcman (2015). *Pressed for Time: The Acceleration of Life in Digital Capitalism*. Chicago: Chicago University Press.

9. Age UK (no date). *Technology and Older People Evidence Review*. London: Age UK. See <http://www.ageuk.org.uk/documents/en-gb/for-professionals/computers-and-technology/evidence_review_technology.pdf?dtrk=true>.

10. Age UK (no date). *Technology and Older People Evidence Review*.

11. S. West (2015). *Later Life in a Digital World*. London: Age UK. See <http://www.ageuk.org.uk/globalassets/age-uk/documents/reports-and-publications/reports-and-briefings/active-communities/later_life_in_a_digital_world.pdf>.

12. Office for National Statistics (2008; 2014). *Internet Access – Households and Individuals*.

13. From the UK Time Use Survey 2000–2001, 45 per cent of households had a computer at home, and 32 per cent had internet access at home. From the UK Time Use Survey 2014–2015 85 per cent of households has a computer at home, and internet access at home.

14. Together these sum to 52 minutes on average, or 81 per cent of average leisure time with a device. The remaining time spreads thinly across a range of other leisure and personal activities including sport, activities relating to hobbies, education and creative activities, and personal care.

15. Additional analysis showed that there were significant differences in time using computers and mobile devices related to education. Specifically, adults with a degree qualification averaged significantly more time using these devices than those without.

16. Analysis also did not reveal significant differences in time using devices related to time pressure or subjective wellbeing across age groups.

17. The analysis is based on a sample of 2,103 adults aged 60 and over. Of these, 22.3 per cent are non-retirees (n=468), and the remainder are retired (n=1,635).

18. West (2015). *Later Life in a Digital World*; Office for National Statistics (2014). *Internet Access – Households and Individuals*.

19. On the specific question of watching TV while travelling, less than 1 per cent of diaries contain any time in this activity in both 2000 and 2015, though it does increase from 0.24 per cent in 2000 to 0.62 per cent in 2015.

20. Multivariate analysis shows that routine/manual workers who report stress or dissatisfaction with life spend significantly more time using devices.

CHAPTER 12: TIME USE AND WELLBEING IN LATER LIFE

1. The population projection is based on the national population projections. Available at <https://www.ons.gov.uk/peoplepopulationandcommunity/populationandmigration/populationprojections>.

2. Cathleen D. Zick, Robert B. Stevens and W. Keith Bryant (2011). 'Time Use Choices and Healthy Body Weight: A Multivariate Analysis of Data from the American Time Use Survey'. *International Journal of Behavioral Nutrition and Physical Activity* 8(84): 1–14.

3. Larry A. Tucker and Glenn M. Friedman (1989). 'Television Viewing and Obesity in Adult Males.' *American Journal of Public Health* 79(4): 516–18; Zick, Stevens and Bryant (2011). 'Time Use Choices and Healthy Body Weight'.

4. Maria Mireault and Anton de Man (1996). 'Suicidal Ideation among Older Adults: Personal Variables, Stress, and Social Support'. *Social Behavior and Personality* 24(4): 385–92; Patricia A. Thomas (2011). 'Trajectories of Social Engagement and Limitations in Late Life'. *Journal of Health and Social Behavior* 52(4): 430–43.

5. J. Jun (2014). 'Balance beyond Work Life: An Empirical Study of Older People's Time Use in the UK'. Unpublished DPhil thesis. University of Oxford, UK.

6. Gershuny (2003). *Changing Times*.

7. This classification owes its origin to Dagfinn Ås's four-fold typology of activities: D. Ås (1978). 'Studies of Time-use: Problems and Prospects'. *Acta Sociologica* 21(2): 125–41.

8. Jun (2014). 'Balance beyond Work Life'.

9. P. Laslett (1996). *A Fresh Map of Life: The Emergence of the Third Age* (2nd edn). Cambridge, MA: Harvard University Press.

10. R. Illsley (1991). 'Review of "Peter Laslett, *A Fresh Map of Life*"'. *Ageing and Society* 11(01): 85–6.

11. For more discussion about the importance of time structure in later life, see Jun (2014).

12. Jun (2014). 'Balance beyond Work Life'.

13. Jun (ibid.) examined the relationship between the time balance and health, controlling for other factors such as long-term illness, and found that the relationship was still significant.

14. Note that 1,577 cases were missing for this variable, so the result may not properly represent the actual trend.

15. Peter Elwood et al. (2013). 'Healthy Lifestyles Reduce the Incidence of Chronic Diseases and Dementia: Evidence from the Caerphilly Cohort Study'. *PloS One* 8(12).

16. Jun (2014). 'Balance beyond Work Life'.

17. D. Paterson, G. Jones, C. Rice and R. Sheperd (2007). 'Ageing and Physical Activity: Evidence to Develop Exercise Recommendations for Older Adults'. *Applied Physiology, Nutrition and Metabolism* 32(S2E): S69–S108; W. Nusselder, C. Looman, O. Franco, A. Peeters, A. Slingerland and J. Mackenbach (2008). 'The Relation between Non-occupational Physical Activity and Years Lived with and without Disability'. *Journal of Epidemiology and Community Health* 62(9): 823–8.

18. NHS (2015). See <http://www.nhs.uk/Livewell/fitness/Pages/physical-activity-guidelines-for-older-adults.aspx#moderate>.

19. M. E. Nelson et al. (2007). 'Physical Activity and Public Health in Older Adults: Recommendation from the American College of Sports Medicine and the American Heart Association'. *Medicine and Science in Sports and Exercise* 39(8): 1435.

20. M. T. Hamilton, D. G. Hamilton and T. W. Zderic (2007). 'Role of Low Energy Expenditure and Sitting in Obesity, Metabolic Syndrome, Type 2 Diabetes, and Cardiovascular Disease'. *Diabetes* 56(11): 2655–67. doi:10.2337/db07-0882; K. R. Westerterp (2001). 'Pattern and Intensity of Physical Activity'. *Nature* 410(6828): 539.

21. Y. Hao (2008). 'Productive Activities and Psychological Well-being among Older Adults'. *Journals of Gerontology Series B: Psychological Sciences and Social Sciences* 63(2): S64–S72; M. Wahrendorf, O. von dem Knesebeck and J. Siegrist (2006). 'Social Productivity and Well-being of Older People: Baseline Results from the SHARE Study'. *European Journal of Ageing* 3(2): 67–73; A. McMunn, J. Nazroo, M. Wahrendorf, E. Breeze and P. Zaninotto (2009). 'Participation in Socially Productive Activities, Reciprocity and Wellbeing in Later Life: Baseline Results in England'. *Ageing and Society* 29(5): 765.

22. In particular, it would be important to investigate how much time older people spend alone.

23. P. Hicks (2002). 'Preparing for Tomorrow's Social Policy Agenda: New Priorities for Policy Research and Development that Emerge from an Examination of the Economic Well-being of the Working-age Population'. (Report No. SRDC Working Paper Series 02-04). Ottawa, ON: Social Research and Demonstration Corporation. Available at <http://www.srdc.org/publications/Preparing-for-Tomorrows-Social-Policy-Agenda-New-Priorities-for-Policy-Research-and-Development-That-Emerge-From-an-Examination-of-the-Economic-Well-Being-of-the-Working-Age-Population-details.aspx>.

24. John R. Kelly (1997). 'Activity and Ageing: Challenge in Retirement'. In J. T. Haworth (ed.), *Work, Leisure and Well-being* (pp. 165–79). London: Routledge.

CHAPTER 13: FEELING RUSHED: IS OUR DAILY LIFE REALLY SPEEDING UP?

1. Popular and academic accounts include Jonathan Crary (2013). *24/7: Late Capitalism and the Ends of Sleep.* London: Verso Books; Hartmut Rosa (2013). *Social Acceleration: A New Theory of Modernity.* New York: Columbia University Press; Brigit Schulte (2014). *Overwhelmed: Work, Love and Play when No-one has the Time.* New York: Sarah Crichton Books.

2. E.g. Judy Wajcman, (2015). *Pressed for Time: The Acceleration of Life in Digital Capitalism.* Chicago: University of Chicago Press.

3. Shira Offer and Barbara Schneider (2011). 'Revisiting the Gender Gap in Time-use Patterns: Multitasking and Well-being among Mothers and Fathers in Dual-earner Families'. *American Sociological Review* 76(6): 809–33; Liana Sayer (2007). 'More Work for Mothers? Trends and Gender Differences in Multitasking' in T. van der Lippe and P. Peters (eds.), *Competing Claims in Work and Family Life*, pp. 41–55. Cheltenham: Edward Elgar; Oriel Sullivan and Jonathan Gershuny (2013). 'Domestic Outsourcing and Multitasking: How Much Do they Really Contribute?' *Social Science Research* 42(5): 1311–24.

4. Wajcman (2015). *Pressed for Time.*

5. Michael Bittman, Judith E. Brown and Judy Wajcman (2009). 'The Mobile Phone, Perpetual Contact and Time Pressure'. *Work, Employment & Society* 23(4): 673.

6. These occupational-based status groups are defined according to current or previous employment. Very few respondents had never had a job, so the figures include most of the sample.

7. The occupational status categories used in this chapter are derived from the National Statistics Socio-Economic Classification (SEC), based on occupational 'employment relations'.

8. Offer and Schneider (2011). 'Revisiting the Gender Gap in Time-use Patterns'; Sayer (2007). 'More Work for Mothers?'

9. E.g. Jerry A. Jacobs and Kathleen Gerson (2005). *The Time Divide: Work, Family and Gender Inequality.* Cambridge: Harvard University

Press; John Robinson and Geoffrey Godbey (1997). *Time for Life: The Surprising Ways Americans Spend their Time*. University Park, PA: Penn State University Press; Jonathan Gershuny (2003). *Changing Times*; Oriel Sullivan and Jonathan Greshuny (2001). 'Cross-national Changes in Time-use: Some Sociological (Hi)Stories Re-examined'. *British Journal of Sociology* 52(4): 331–47.

10. Jacobs and Gerson (2005). *The Time Divide*, p. 39.

11. Staffan B. Linder (1970). *The Harried Leisure Class*. New York: Columbia U.P.

12. Oriel Sullivan and Tally Katz-Gerro (2007). 'The Omnivorousness Thesis Revisited: Voracious Cultural Consumers'. *European Sociological Review* 23(2): 123–37.

13. Jonathan Gershuny (2005). 'Busyness as the Badge of Honor for the New Superordinate Working Class'. *Social Research* 72(2): 287–314; Oriel Sullivan (2008). 'Busyness, Status Distinction and Consumption Strategies of the Income-rich, Time-poor'. *Time & Society* 17(1): 71–92.

14. We repeated these analyses using educational level in place of occupational status and found very similar results.

15. E.g. Suzanne M. Bianchi, John P. Robinson and Melissa A. Milkie (2006). *The Changing Rhythm of American Family Life*. New York: Russell Sage Foundation; Scott Coltrane (2000). 'Research on Household Labor'. *Journal of Marriage and Family* 62(4): 1209–33; Claudia Geist and Philip Cohen (2011). 'Headed toward Equality? Housework Change in Comparative Perspective'. *Journal of Marriage and Family* 73(4): 832–44; Arlie Hochschild (1989). *The Second Shift: Working Parents and the Revolution at Home*. Berkeley: University of California Press; Robinson and Godbey (1997). *Time for Life*; Liana Sayer, Paula England, Michael Bittman and Suzanne M. Bianchi (2009). 'How Long is the Second (Plus First) Shift? Gender Differences in Paid, Unpaid, and Total Work Time in Australia and the United States'. *Journal of Comparative Family Studies* 40(4): 523–44; Oriel Sullivan (1997). 'Time Waits for no (Wo)man: An Investigation of the Gendered Experience of Domestic Time', *Sociology* 31(2): 221–39.

16. See Dale Southerton (2006). 'Analysing the Temporal Organization of Daily Life: Social Constraints, Practices and their Allocation'. *Sociology* 40(3): 435–54; Dale Southerton and Mark Tomlinson (2005). '"Pressed for Time" – the Differential Impacts of a "Time Squeeze"'. *Sociological Review* 53(2): 215–39.

CHAPTER 14: TIME AND ENJOYMENT: MEASURING NATIONAL HAPPINESS

1. J. E. Stiglitz et al. (2009). *The Measurement of Economic Performance and Social Progress Revisited*. OFCE 2009: 33.

2. In the UK this demand for wider measures of quality of life, including wellbeing measures for use in the policymaking process, has led to the recent establishment of a government-supported UK programme within the Office for National Statistics aimed at producing statistics relating to personal and national wellbeing.

3. The idea of using an enjoyment column in a time-use diary to collect information on objective happiness dates back to the mid-1980s, invented, as far as we can tell, independently and simultaneously in a small-scale UK study and US national sample, by John Robinson (J. P. Robinson and G. Godbey (1998). *Time for Life: The Surprising Ways that Americans Use Their Time*. University Park, PA: Penn State University Press and Alma Erlich (A. Erlich (1987). 'Time Allocation: Focus on Personal Care Household Research Project'. TIS no. G87002. London: Unilever Research). It originated from discussions from the mid-1960s onwards at the Institute for Social Research at the University of Michigan (where Daniel Kahneman was a post-doctoral researcher). Other time-use researchers (e.g. William Michaelson and Ignace Glorieux) used the same or similar techniques during the 1990s. Kahneman et al.'s very widely cited 2004 article (D. Kahneman, A. B. Krueger, D. Schkade, N. Schwarz and A. Stone (2004). 'A Survey Method for Characterizing Daily Life Experience: The Day Reconstruction Method'. *Science* 306(5702): 1776–80) mistakenly claims credit for the invention of this technique, renaming the long-established time-diary method (e.g. Hildegarde Kneeland (1929). 'Woman's Economic Contribution in the Home'. *Annals of the American Academy of Political and Social Science* 143: 33–40; Alexander Szalai (1972). *The Use of Time: Daily Activities of Urban and Suburban Populations in Twelve Countries*. The Hague: Mouton) as the 'Day Reconstruction Method' (DRM).

4. E.g. Daniel Kahneman, in the introduction to D. Kahneman, E. Diener and N. Schwarz (eds.) (1999). *Well-being: The Foundations of Hedonic Psychology*. New York: Russell Sage Foundation.

5. In order to compare these responses to the more standard survey-type questions, in the 2014–15 UK diary we also asked our diarists some of these sorts of more general questions about the enjoyment of particular activities, allowing us to compare their answers to their 'objective' diary

results. The correlation between these measures ranges from less than 0.2 (for shopping) to 0.46 (for paid work), indicating that there is some value in asking such questions where diaries are not used, but that they are not particularly accurate. The 2014–15 survey includes eleven questionnaire-type 'predicted' enjoyment questions. We ask respondents how satisfied they are with their jobs, and how much they enjoy cooking (separately for an ordinary family meal and a special occasion), shopping (for food and non-food items), home maintenance, decorating/DIY, tidying and cleaning the house, washing and ironing clothes, physical care and comforting children, and helping children with homework. We can match these question items reasonably closely with particular activities as reported in the diaries, and hence compare levels of enjoyment of these activities reported in each source. It is not entirely clear what levels of association we should expect between the questionnaire-based predicted measures and the diary-based experienced measures. A .46 correlation between predicted (question-based measure) and experienced enjoyment of the job (diary-based measure) indicates more than 20 per cent joint variation between the two measures, and the correlations for gardening, tidying the house and laundry similarly indicate around 10 per cent joint variation. So, although these percentages of joint variation are not particularly high, the questionnaire items in this case appear to be giving some sort of informative signal about the enjoyment of the activity.

6.   To arrive at these mean enjoyment scores we multiply the duration of each episode where the activity category concerned is the primary activity recorded by the enjoyment level to arrive at the total enjoyment score for that episode. We then *sum* these total enjoyment scores for each category of activity across the day, and finally divide these daily enjoyment total scores for each activity by the amount of time devoted to the activity. In this way, we arrive at an appropriately weighted mean enjoyment level for each activity across all those who engage in it.

7.   The length of these confidence bars depends on both the number of people who engage in the activity during the diary day, and the variability of the enjoyment level among the participants. The larger the number of participants and the smaller the variability, the less the uncertainty about the estimate of the mean, and hence the shorter the error bar. One simple and rather conservative way of reading these confidence intervals is to say that if the bottom of the 95 per cent confidence bar for one activity is above the top of the confidence bar for another activity, then we can be quite certain that the difference between the means for the two activities is

statistically significant. (That is to say, if the bottom of one bar just touches the top of another, there are still fewer than 3 chances out of 1,000 that the means are the same.)

8. The Unilever survey used a different recording methodology (a small fixed activity list and a five-point negative scale instead of the 7-point positive scale used in the 2014–15 survey).

9. **Group 1**, described under the general heading of 'doing housework', includes doing school homework (which achieves by far the lowest mean enjoyment score – 4.14 – of all activities), looking for a job, laundry, house cleaning and doing the washing-up, with a mean score of 4.47. **Group 2**, 'paid work' (with a range of mean enjoyment scores from 4.58 to 4.93) includes other domestic work, commuting, main job (score 4.68), work travel, time at school and education travel, paid work at home and other workplace activities, adult care, time in bed but not asleep and voluntary work. Then we have **Group 3**, the 'shopping' group (range 5.03 to 5.24) which also includes attending courses for leisure purpose (perhaps surprisingly low-valued at 5.09, writing letters and self-care (washing, dressing), cooking and pet care. **Group 4**, the 'intermediate' category (range 5.26 to 5.69 – so described because the activities in it include more enjoyable work activities and some childcare and leisure activities), includes various sorts of travel, work breaks, time in second job (at 5.37 scoring much higher than main job), DIY, other outdoor work, emailing and internet use (around 5.45), meals at work, childcare, listening to radio, gardening, reading to children, walking, and accompanying children. **Group 5** consists of activities referred to as 'relaxation' (range 5.79 to 6.21). This cluster contains the main leisure activities conducted at (or starting from) home: talking, relaxing or doing nothing, watching television or other video materials, as well as ordinary meals at home, reading, walking dogs, listening to music, cycling, playing sport, visits from (or to) friends, parties, hobbies and playing computer or other games. **Group 6** is the single activity 'sleep', with a high enjoyment score (6.24). **Group 7** is the most enjoyed of all (with a range of mean enjoyment scores from 6.25 to 6.56); the 'going out' category (which also includes playing with children) includes going to restaurants and pubs, to sports events, and to theatres, cinema and concerts.

10. Daniel Kahneman and Alan B. Krueger. (2006.) 'Developments in the Measurement of Subjective Well-Being'. *Journal of Economic Perspectives* 20 (1): 3–24.

11. At the ISR at the University of Michigan. Dow and Juster, in F. T. Juster and T. Stafford (eds) (1985). *Time, Goods and Wellbeing*. Michigan: ISR.

12. In fact, since they only had questionnaire-type enjoyment information, Dow and Juster had a non-exhaustive representation of the day, weighting the enjoyment scores for those specific activities for which this information was collected, by the mean time spent in the activities.

13. J. S. Mill (1863). *Utilitarianism*. London: Parker, Son and Bourn.

14. The inclusion of sleep in this list reflects the convention by which the amenity of bedrooms in private households is included in conventional GNP measures. The UK Office for National Statistics, in its pioneering experimental extension of national accounts, estimated the value of a night's sleep in a private home by the equivalent cost of a basic hotel room. See S. Holloway, S. Shortand and S. Tamplin (2002). *Household Satellite Account (Experimental) Methodology*. London: ONS.

Index

PELICAN BOOKS

PELICAN BOOKS

PELICAN BOOKS